Microsoft® Windows® Me

Millennium Edition

At a Glance

Your fast-answers guide to Windows Me!

Jerry Joyce and
Marianne Moon

PUBLISHED BY
Microsoft Press
A Division of Microsoft Corporation
One Microsoft Way
Redmond, Washington 98052-6399

Library of Congress Cataloging-in-Publication Data
Joyce, Jerry, 1950–
Microsoft Windows Millennium Edition At a Glance / Jerry Joyce, Marianne Moon
p. cm.
ISBN 0-7356-0970-5
1. Microsoft Windows (Computer file) 2. Operating systems (Computers) I. Moon, Marianne. II. Title.

QA76.76.O63 J6938 2000
005.4'469--dc21 00-038672

Printed and bound in the United States of America.

2 3 4 5 6 7 8 9 QWTQWT 5 4 3 2 1 0

Distributed in Canada by Penguin Books Canada Limited.

A CIP catalogue record for this book is available from the British Library.

Microsoft Press books are available through booksellers and distributors worldwide. For further information about international editions, contact your local Microsoft Corporation office or contact Microsoft Press International directly at fax (425) 936-7329. Visit our Web site at mspress.microsoft.com. Send comments to *mspinput@microsoft.com*.

Acquisitions Editor: Christey Bahn
Project Editor: Kim Fryer
Technical Editor: Dail Magee Jr.

Contents

4 Networking 35

5 Running Programs 53

6 Playing Games 67

9 Connecting 109

10 Customizing 131

12 Managing Windows Me 169

i Index 189

1 About This Book

In this section

If you want to get the most from your computer and your software with the least amount of time and effort—and who doesn't?—this book is for you. You'll find *Microsoft Windows Millennium Edition At a Glance* to be a straightforward, easy-to-read reference tool. With the premise that your computer should work for you, not you for it, this book's purpose is to help you get your work done quickly and efficiently so that you can get away from the computer and live your life.

No Computerese!

Let's face it—when there's a task you don't know how to do but you need to get it done in a hurry, or when you're stuck in the middle of a task and can't figure out what to do next, there's nothing more frustrating than having to read page after page of technical background material. You want the information you need—nothing more, nothing less—and you want it now! *And* it should be easy to find and understand.

That's what this book is all about. It's written in plain English—no technical jargon and no computerese. There's no single task in the book that takes more than two pages. Just look the task up in the index or the table of contents, turn to the page, and there's the information you need, laid out in an illustrated step-by-step format. You don't get bogged down by the whys and wherefores: just follow the steps and get your work done with a minimum of hassle.

Occasionally you might have to turn to another page if the procedure you're working on is accompanied by a "See Also." That's because there's a lot of overlap among tasks, and we didn't want to keep repeating ourselves. We've scattered some useful Tips here and there, and thrown in a "Try This" once in a while, but by and large we've tried to remain true to the heart and soul of the book, which is that the information you need should be available to you at a glance.

Useful Tasks...

Whether you use Windows Me at home or on the road, we've tried to pack this book with procedures for everything we could think of that you might want to do, from the simplest tasks to some of the more esoteric ones.

...And the Easiest Way to Do Them

Another thing we've tried to do in this book is find and document the easiest way to accomplish a task. Windows Me often provides a multitude of methods to accomplish a single end result—which can be daunting or delightful, depending on the way you like to work. If you tend to stick with one favorite and familiar approach, we think the methods described in this book are the way to go. If you like trying out alternative techniques, go ahead! The intuitiveness of Windows Me invites exploration, and you're likely to discover ways of doing things that you think are easier or that you like better than ours. If you do, that's great! It's exactly what the developers of Windows Me had in mind when they provided so many alternatives.

A Quick Overview

Your computer probably came with Windows Me preinstalled, but if you do have to install it yourself, the Setup Wizard makes installation so simple that you won't need our help anyway. So, unlike many computer books, this one doesn't start with installation instructions and a list of system requirements.

Next, you don't have to read this book in any particular order. It's designed so that you can jump in, get the information you need, and then close the book and keep it near your computer until the next time you need to know how to get something done. But that doesn't mean we scattered the information about with wild abandon. We've organized the book so that the tasks you want to accomplish are arranged in two levels—you'll find the overall type of task you're looking for under a main section title such as "Accessing and Organizing," "Playing Games," "Running Programs," and so on. Then, in each of those sections, the smaller tasks within the main task are arranged in a loose progression from the simplest to the more complex.

Sections 2 and 3 cover the basics: starting Windows Me and shutting it down, changing users if more than one person uses your computer, starting programs and working with program windows, using shortcut menus, taking a class at Mouse School, and getting help if you need it. There's also a lot of useful information about accessing and organizing your documents, files, and folders: moving or copying files and creating a system of folders in which to keep them, recovering deleted items, using compressed folders to minimize large files, and arranging the items on your Desktop. You'll also learn about exploring the Internet, setting your home page, and saving your favorite Internet locations so that you can get back to them quickly.

Section 4 is all about networking—the different types of networks you're likely to encounter, how to find what you need on your network, and how to use the power of a network to your best advantage. You'll find the information helpful whether you have two computers connected to share a printer, a multicomputer household that shares a single Internet connection, or a home office where you want to share certain files. We'll show you, among other things, how to set up your network, how to share files and folders, and how to connect to your network.

Section 5 focuses on running programs, including some of the programs that come with Windows Me. Here's where you'll find information about your everyday tasks: composing, editing, and printing documents; copying material between documents; using the Calculator; even what to do if your computer "freezes up." There's also a short section here for all you MS-DOS fans!

Sections 6, 7, and 8 are all about having fun—playing games, either by yourself or with an international group of opponents via the Internet; working with different types of pictures, including drawings and photographs; creating and listening to your own music playlist; assembling slide shows; and making movies with narration, soundtracks, and fade-in/fade-out transitions between clips. The possibilities are endless, and we know you'll be thrilled by the professional results you can achieve with the combination of your own imagination and the Windows Me tools—among them Media Player and Movie Maker—which let you give free rein to your creativity.

Section 9 is about connecting to and communicating with co-workers and friends and using Windows Me as your window on the world at large: sending and receiving e-mail, perusing and taking part in newsgroup discussions, and using some of the tools that go along with working and playing in cyberspace, including sending and receiving instant messages and videoconferencing directly from your computer.

The final sections, 10 through 12, deal with more advanced topics: reorganizing and restructuring the Start menu; customizing your Desktop, your folder windows, your mouse, the toolbars, and even the way you enter information, so that everything on your computer looks and works exactly the way you want it to; improving your computer's security; protecting your files and folders by specifying who is allowed to access them; adding and removing software or hardware components; updating your system and maintaining the drives; and diagnosing and taking care of problems. If you think these tasks sound complex, rest assured that they're not—Windows Me makes them so easy that you'll sail right through them.

A Few Assumptions

We had to make a few educated guesses about you, our audience, when we started writing this book. Perhaps your computer is solely for personal use—e-mail, surfing the Internet, playing games, and so on. Perhaps your work allows you to telecommute. Or maybe you run a small home-based business. Taking all these possibilities into account, we assumed that you'd either be using a stand-alone home computer or that you'd have two or more computers connected so that you could share files, a printer, and so on. We also assumed that you had an Internet connection.

Another assumption we made is that—initially, anyway—you'd use Windows Me just as it came, meaning that you'd view folder windows showing web content and that you'd use your little friend the mouse in the traditional way: that is, point and click to select an item, and then double-click to open it. If you'd prefer using the mouse as if you were working on a web page—pointing to an item to select it and then opening it with a single click—you can easily do so. You'll find the necessary information in "Setting Your Click" on page 148. However, because our working style is somewhat traditional, and because Windows Me is set up to work in the traditional style, that's what we've described in the procedures and graphics throughout this book.

A Final Word (or Two)

We had three goals in writing this book:

- Whatever you want to do, we want the book to help you get it done.
- We want the book to help you discover how to do things you *didn't* know you wanted to do.
- And, finally, if we've achieved the first two goals, we'll be well on the way to the third, which is for our book to help you *enjoy* using Windows Me. We think that's the best gift we could give you to thank you for buying our book.

We hope you'll have as much fun using *Microsoft Windows Millennium Edition At a Glance* as we've had writing it. The best way to learn is by *doing,* and that's how we hope you'll use this book.

Jump right in!

Jump Right In

In this section

Microsoft Windows Millennium Edition is designed to work for you, not you for it. Don't be afraid to jump right in and try out some features. You'll find that there are often several ways to accomplish one task. Why? Because people work differently. Because different tasks have different requirements. And because you want to find the way that works best for you, get your work done quickly, and get away from the computer!

You'll find that the procedures are simple and straightforward and that you can often use automated methods to get the more complex tasks done easily. This doesn't mean that you can't get stuck or get into trouble, but there are so many safeguards built into Windows Me and so many places to get help that you'll have to work pretty hard to get into *real* trouble.

This section of the book covers the basics: starting Windows Me and shutting it down, starting programs, getting online help, and so on. There's also a handy visual glossary on the following two pages that will help you become familiar with the various components of the Windows Me environment.

Don't change or delete anything just yet—you want to feel comfortable with the basics before you do any customizing. The best way to learn about running programs, managing windows, and getting help if you *do* get into trouble is to jump right in and try things out.

Windows Me at a Glance

Microsoft Windows Millennium Edition is your working headquarters—the *operating system* that lets you run different programs simultaneously and share information between programs if you need to. Most of the programs you'll use have common characteristics that were designed to work together in the Windows Me environment so that once you learn how to do something in one program, you know how to do it in other programs.

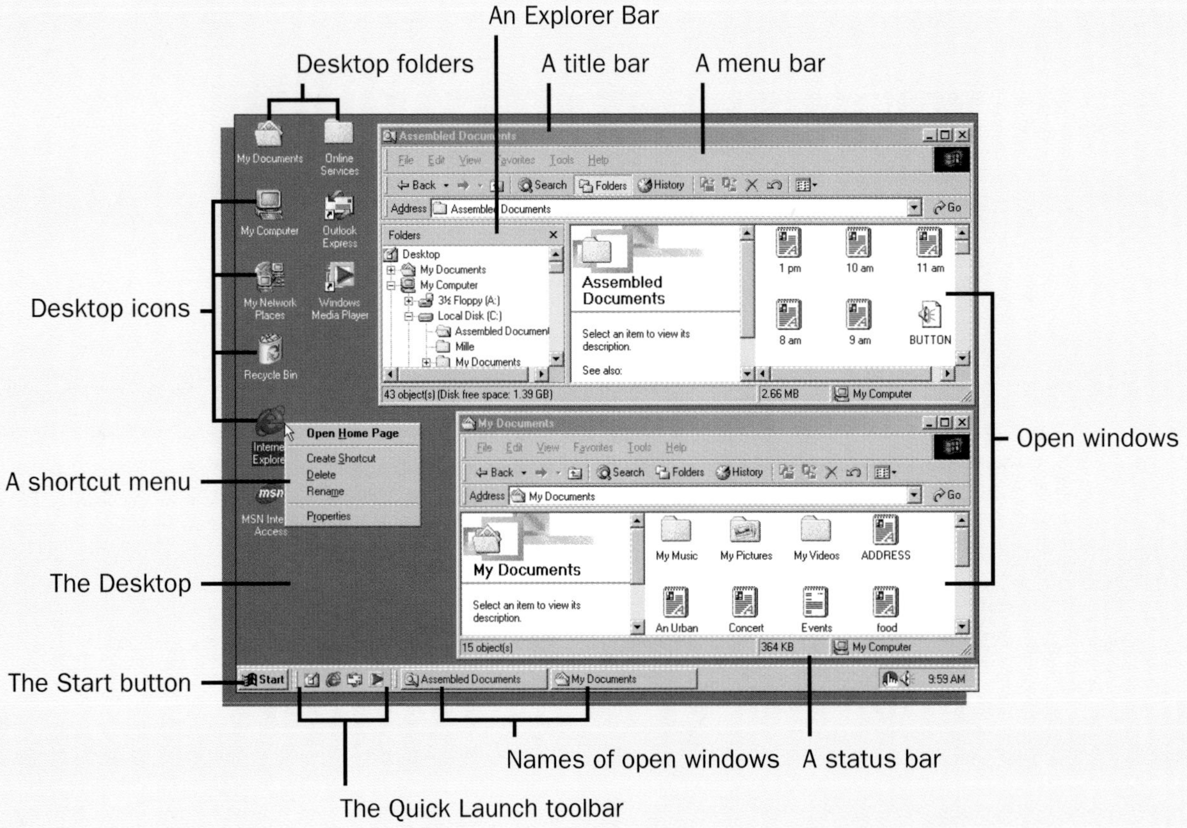

Take a look at the different parts of the Windows Me environment displayed on these two pages—what they do and what they're called—and you'll be on the road to complete mastery. As you use Windows Me, you might change the way some of these items look and work, but the basic concepts are the same. And if you need to, you can always come back to this visual glossary for a quick refresher on Windows Me terminology.

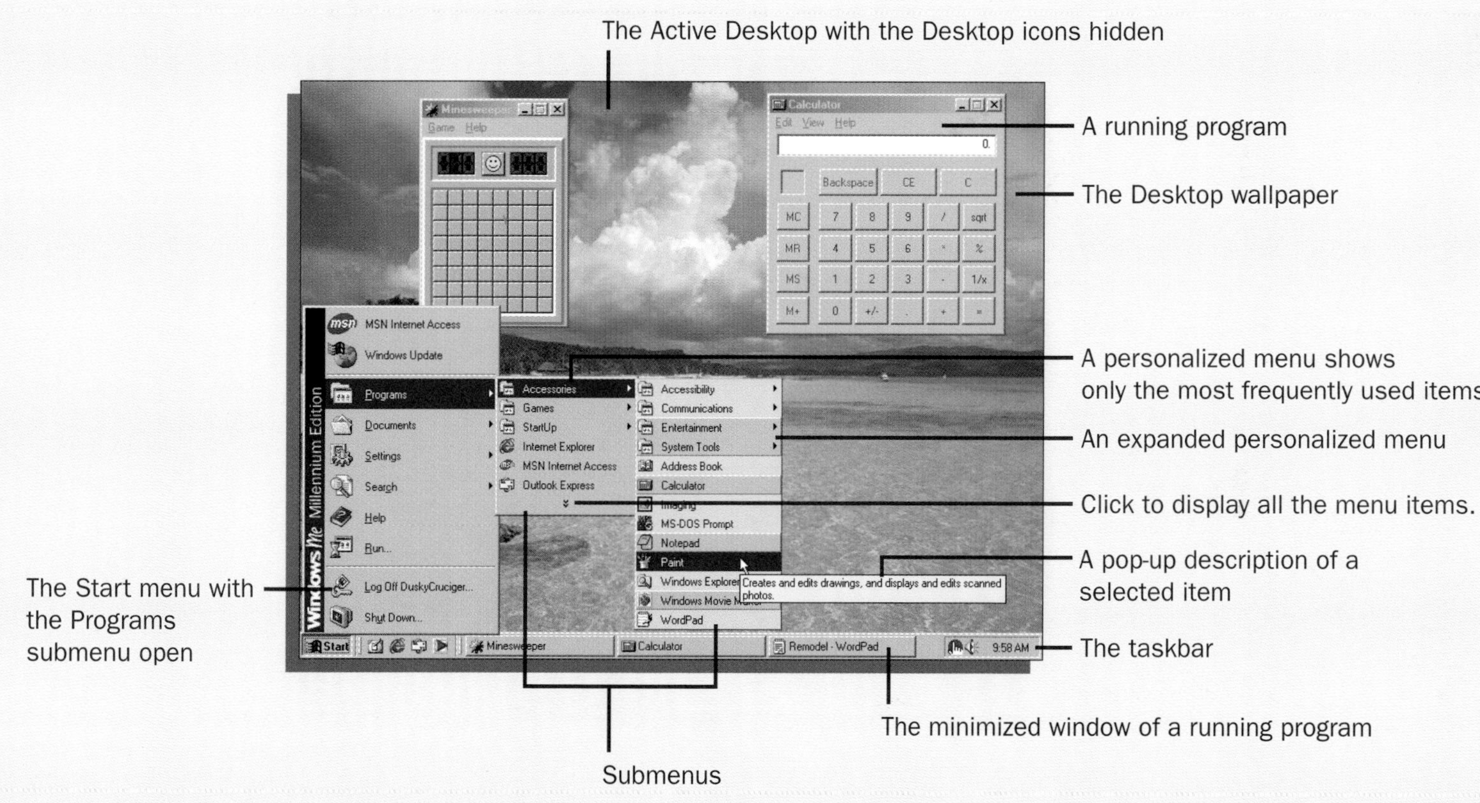

Starting Up and Shutting Down

When you turn on your computer, you're also starting Windows Me. Startup time depends on your computer's speed, configuration, and connections, and on the programs that are set up to start automatically. If someone else wants to use the computer, you simply log off so that the other person can log on and use his or her own settings. When you've finished your work, don't just turn off the computer! Windows Me needs a little time to close any open programs or connections and to save your current settings.

TIP: Your computer can have several states of resting other than simply being turned off. Before you touch the On/Off switch, try pressing a key to see whether the computer comes to life.

TIP: You'll probably want to restart Windows Me after you've made changes to the computer's configuration or if you're having any software problems.

Start Windows Me

1. Turn on your computer, your monitor, and any peripheral devices—your printer, for example.
2. Wait for Windows Me to load.
3. If a password dialog box appears, type (if it's not already there) or select the name you've been assigned in the User Name box, and press the Tab key.
4. Type your password in the Password text box.
5. Click OK.

The standard Windows Me Logon

The Microsoft Family Logon

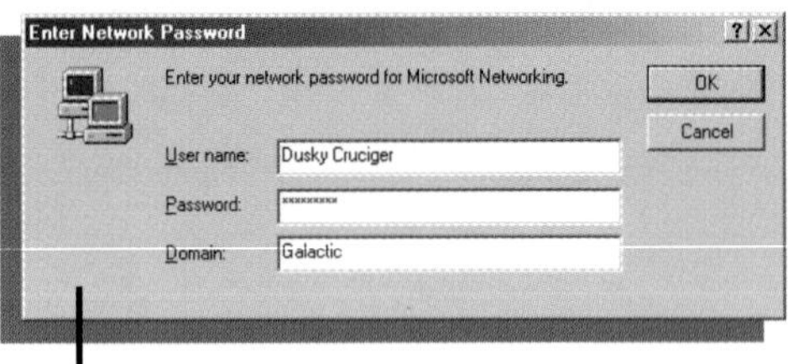

The Network Logon. The Domain name won't be shown if the computer isn't configured to connect to a client-server network.

SEE ALSO: For information about what to do if you're having problems when you try to quit Windows Me, see "Quitting When You're Stuck" on page 66.

For information about changing the way you log on, see "Changing the Logon" on page 182.

Change Users

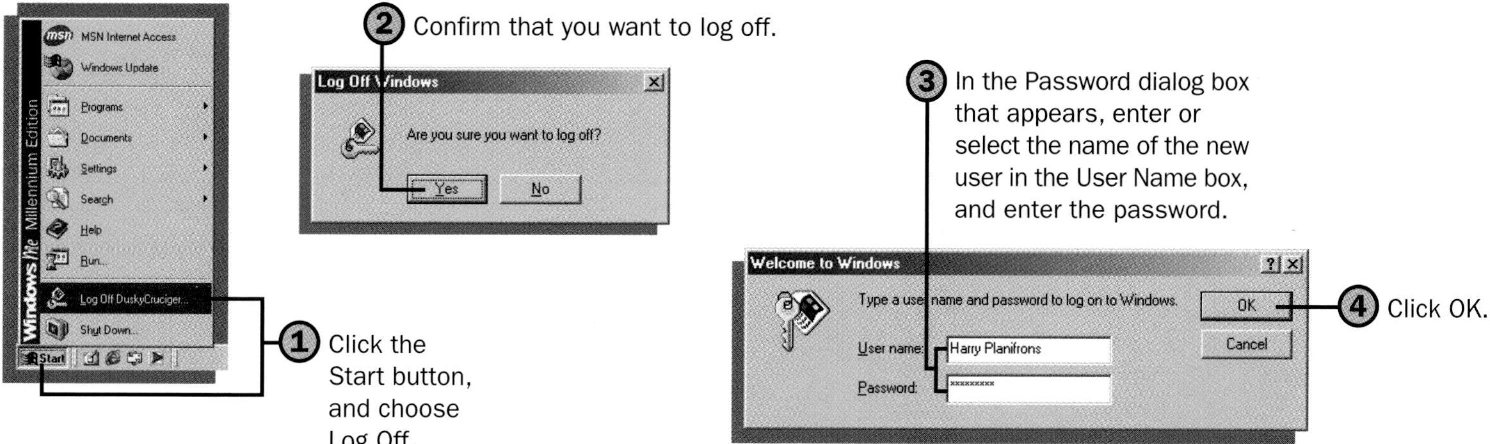

1. Click the Start button, and choose Log Off.
2. Confirm that you want to log off.
3. In the Password dialog box that appears, enter or select the name of the new user in the User Name box, and enter the password.
4. Click OK.

Shut Down Your Computer

1. Click the Start button, and choose Shut Down.
2. Click to select the appropriate option. The options available depend on the configuration of your computer.

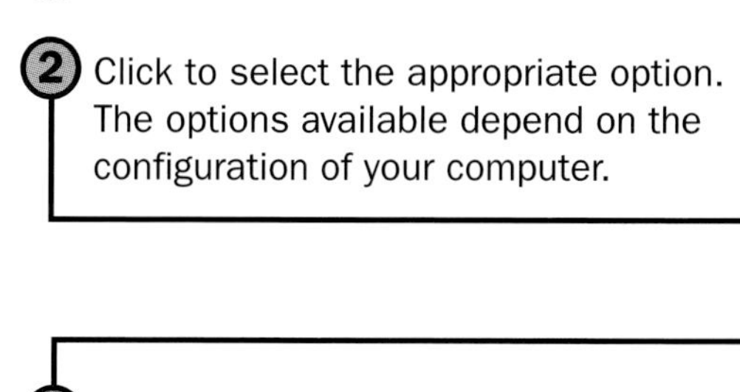

Shut down: Exits Windows Me and prepares the computer to be turned off.

Restart: Exits and then restarts the computer.

Stand by: Switches the computer to low-power mode.

Hibernate: Records onto the hard disk all the items contained in the computer's memory and then shuts down the computer. All items are restored when the computer is restarted.

3. Click OK. If you chose to shut down, the computer will probably shut itself down. If it doesn't, wait for the message that tells you it's safe to turn off your computer, and then turn it off.

Starting a Program

The real work of an operating system is to run software programs. Windows Me comes with a wide variety of programs, and you can install additional (and often more powerful) ones. Most programs are listed on the Start menu, but Windows Me gives you several ways to start your programs, so you can choose the way that's easiest for you or the one you like best.

Start a Program

1. Do any of the following:
   - Click the Start button, point to Programs, point to any relevant program groups to display additional submenus, and choose the program you want.
   - Point to and then double-click the program icon on the Desktop.
   - Open the My Computer folder, navigate to the folder that contains the program you want, and double-click the program.
   - Insert the CD that contains a program that's designed to run from the CD, and wait for the program to start.
   - Click the Start button, choose Run, type the full path and filename of the program, and click OK.
2. Use the program, and close it when you've finished.

TIP: The programs listed in the table at the right are only some of the programs that come with Windows Me. You'll find descriptions of some of the other useful or popular programs elsewhere in this book.

Frequently Used Windows Me Programs

Program	Purpose
Address Book	Stores names, addresses, and other contact information
Calculator	Does arithmetic calculations and complex mathematical calculations.
Character Map	Inserts special characters from installed fonts.
Imaging	Views, scans, annotates, and prints images.
Internet Explorer	Functions as a web browser and an HTML document viewer.
Magnifier	Magnifies sections of the screen.
Narrator	Describes and reads aloud the screen contents.
NetMeeting	Facilitates teleconferencing over the Internet or over a network.
Notepad	Creates, edits, and views text documents.
On-Screen Keyboard	Allows keyboard input using the mouse or other pointing device.
Outlook Express	Provides e-mail, newsgroup, and directory services.
Paint	Creates and edits bitmap pictures; imports and edits scanned images and digital pictures.
Sound Recorder	Creates and plays digital sound files.
Windows Media Player	Plays sound, music, and video.
Windows Movie Maker	Converts, edits, organizes, and distributes audio and video files.
WordPad	Creates, edits, and views text, Rich Text Format, and Word documents.

Managing a Program Window

"Managing" a window means bossing it around: you can move it, change its size, and open and close it. Most programs are contained in windows. Although these windows might have some different features, most program windows have more similarities than differences.

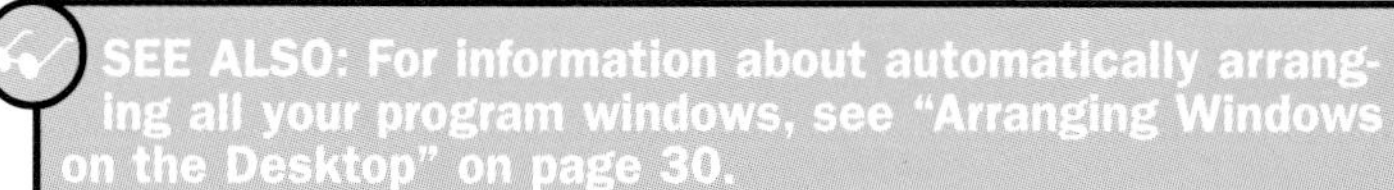

Use the Buttons to Switch Between Sizes

The program's title bar

Buttons for switching between window sizes

1. Click the Maximize button, and the window enlarges and fills the screen. (If the window is already maximized, you won't see the Maximize button.)
2. Click the Restore button, and the window gets smaller. (If the window is already restored, you won't see the Restore button.)
3. Click the Minimize button, and the window disappears but you can see its name on a button on the taskbar.
4. Click the window's name on the taskbar, and the window zooms back to the size it was before you minimized it.

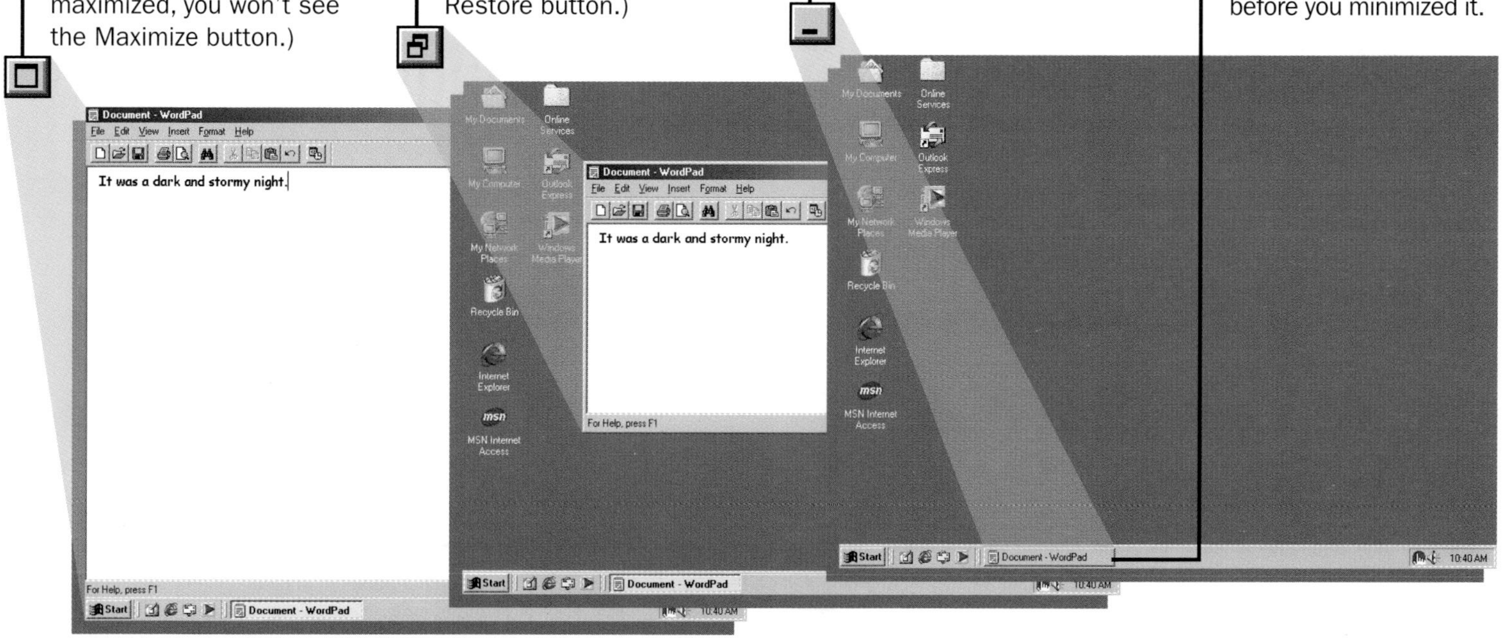

SEE ALSO: For information about dragging items with the mouse, see "Mouse Maneuvers" on page 14.

TIP: To see the contents of a window when you move it rather than seeing a blank placeholder rectangle, right-click the Desktop, choose Properties from the shortcut menu, and, on the Effects tab, turn on the Show Window Contents While Dragging check box.

TIP: You can't manually resize a maximized window, so if the window you want to resize is currently maximized, click the Restore button.

TIP: Move your mouse over a side border to change the window's width, over a top or bottom border to change the window's height, and over a corner to change both height and width.

Use the Mouse to Resize a Window

1. Move the mouse over one of the borders of the window until the mouse pointer changes into a two-headed arrow. Drag the window border until the window is the size you want. The directions of the arrowheads show you the directions in which you can move the window border.

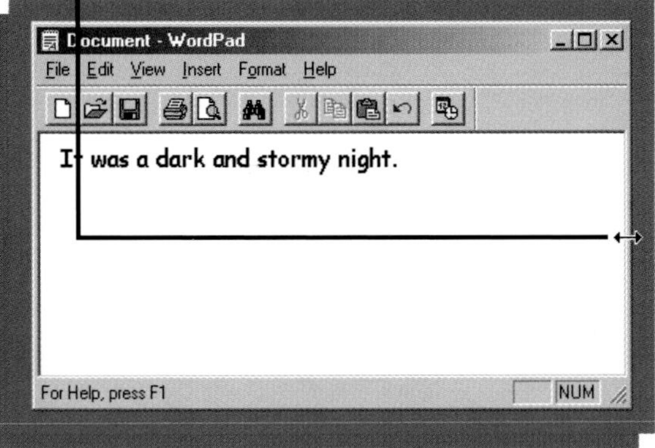

Move a Window

1. Point to the title bar.

2. Drag the window to a new location.

TRY THIS: Double-click the title bar of a maximized window to restore the window to its original size. Double-click the title bar again to return the window to its maximized size. Now press Alt+Spacebar to open the window's Control menu, and choose the action you want from the menu.

Using Shortcut Menus for Quick Results

Windows Me and the programs that work with it were designed to be intuitive—that is, they anticipate what you're likely to want to do when you're working on a particular task, and they place the appropriate commands on a shortcut menu that you open by clicking the *right* mouse button. These shortcut menus are *dynamic,* which means that they change depending on the task in progress.

Use a Shortcut Menu Command

1. Right-click an item.

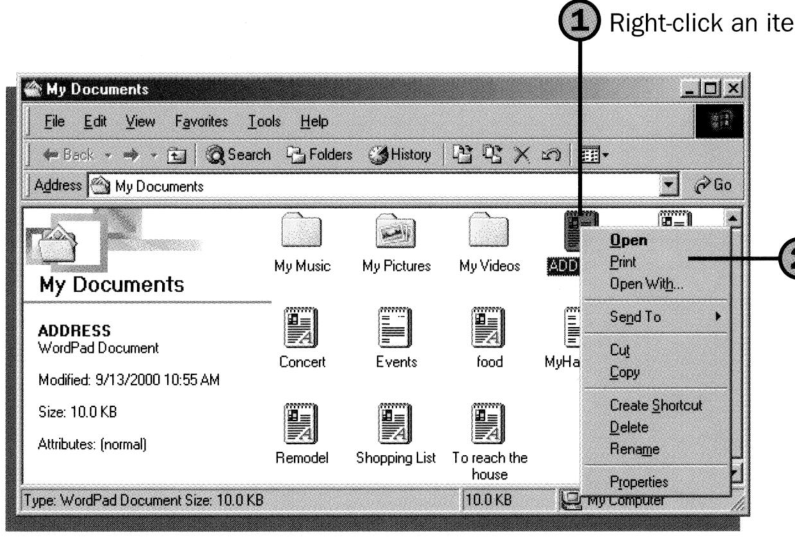

2. Choose a command from the shortcut menu to accomplish the task at hand. If the item or action you want isn't on the shortcut menu, do any of the following:

- From the shortcut menu, choose any items whose names have arrows next to them to see whether the item or action you want is on one of the shortcut menu's submenus.
- Check to be sure that you right-clicked the proper item.
- Verify that what you want to do can be accomplished from the item you right-clicked.

TIP: If you're not sure how to accomplish what you want to do, right-click the item in question, and you'll often see an appropriate command on the shortcut menu.

Mouse Maneuvers

Navigating with a mouse is like traveling in a helicopter: you can lift off from any spot and set down wherever you want. Using the keyboard is like taking the scenic route—you get to explore the road less traveled, and you might even come across features and techniques that are new to you. But to finish your tasks as quickly as possible—and to take advantage of some of the best features of Windows Me—give your mouse the job!

Before you fly off on your mouse wings, you might need some Mouse Basics. Here at Mouse School you'll learn to point, click, double-click, right-click, select, multiple-select, and drag with your mouse. Don't be too surprised if the mouse acts a bit differently from the way you expect it to. Windows Me gives you numerous options for customizing the way your mouse works, so be patient, experiment a bit, and read "Customizing Your Mouse" on page 146 for information about setting up Windows Me so that your mouse works the way you want it to.

Point: Move the mouse until the mouse pointer (either a small arrow-shaped pointer or a tiny hand) is pointing to the item you want.

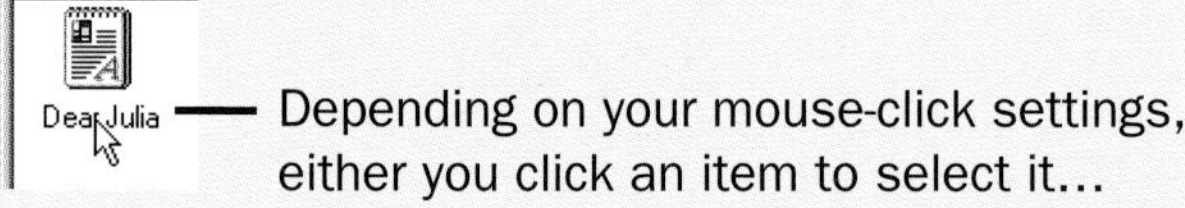

Depending on your mouse-click settings, either you click an item to select it...

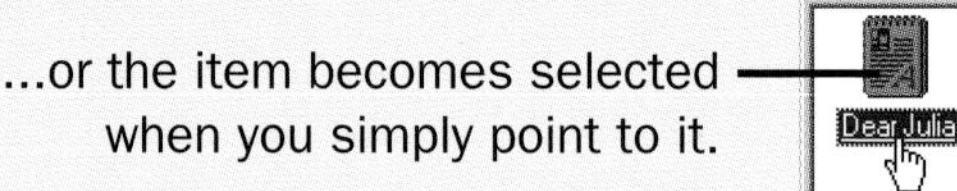

...or the item becomes selected when you simply point to it.

Click: Point to the item you want, and then quickly press down and release the left mouse button.

Double-click: Point to the item you want, and then quickly press down and release the left mouse button twice, being careful not to move the mouse between clicks.

Right-click: Point to the item you want, and then quickly press down and release the right mouse button.

Select: Point to an item, and click to select it. To select a web-style icon, point to it but don't click. A selected item is usually a different color from other similar items or is surrounded by a frame.

Multiple-select: To select a list of adjacent or sequential items, click the first item, hold down the Shift key, and click the last item. To select or deselect *nonadjacent* items, hold down the Ctrl key and click each item you want. (Only certain windows and dialog boxes permit multiple selection.)

Drag: Select the item you want. Keeping the mouse pointer on the selected item, hold down the left mouse button and move the mouse until you've "dragged" the item to the desired location; then release the left mouse button.

Point to the item...

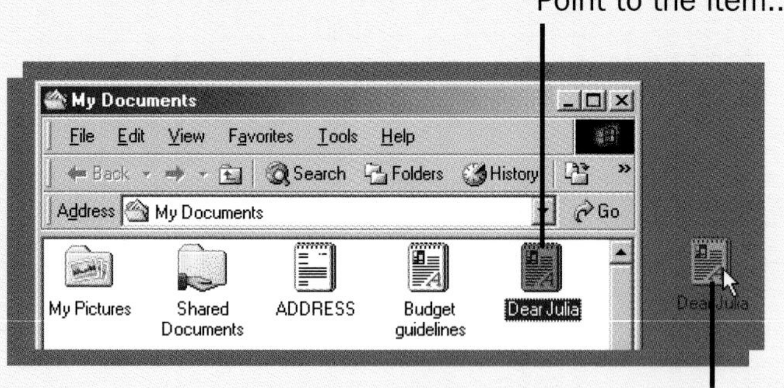

...and drag it to a new location.

Getting Help

What are big and colorful; packed with information, procedures, shortcuts, and links to online information; and sadly underutilized? The Help programs! Of course, they couldn't possibly replace this book, but you can use them to find concise step-by-step procedures for diagnosing and overcoming problems, and to explore many aspects of managing Windows Me. There are three basic types of help: the Help And Support Center, Program Help, and dialog box Help.

Use the Help And Support Center

1. Click the Start button, and choose Help to open the Help And Support Center.

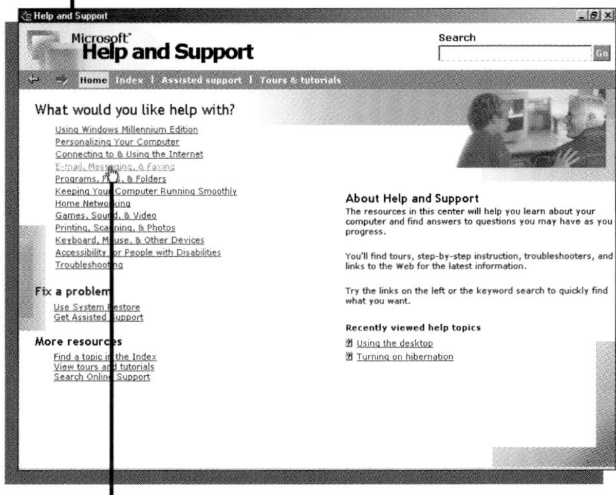

2. Click a link to the main topic of interest. Continue clicking links until you see the topic you want to explore.
3. Click the item of interest.
4. Read the information.

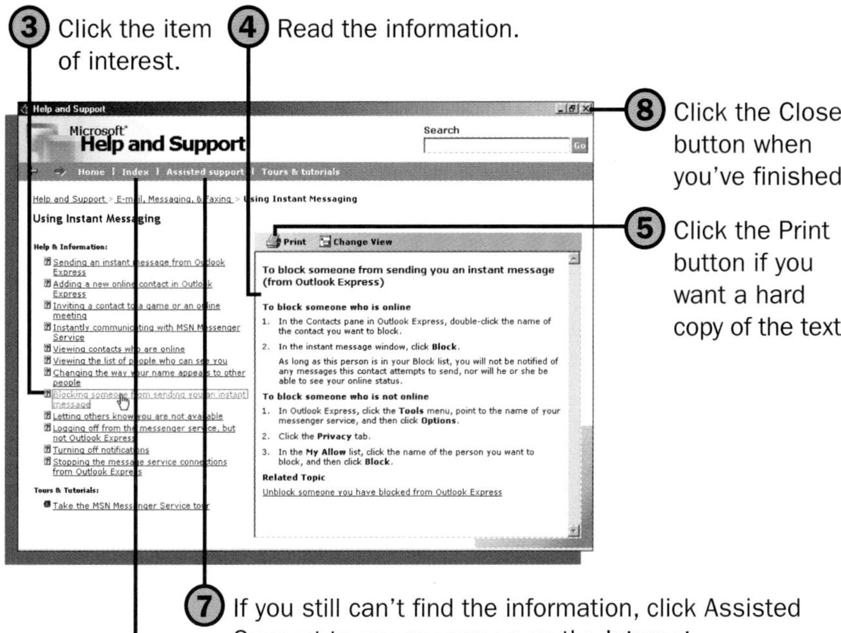

5. Click the Print button if you want a hard copy of the text.
6. If you can't find the information you need, click Index, and search for help using keywords.
7. If you still can't find the information, click Assisted Support to use resources on the Internet.
8. Click the Close button when you've finished.

TIP: Once you've found the information you want to read as you step through procedures, click the Change View button to display only the relevant information and hide all the extra material.

Use Program Help

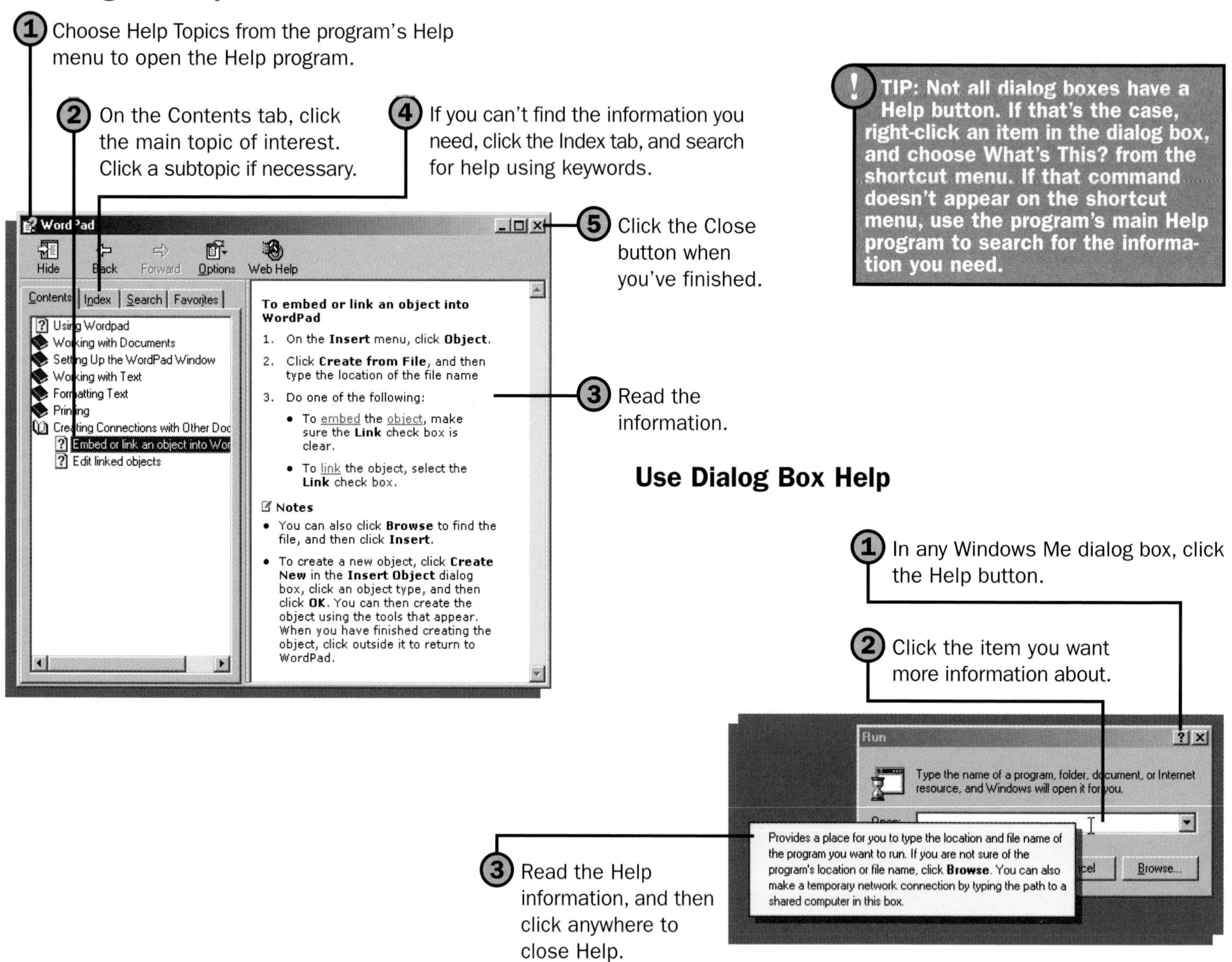

1. Choose Help Topics from the program's Help menu to open the Help program.
2. On the Contents tab, click the main topic of interest. Click a subtopic if necessary.
3. Read the information.
4. If you can't find the information you need, click the Index tab, and search for help using keywords.
5. Click the Close button when you've finished.

TIP: Not all dialog boxes have a Help button. If that's the case, right-click an item in the dialog box, and choose What's This? from the shortcut menu. If that command doesn't appear on the shortcut menu, use the program's main Help program to search for the information you need.

Use Dialog Box Help

1. In any Windows Me dialog box, click the Help button.
2. Click the item you want more information about.
3. Read the Help information, and then click anywhere to close Help.

Accessing and Organizing

In this section

The Microsoft Windows Millennium Edition Desktop is a "gateway" through which you can access your files and folders, your computer's drives, the computers that are part of your network, and, of course, the Internet itself. Among the items on your Desktop are the My Documents folder, where you can store and access all your documents; the My Computer icon, from which you can explore as deep into your computer's drives as you want to go; and, of course, Internet Explorer, through which you can connect to the Internet.

Windows Me supplies the framework—a basic file structure of drives and folders, which you can leave as is if it's compatible with the way you work. Otherwise, reorganize! Create your own system of folders and subfolders. Organize the files within those folders—alphabetically, or by size, type, or date—and view them with large or small icons, as detailed lists, and so on. If you delete a file or folder by mistake, you can easily recover it. And if you can't find a document that you know is somewhere in your computer, let Windows Me find it for you! Reduce the file size of your documents by using compression folders, which are invaluable if you have large graphics files. Organize your Desktop by specifying how you want your windows to be arranged; keep the Desktop uncluttered by rearranging icons or *minimizing* windows and storing them on the taskbar. Locate people or businesses on the Internet, set your home page, and save and organize in your Favorites list the sites you want to revisit.

Exploring Your Computer

Sitting on your Desktop are the My Documents folder—a personal storage area where you can store and access your documents—and the My Computer folder, which is the gateway to your computer's contents. The My Computer folder contains icons for all your local storage areas: removable disk drives, hard disks, CD drives, and so on. From here you can venture as deep into the folder structure of your computer as you dare.

SEE ALSO: For information about creating personalized settings for each user, see "Adding Users" on page 183.

For information about changing the way folders are displayed, see "Windows Views" on page 22, "Organizing with Folders" on page 25, and "Customizing a Folder Window" on page 144.

For information about accessing files and folders that are located on a network, see "Exploring Your Network" on page 38.

Open My Documents

1. Double-click My Documents on the Desktop.
2. Click a file to select it. 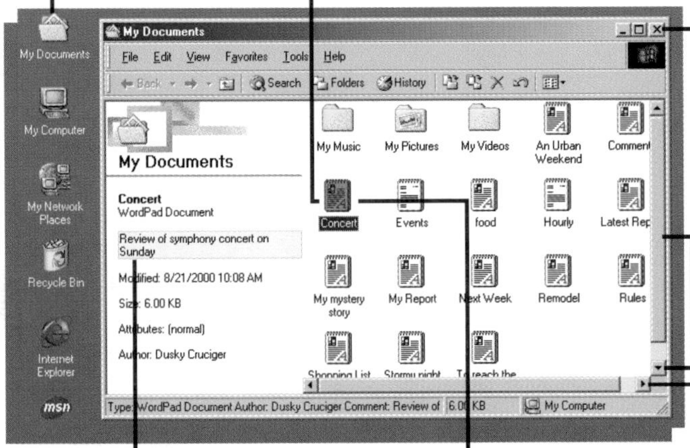
3. Read the description of the selected file. If you can't see all the information, increase the size of the window until the information is visible.
4. Open, move, copy, delete, or rename the file if you want.
5. Use the scroll bars, if necessary, to view all the documents. Click the scroll arrows to scroll a small increment at a time, or drag the scroll box to scroll a greater distance.
6. Click the Close button when you've finished.

TIP: If more than one person uses your computer, each user can have a separate My Documents folder, as well as other personalized settings.

TIP: The My Music folder is automatically created to hold music you've copied using the Windows Media Player. The My Videos folder is automatically created to hold movies you've created using the Windows Movie Maker.

Open Any Folder

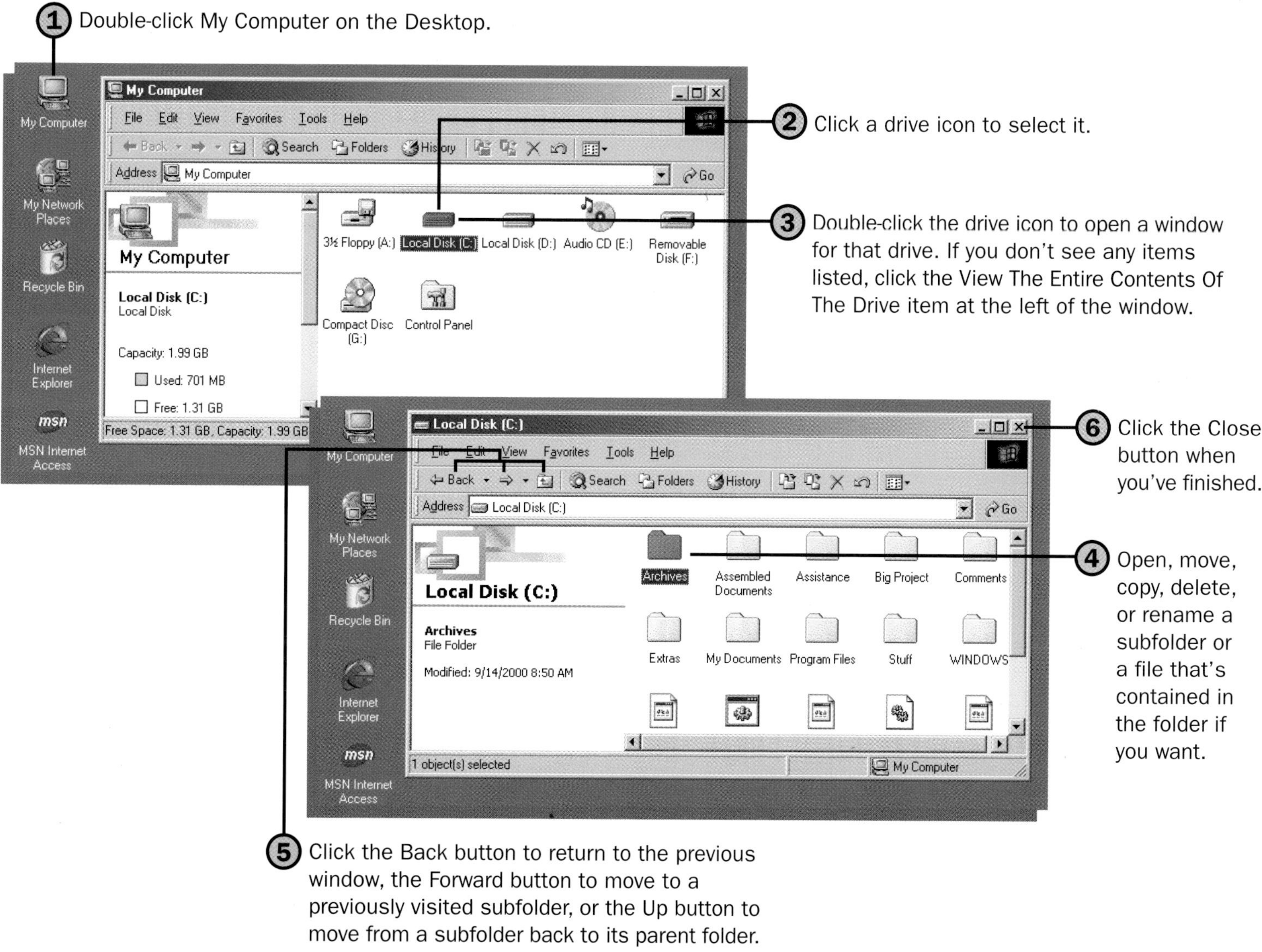

1. Double-click My Computer on the Desktop.
2. Click a drive icon to select it.
3. Double-click the drive icon to open a window for that drive. If you don't see any items listed, click the View The Entire Contents Of The Drive item at the left of the window.
4. Open, move, copy, delete, or rename a subfolder or a file that's contained in the folder if you want.
5. Click the Back button to return to the previous window, the Forward button to move to a previously visited subfolder, or the Up button to move from a subfolder back to its parent folder.
6. Click the Close button when you've finished.

Opening a Document

Documents are the files that contain your data—formatted or plain text, numbers, pictures, even complex databases—and they work within specific programs. When you open a document, Windows Me starts the associated program (if it's not already running) and opens the document in that program. You can also tell Windows Me to open the document in a different program.

SEE ALSO: For information about displaying file extensions, see "Customizing a Folder Window" on page 144.

Open a Document

1. Open the folder (My Documents or My Computer, for example) that contains the document.
2. Double-click the document to open it. The type of icon that's displayed indicates the program in which the document will open.
3. Wait for the program to start and the document to load.
4. Work on the document.
5. Use the program's File menu commands to save (if necessary) and close the document, and to open any other documents you want to work on in that program.

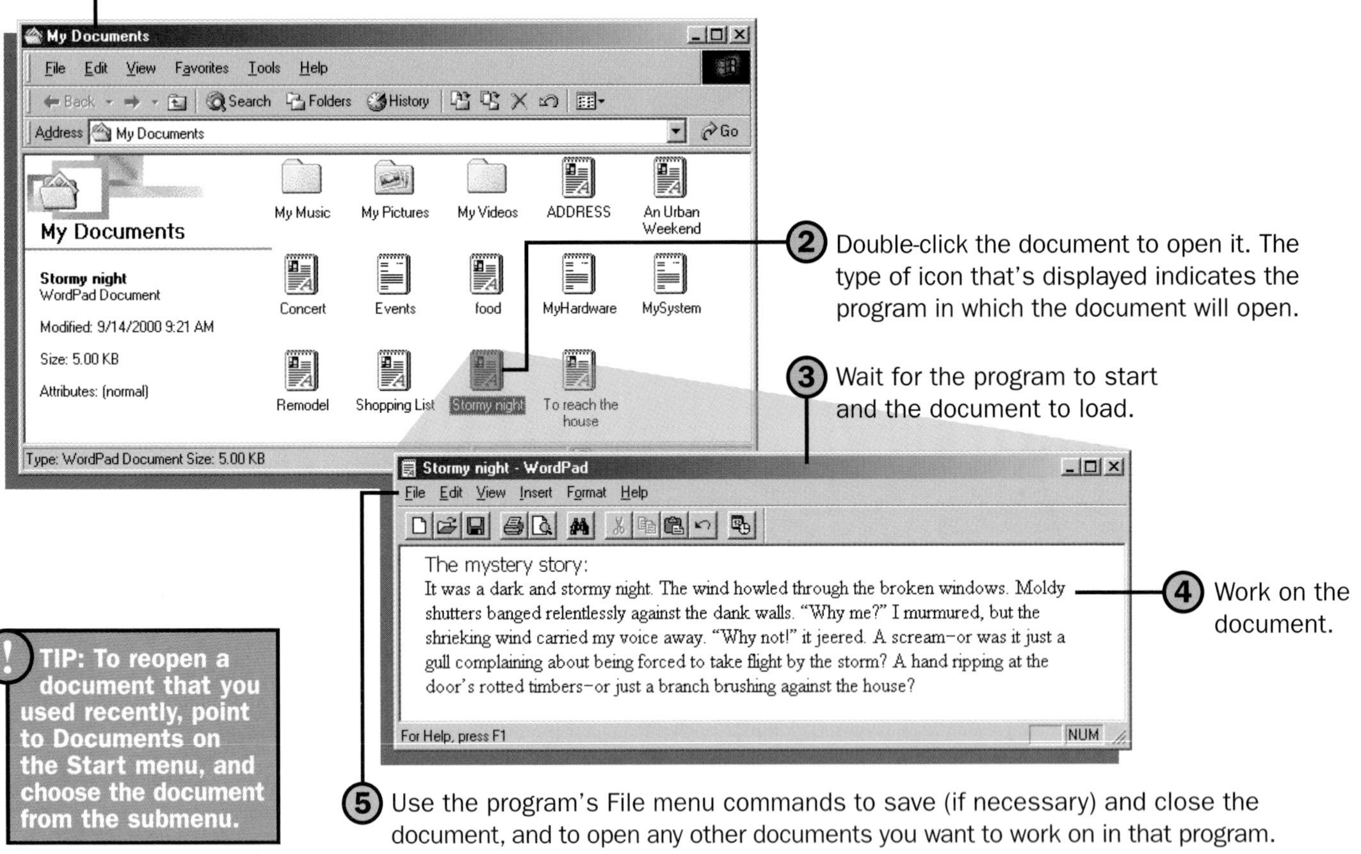

TIP: To reopen a document that you used recently, point to Documents on the Start menu, and choose the document from the submenu.

Open a Document in a Different Program

1. Open the folder that contains the document.

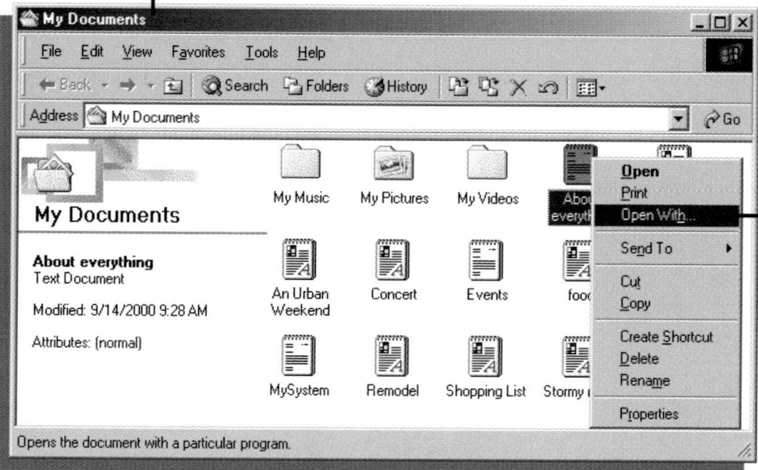

2. Right-click the document, and choose Open With from the shortcut menu. If the Open With command displays a submenu, either select a program from the list or click the Open With command.

TIP: Windows Me uses the file extension (the last two or three characters after the period in the filename) to determine which program is used. If a document has no extension or one that Windows Me doesn't recognize, Windows Me will ask you which program should be used. Most file extensions aren't visible in folder windows unless you change the way information is displayed.

TRY THIS: Locate the text document you want, right-click it, and choose Open With. Find WordPad in the list, and click OK. Close WordPad, right-click the document again, and point to Open With. Notice that there's now a submenu listing the default program (Notepad) and the program you chose to use (WordPad). From the submenu, click Choose Program, select Internet Explorer, and click OK. Close the program when you've finished. Note that from now on, all you need to do is choose the program from the Open With submenu.

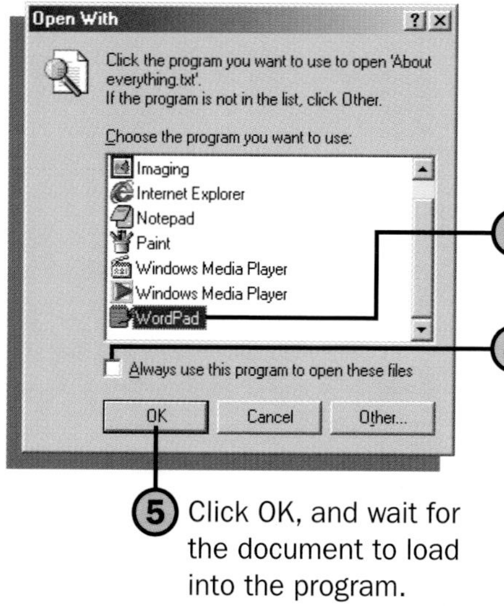

3. Select the program in which you want to open the document.
4. Turn on this check box if you always want all documents of this type to open using the program you specify, or turn off the check box if you want to open the document this time only in this program.
5. Click OK, and wait for the document to load into the program.

Windows Views

Windows Me can display the contents of a folder window in one of five available views. You can choose the view you want from the View menu or by clicking the View button on the Standard Buttons toolbar. You'll probably want to experiment to see which view is best suited for your work and for the contents of the folder. For example, you might want to use Large Icons view in a folder that contains only a few files of different types, Details view when you're looking for files that were created on a specific date, or Thumbnails view when you're working with pictures.

Thumbnails view is quite different from the other views. Some folders—My Computer and Control Panel, for example—don't offer this view because it's not a useful view in these folders. Thumbnails view also displays an icon instead of a preview if Windows Me doesn't have the appropriate graphics-conversion filters installed or if a preview of a document wasn't saved with the document.

Once you've selected a view, Windows Me offers more options. In each view, you can arrange the way the files are sorted—for example, you can group them by file type or order them by date. In all views, you do this by choosing the arrangement you want from the View menu. In Details view, you can also click the top of a column to sort by that column.

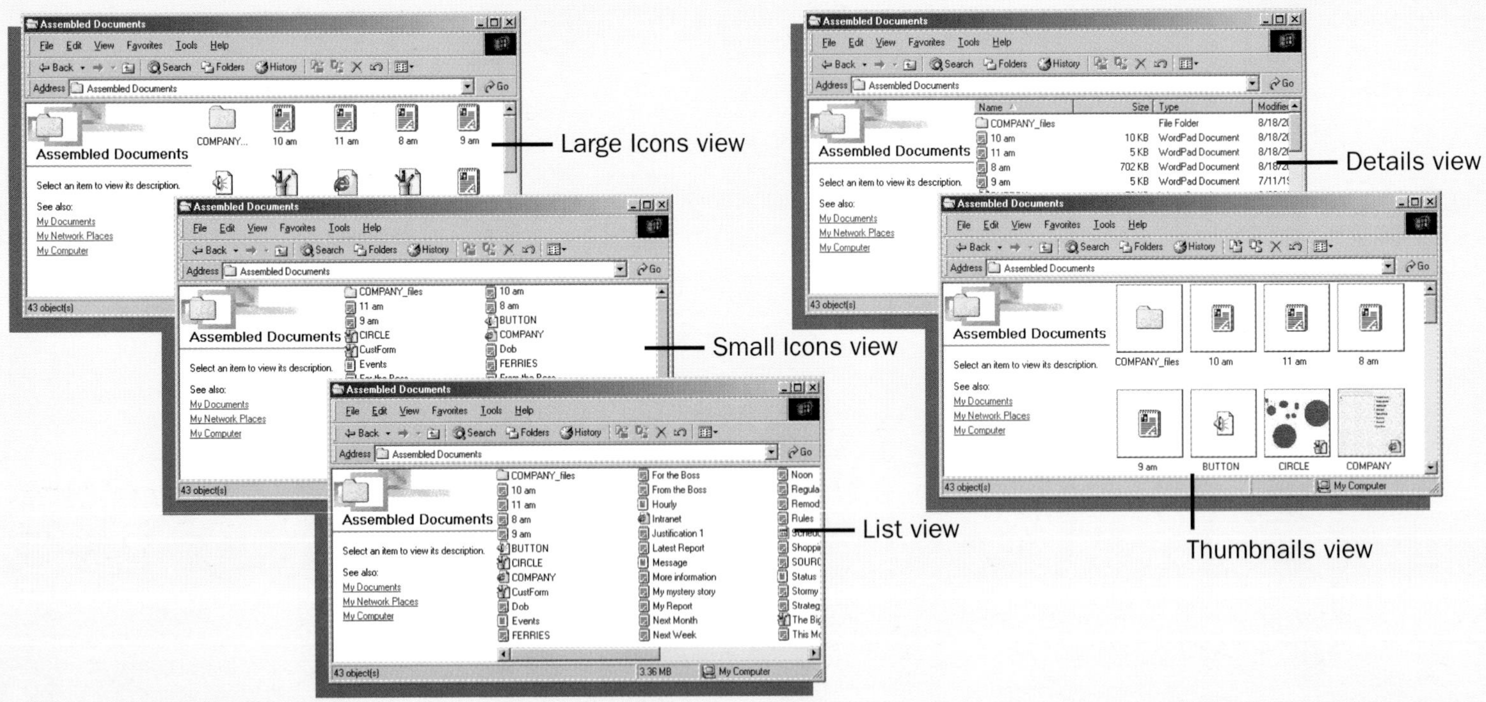

Organizing Your Files

If you have a limited number of files, you can easily keep them all in a single folder, such as the My Documents folder. However, if you have many files, or files dealing with different projects, you'll probably want to organize them by placing them in individual folders.

TIP: To select multiple files, hold down the Ctrl key as you click each file to be selected.

TIP: To delete a file or a group of files, select the file or the group of files, and press the Delete key.

Move or Copy a File

1. Open the window containing the file or files you want to move or copy.

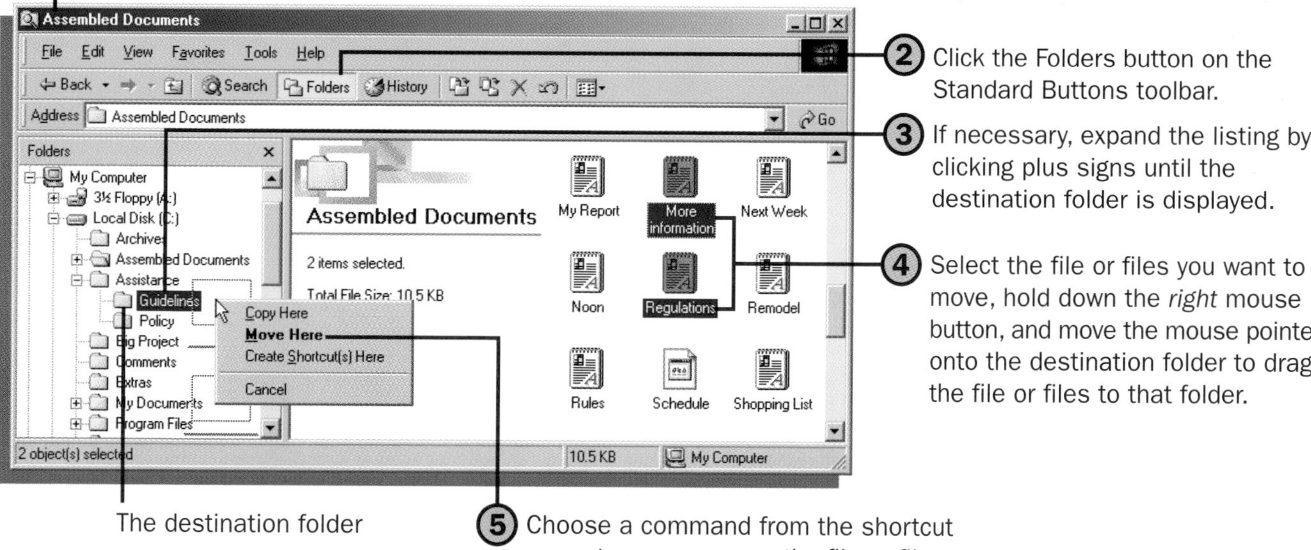

2. Click the Folders button on the Standard Buttons toolbar.
3. If necessary, expand the listing by clicking plus signs until the destination folder is displayed.
4. Select the file or files you want to move, hold down the *right* mouse button, and move the mouse pointer onto the destination folder to drag the file or files to that folder.

The destination folder

5. Choose a command from the shortcut menu to move or copy the file or files.

TIP: If you drag a file while holding down the left mouse button, the file will be *moved* if both its source and destination are on the same drive, but the file will be *copied* if its source and destination are on different drives or in a network folder.

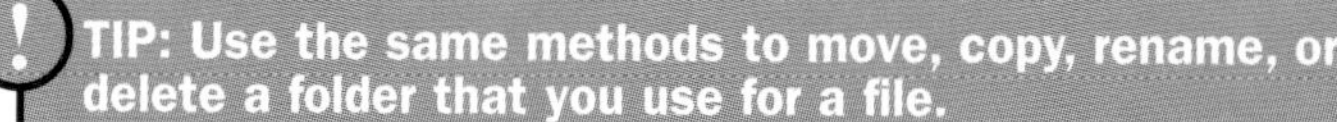

TIP: Use the same methods to move, copy, rename, or delete a folder that you use for a file.

Rename a File

1. Right-click the file.

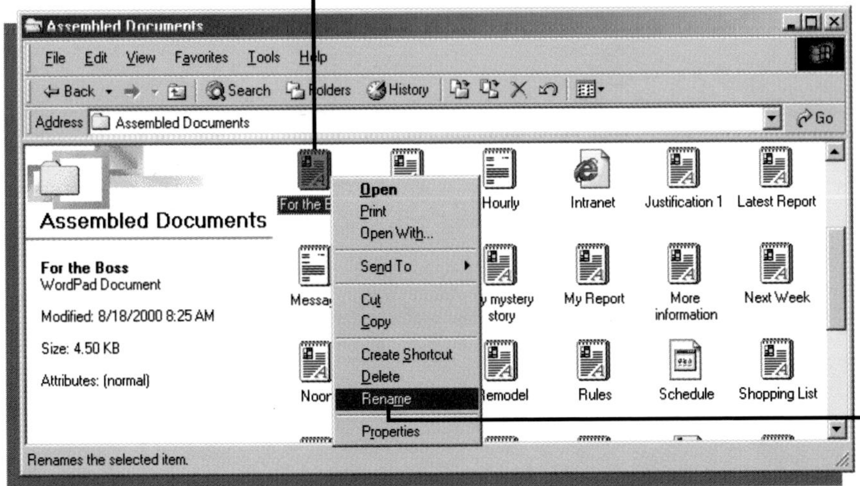

2. Choose Rename from the shortcut menu.

TIP: Filenames (or folder names) can be as long as 255 characters, but, because a long name is often truncated by a program, a descriptive short name is a better choice. You can use spaces and underscores in names, but you can't use the * : < > | ? " \ or / characters.

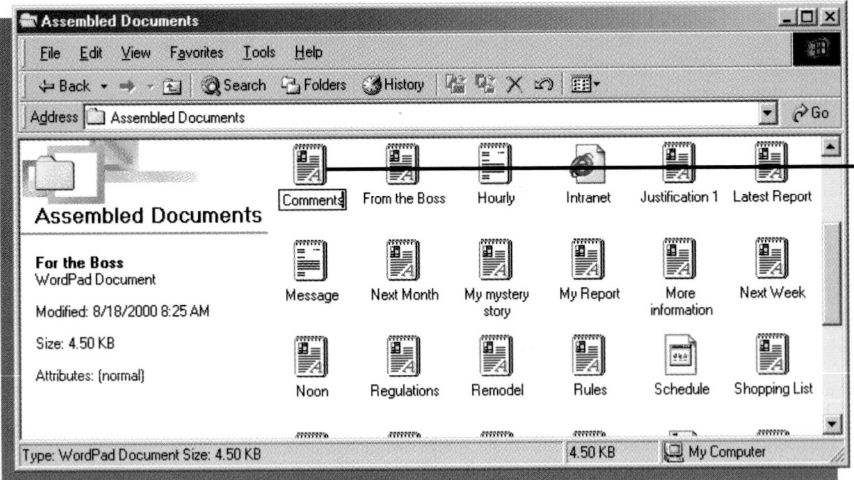

3. With the filename selected, type a new name, or click to position the insertion point and then edit the name. Press Enter when the name is correct.

TRY THIS: Select a file whose name you want to edit, and press the F2 key. Use the arrow keys to move the insertion point within the filename, and edit the name the way you want. Press Enter when the name is correct.

Organizing with Folders

Windows Me provides the basic filing structure—drives and ready-made folders such as My Documents and Program Files. You can customize the filing system by adding your own folders and then moving files into the folders.

SEE ALSO: For information about renaming files or folders, and moving files into a folder, see "Organizing Your Files" on page 23.

Create a Folder

TRY THIS: In a folder in which you want to create a subfolder, press the Alt, F, W, and F keys in succession to create the new folder, and then name it.

1. Open the window of the folder, drive, or other location that is to contain the folder, point to a blank part of the window, and right-click.

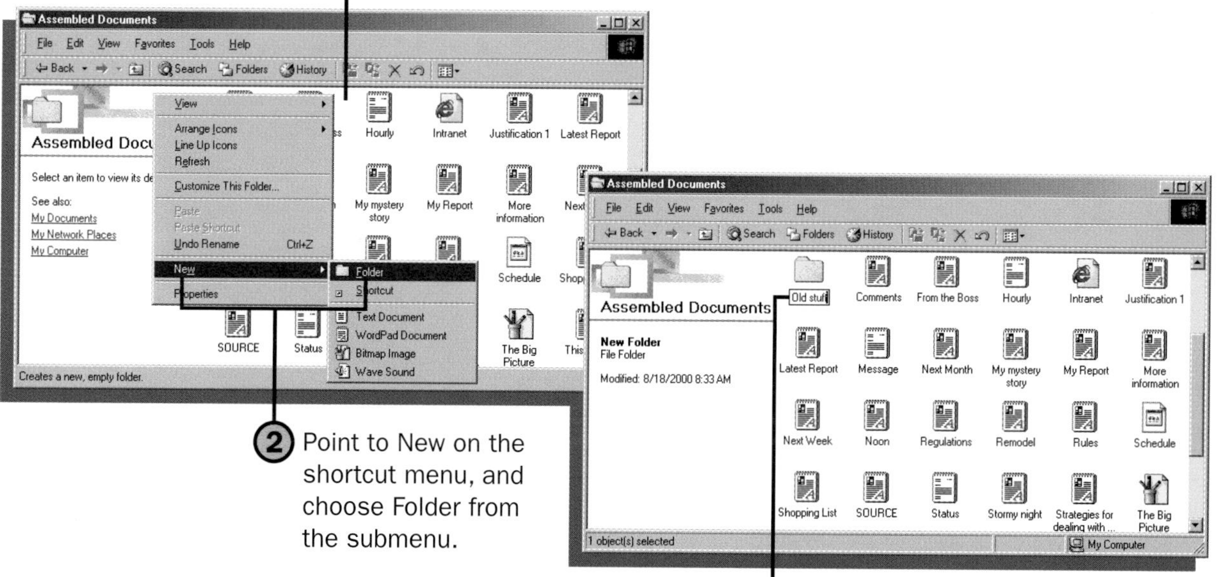

2. Point to New on the shortcut menu, and choose Folder from the submenu.

3. Type a name for the new folder, and press Enter when the name is correct.

TIP: There are some locations in which you can't create your own folders—the Printers and the Control Panel folders, for example. In those cases, there won't be a New command on the shortcut menu that appears when you right-click.

TIP: To delete a folder, select it and press the Delete key. The folder and all its contents will be deleted.

Recovering a Deleted Item

If you accidentally delete a file, folder, or shortcut from your computer's hard drive, you can quickly recover the item either by undoing your action immediately or by restoring the deleted item from the Recycle Bin. The Recycle Bin holds all the files you've deleted from your hard disk(s) until you empty the bin or until it gets so full that the oldest files are deleted automatically. You can't recover files that you've deleted from a floppy disk.

TIP: When you've deleted a folder, you have to restore the entire folder. You can't open a deleted folder in the Recycle Bin and restore selected files.

Restore an Item

1. Double-click the Recycle Bin icon on the Desktop to open the Recycle Bin window.
2. Select the item or items to be recovered, and right-click.
3. Choose Restore from the shortcut menu.
4. Click the Close button to close the Recycle Bin.

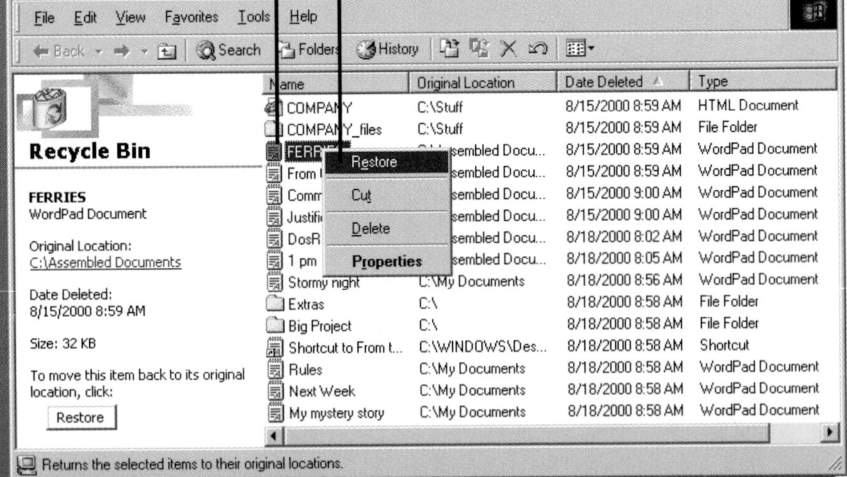

Undo a Deletion

1. Point to a blank part of the Desktop or to a blank part of any folder window, and right-click.
2. Choose Undo Delete from the shortcut menu.

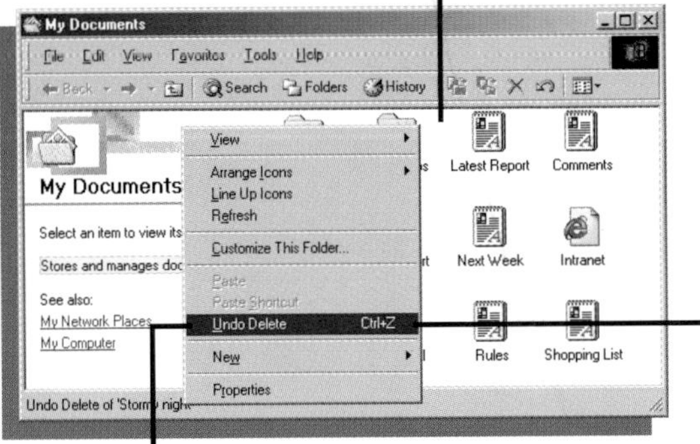

The command is available only if the deletion was your most recent action.

TIP: Windows Me remembers as many as three of your most recent actions, so if you executed an action after you deleted something, undo the action first and then undo the deletion.

Compressing Files

Compressed folders are special folders that use compressing software to decrease the size of the files they contain. Compressed folders are useful for reducing the file size of standard documents and programs, but they're invaluable when you're storing large graphics files such as bitmaps or when you're transferring large files by e-mail.

Create and Use a Compressed Folder

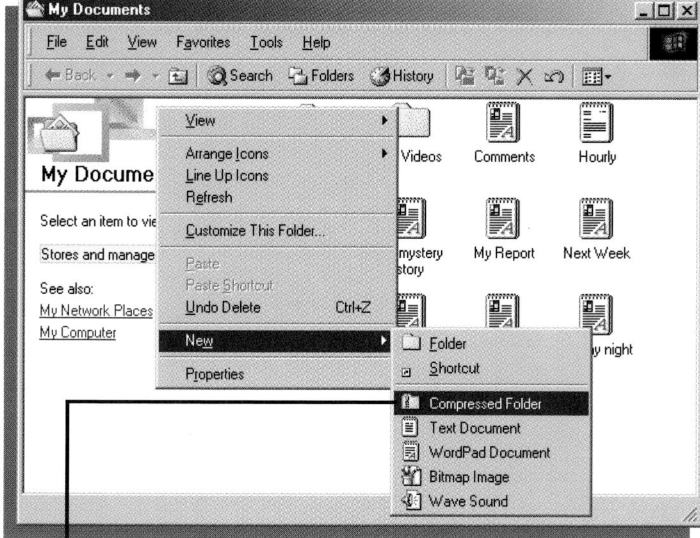

1. Right-click a blank spot in the folder window of the drive or folder into which you want to put the compressed folder, point to New on the shortcut menu, and choose Compressed Folder from the submenu.

SEE ALSO: For information about installing the Compressed Folders component if it's not on the shortcut menu, see "Adding or Removing Windows Me Components" on page 170.

For information about encrypting compressed folders for increased security, see "Protecting Your Files with a Password" on page 166.

2. Type a name for the compressed folder, and press Enter. (The zippered-folder icon denotes a compressed folder.)

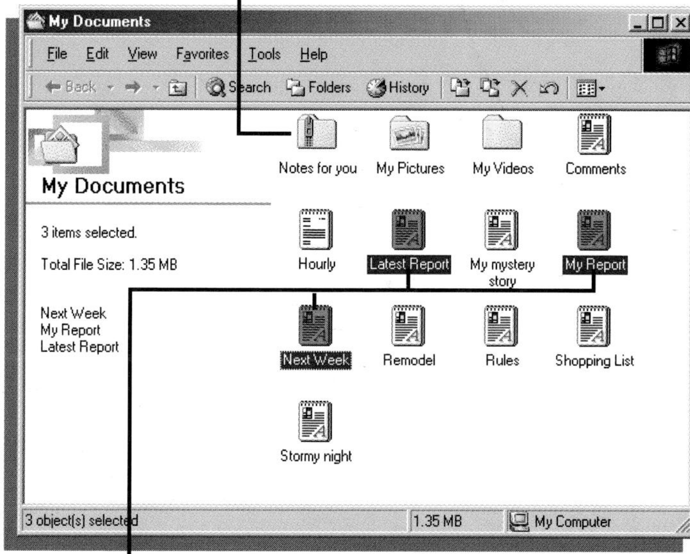

3. Drag selected files onto the compressed-folder icon to copy and compress the files.

Compress a Single File

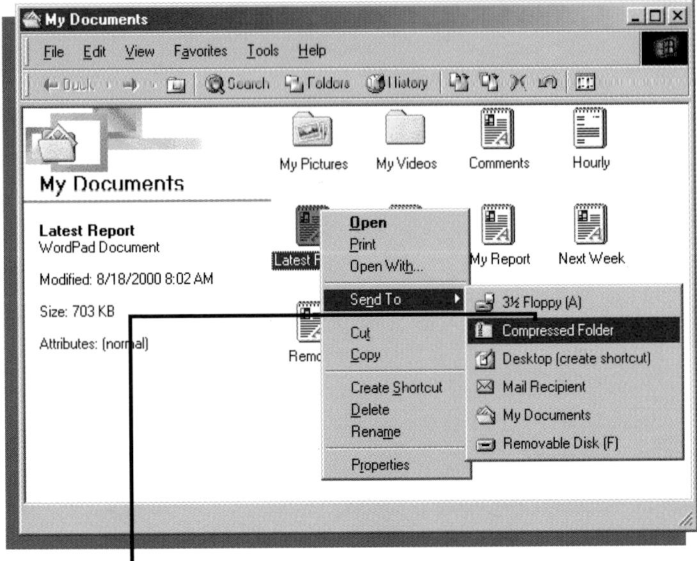

1. Right-click the file, point to Send To, and choose Compressed Folder from the shortcut menu.

TIP: Compressed folders are ZIP-type compressed files and are compatible with compressed files created using a ZIP compression program.

TIP: Compressed folders preserve the contents of most files, but it's possible that you could lose data when you're using certain file formats. It's wise to test your file format in a compressed folder before you move valuable files into that folder.

Finding a Document

When you want to open a document that you know is on your computer but that you just can't find (or don't want to waste the time looking for), let Windows Me do the work for you. All you need to do is provide a hint or two and then wait for Windows Me to return a list of possible documents. Then you can select the document you want from the list.

TIP: Four Explorer bars—Search, Folders, History, and Favorites—can be displayed in folder windows. Only the first three can be displayed from the Standard Buttons toolbar, but all four can be displayed from the Explorer Bar submenu of the View menu. However, only one Explorer bar can be displayed at a time.

Advanced Search Options

Option	Search parameters
Date	The date range during which files or folders were created, modified, or last accessed
Type	The file type based on the file's extension and the programs registered with Windows Me, or the folder type
Size	The minimum or maximum size of the file, in kilobytes
Advanced Options	Searches all of the folder subfolders specified in the Look In box; specifies whether the search must match only the capitalization you used for the filename or folder name

Find a Document

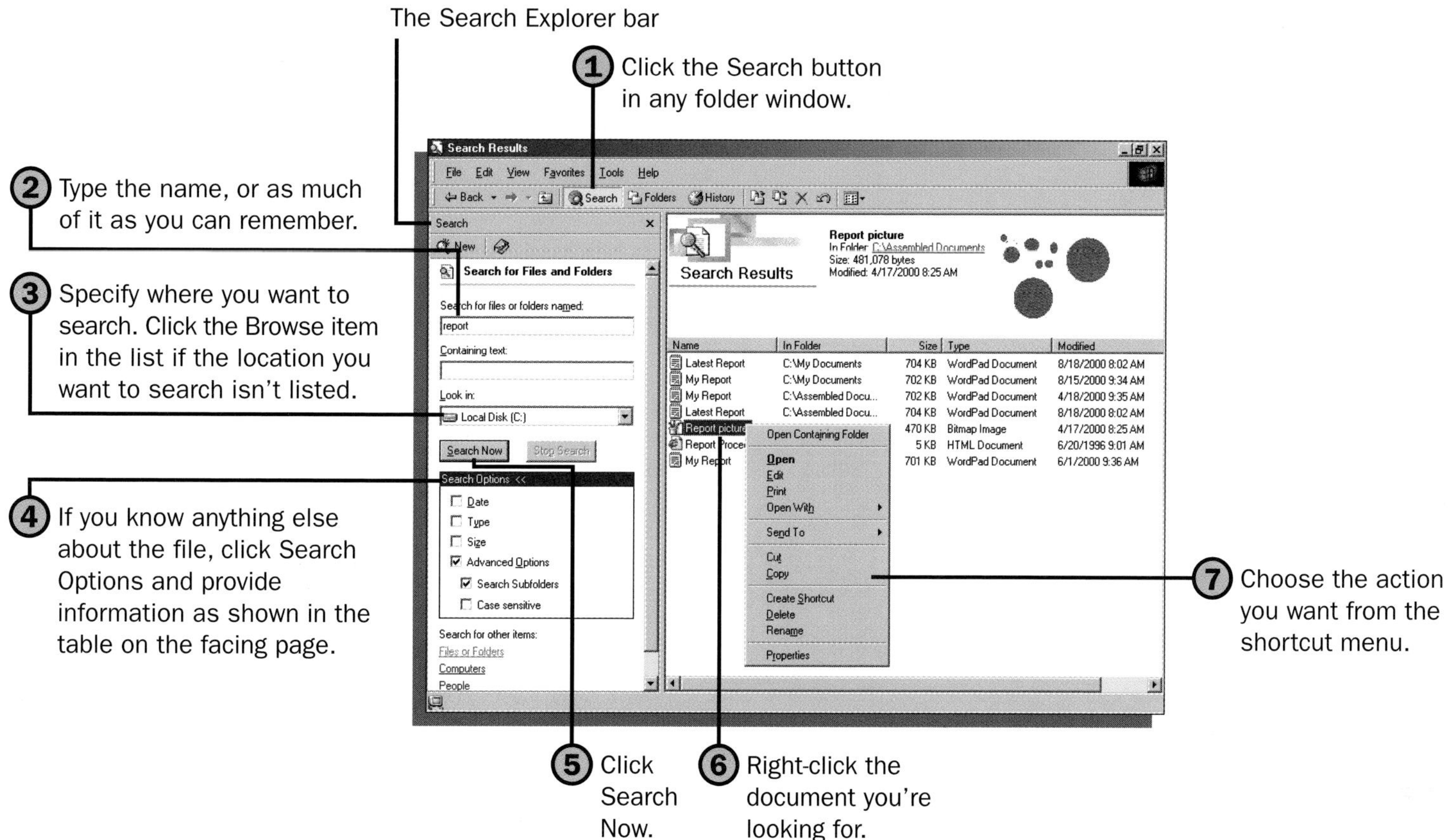

TIP: You can search for a document based on some of its text, but a search of this type is usually very slow.

Arranging Windows on the Desktop

When you have several windows open, your Desktop can become littered with overlapping windows. You can arrange the open windows for easy access, or you can minimize and store some or all of them on the taskbar to keep your Desktop neat and uncluttered.

TIP: If you want to access only one Desktop icon, use the Desktop toolbar. If you want full access to the Desktop, use the Desktop button on the Quick Launch toolbar to minimize all your windows.

Arrange Your Open Windows

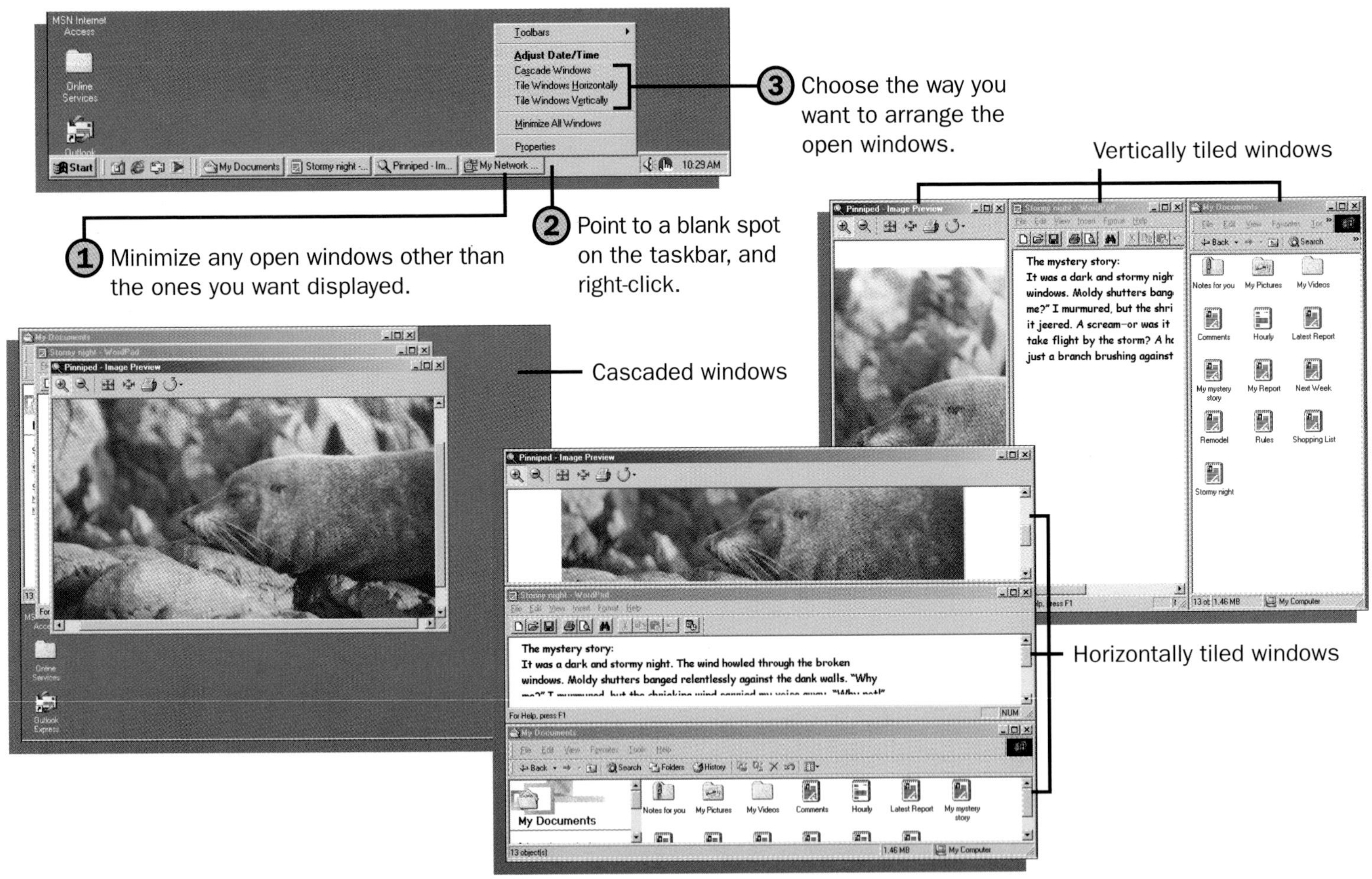

1. Minimize any open windows other than the ones you want displayed.
2. Point to a blank spot on the taskbar, and right-click.
3. Choose the way you want to arrange the open windows.

Vertically tiled windows

Cascaded windows

Horizontally tiled windows

Tidying Up the Desktop

If your Desktop becomes so cluttered with shortcuts, files, or overlapping icons that you can't find what you want at a glance, take a minute or two to do a little housekeeping.

SEE ALSO: For information about hiding the Desktop icons, see "Hide the Desktop Icons" on page 139.

Arrange the Icons

1. Select any items you don't want to keep on the Desktop, and press the Delete key.
2. Right-click in a blank part of the Desktop.
3. Point to Arrange Icons on the shortcut menu, and choose the type of arrangement you want.

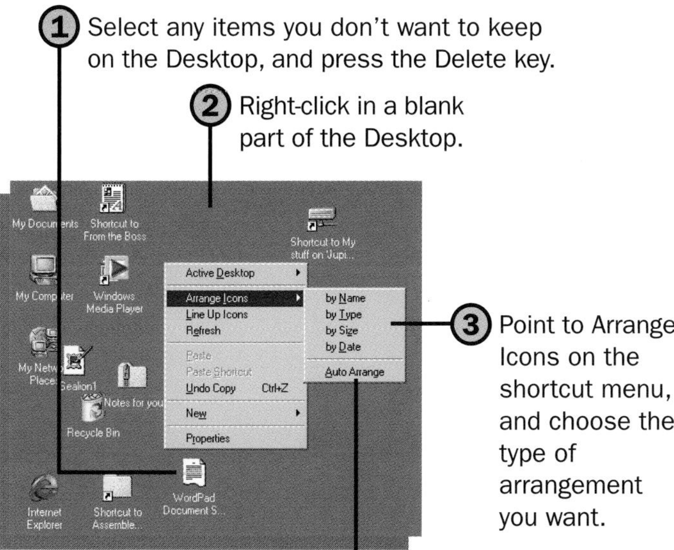

Choose Auto Arrange to have Windows Me automatically arrange the icons after you've created, moved, or deleted them.

Create Your Own Arrangement

1. Drag the icons to the area of the Desktop where you want them.

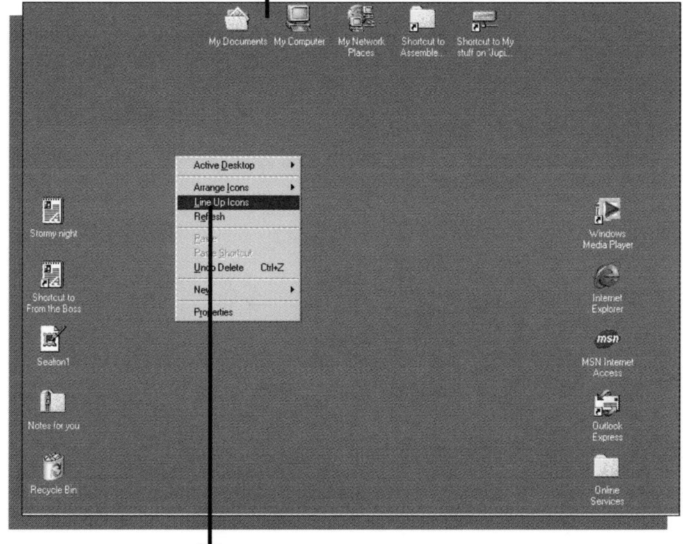

2. Right-click in a blank part of the Desktop, and Choose Line Up Icons from the shortcut menu.

TIP: The Auto Arrange command must be turned off before you can create your own arrangement of icons.

Exploring the Internet

Most of your navigation on the Internet uses links (also called *hyperlinks* or *jumps*) that are located on web pages. When you click a link, an Internet address is sent to your web browser, which looks for the web site and displays the requested page. Once you've located a web page, you can continue to explore.

SEE ALSO: For information about changing your home page, see "Setting the Home Page" on page 34.

For information about controlling and safeguarding your Internet connection, see "Restricting Internet Access" on page 162, "Preventing Cookies" on page 163, and "Protecting Your Personal Information" on page 164.

TIP: If you start Internet Explorer from your Desktop, the Quick Launch toolbar, or the Start menu, Internet Explorer goes to the page you've designated as your home page. If you start Internet Explorer by clicking a link or a menu command, or by using an Internet address, Internet Explorer goes to that specific page, bypassing your home page.

Explore

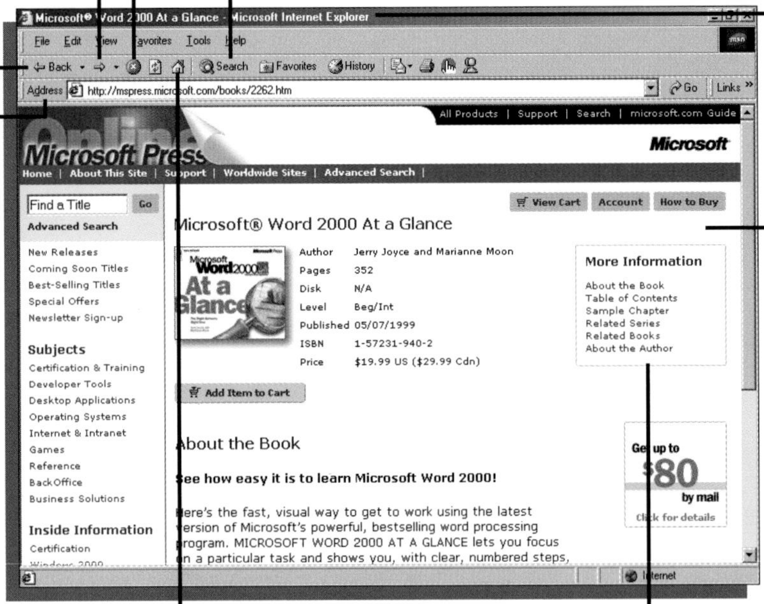

The Stop button

The Forward button

The Search button

The Back button

The Address Bar

1. Start Internet Explorer if it's not already running. If you're using a dial-in connection and aren't already connected to the Internet, connect to your service provider.
2. From your current page, do any of the following:
   - Click the Search button, and search for businesses or individuals or for web pages that contain specific text.
   - Click a relevant link on the page to go to a new page or site.
   - Click the Forward or Back button to return to a previously visited site.
   - Open the Address Bar drop-down list to select and jump to a previously visited site, or type a new address to go to that site.
   - Click the Stop button to stop downloading a site, and then jump to adifferent location.
3. If you get lost, click the Home button to return to your home page.

Use a link to jump to another page.

Returning to Your Favorite Sites

When you find a good source of information or entertainment, you don't need to waste a lot of time searching for that site the next time you want to visit it. You can simply add the site to your Favorites list, and Internet Explorer obligingly creates a shortcut to the site for you.

TIP: If you'll be storing many different favorite locations, click the Create In button in the Add Favorite dialog box, and create a file structure for your pages.

Save a Location

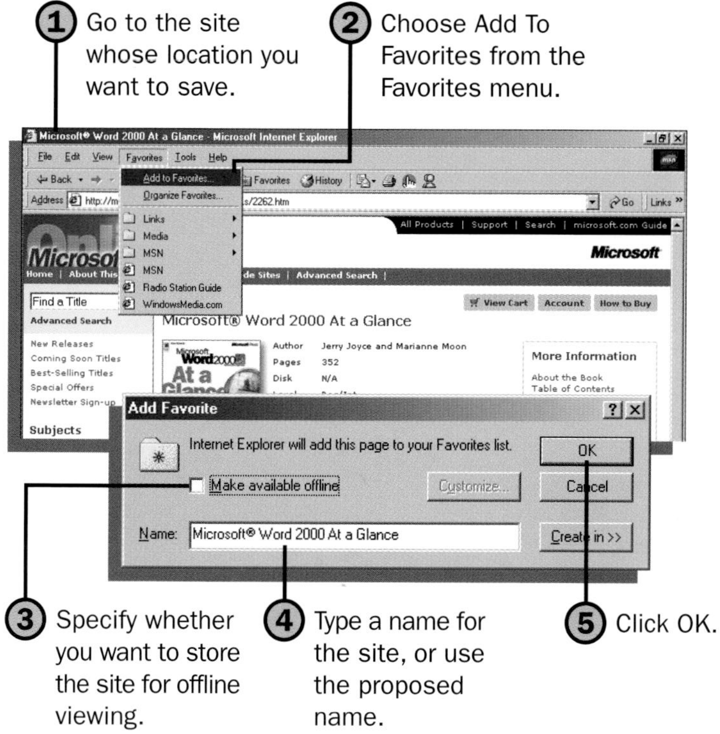

1. Go to the site whose location you want to save.
2. Choose Add To Favorites from the Favorites menu.
3. Specify whether you want to store the site for offline viewing.
4. Type a name for the site, or use the proposed name.
5. Click OK.

Return to a Location

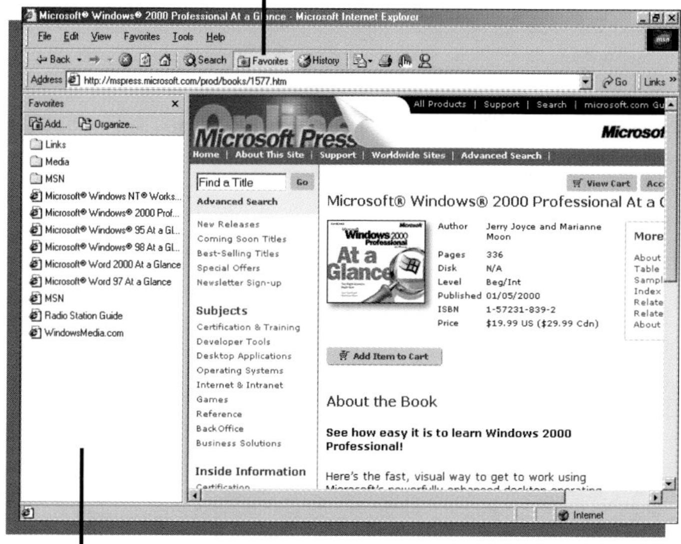

1. Click the Favorites button on the Standard Buttons toolbar.
2. In the Favorites Explorer Bar, click the name of the site you want to return to. If the site is contained in a subfolder, click the folder and then click the site.

TIP: If you want to return to a web page but didn't save it in your Favorites list, click the History button, and search for the page by the time period you visited it.

Setting the Home Page

When you start Internet Explorer, you automatically go to your home page—a page you might have customized or that contains the links and services you want. If you'd rather use a different home page, or if you want to reset the home page after a service or a program changed it, you can designate a new home page with a couple of mouse clicks.

TIP: Some service providers don't allow you to change your home page—you are required to use the service's home page until you're properly logged on. In that case, your only recourse is to complain to that service provider.

Reset the Home Page

1. Use Internet Explorer to go to the page you want to use as your home page.
2. Choose Internet Options from the Tools menu.

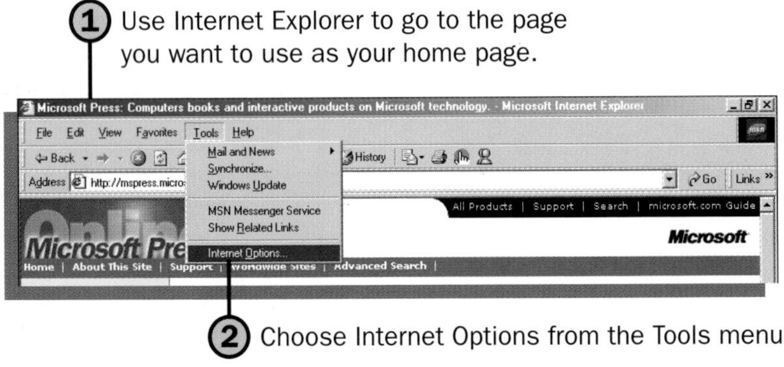

3. Click Use Current.
4. Click OK.

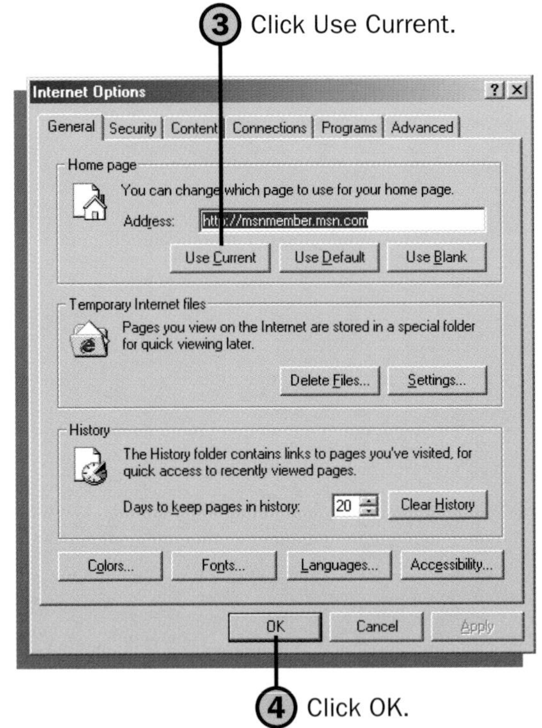

TIP: If a service provider or an installed program has made substantial changes to the way Internet Explorer looks and works, click the Restore Defaults button on the Advanced tab of the Internet Options dialog box to return Internet Explorer to its normal functionality.

TIP: If you don't want anyone else to review the Internet sites that you've visited recently, click the Clear History button on the General tab.

Networking

In this section

Networking—once a requirement only in large corporations—is now almost a necessity in a multi-computer household, a home office, or a small business. With two or more computers connected, you can access files and folders on other computers that are set up for sharing, and you can share the files and folders on your computer with other people. But that's not all—a network also enables you to share printers, to share an Internet connection, to control one computer from another computer, and to communicate over the network by sending and receiving pop-up text messages.

Microsoft Windows Millennium Edition networking isn't necessarily limited to a small home network. Although you can directly connect a computer running Windows Me to a large client-server network, in most business situations you'll probably want to use a more powerful and secure operating system such as Microsoft Windows 2000 Professional. However, if you need to gain access to a large network from your home computer, you can do so via a remote connection: by dialing up a network server, for example, or using the Internet to create a secure connection to a server. Such connections can sometimes be problematic until you get them working properly, but once they're set up, they're no more difficult to use than any other network resource.

For a detailed discussion about various types of networks, see "About Networks" on page 42.

Setting Up a Network

After you've installed a network card in each computer and connected the computers to create a network, your next step is to configure Windows Me to work on that network. Fortunately, a wizard will walk you through the process. The wizard accomplishes three tasks: it identifies the computers to the network; it sets access to files and printers; and, if you so choose, it sets up your computer so that you can share your Internet connection with other computers on the network or so that you can use a different Internet connection that's on someone else's computer. You can also use the wizard to set up on the network any Windows 95 or Windows 98 computers.

Set Up a Windows Me Computer

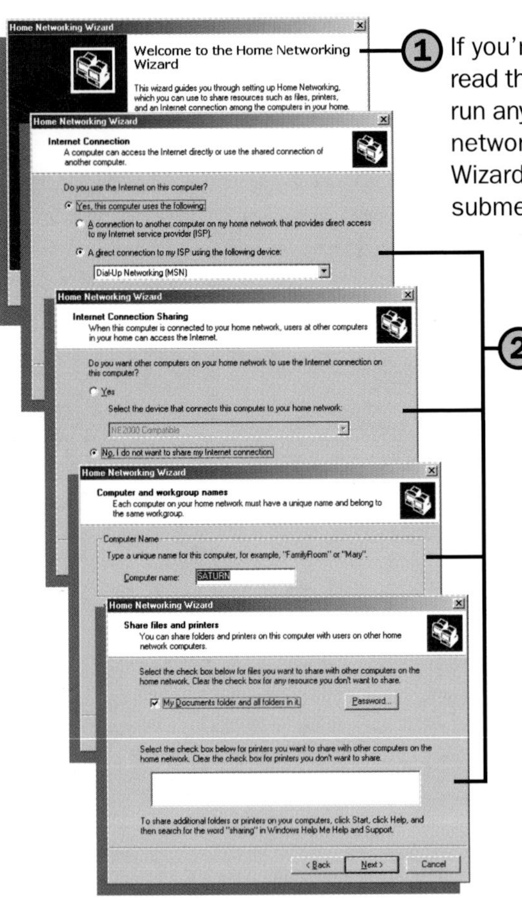

1. If you're using a network installation kit, read the manufacturer's instructions, and run any necessary programs to install the network. Start the Home Networking Wizard from the Communications submenu of the Start menu.

2. Step through the wizard, specifying
   - Whether you want to share an Internet connection with other computers on your network. If you'll be sharing your connection, provide the connection information.
   - A unique and descriptive name for the computer.
   - A name for your workgroup. (On a small network, you'll want all the computers to be in the same workgroup.)
   - Whether you want to share the My Documents folder, and a password to protect access to it.
   - Which printers you want to share.

3. Select the option to create a Home Networking Setup disk if you're going to set up Windows 95 or Windows 98 computers on your network.

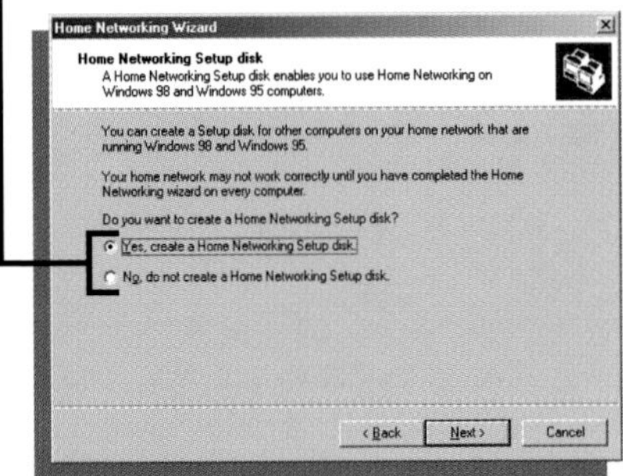

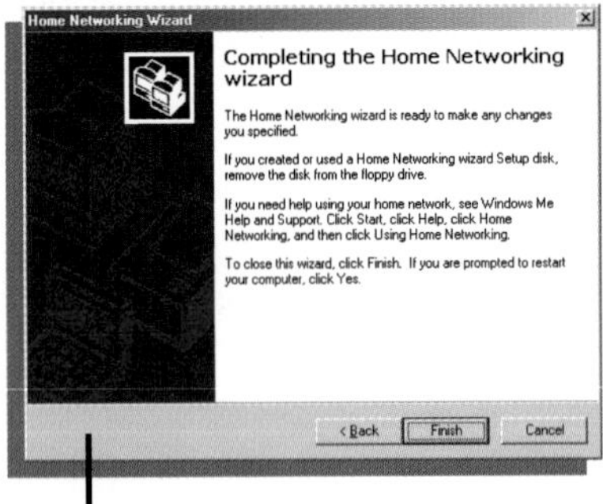

4. Complete the wizard, and restart the computer when prompted.

Set Up a Windows 95 or Windows 98 Computer

1. Insert the Home Networking Setup disk that you created into the disk drive of the computer. Click the Start button, and choose Run.

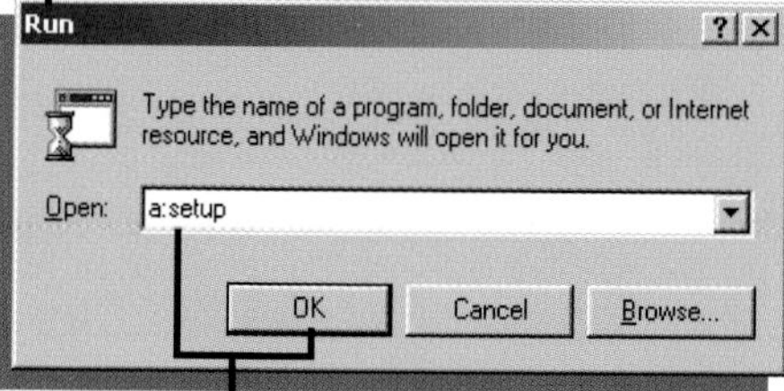

2. In the Open box, type *a:setup*, and click OK. If the floppy disk is in a drive other than the a: drive, substitute the correct drive letter when you type the setup command.

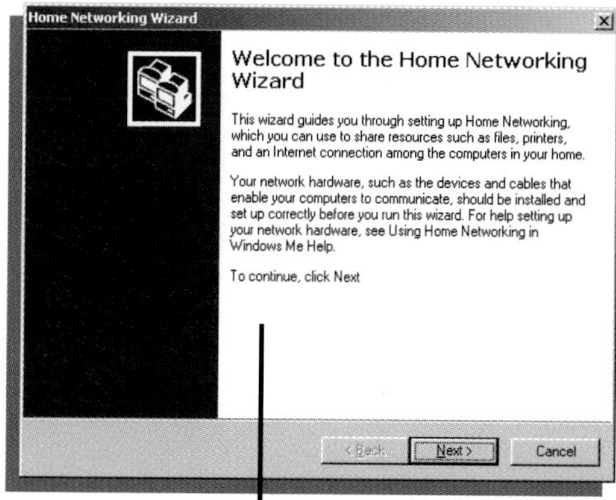

3. Step through the Home Networking Wizard. Remove the floppy disk when you've finished, and restart the computer when prompted.

TIP: To change network settings or to create a new Home Networking Setup disk, rerun the Home Networking Wizard.

TRY THIS: Complete the Home Networking Wizard, and restart your computer. Double-click My Network Places, and then double-click Entire Network. In the Entire Network window, double-click your workgroup. If you chose to share anything (a folder or a printer, for example), you should see your computer listed, and possibly other computers on the network. If your computer is listed, you'll know that it's properly set up for networking. If you receive an error message when you try to access the network, or if your computer isn't listed, there's a problem with your network configuration. If so, right-click My Computer, and choose Properties from the shortcut menu. On the Device Manager tab, under Network Adapters, double-click your network adapter, and investigate the problem. Use the Network Troubleshooter to help you solve the problem.

TIP: If you want to share an Internet connection, set up the computer that has the Internet connection before you set up the other computers. For the best functionality, the connection should be on a computer that's running Windows Me.

SEE ALSO: For information about sharing other files or folders, see "Sharing Files and Folders on the Network" on page 40.

For information about disabling sharing, see "Securing Your Files" on page 160 and "Restricting Access to Files" on page 161.

Exploring Your Network

Windows Me automatically searches for the shared folders, printers, and whatever other items are shared on your network's computers. You can also open a window to all the shared folders on a specific computer and connect to a computer that's in a different workgroup or domain.

SEE ALSO: For information about creating a shortcut to a file, folder, or computer see "Creating a Shortcut to a File or Folder" on page 140.

For information about treating a network folder as a drive for quick access to its contents, see "Creating a Connection to a Network Folder" on page 43.

Connect to a Shared Folder

1. Double-click My Network Places.

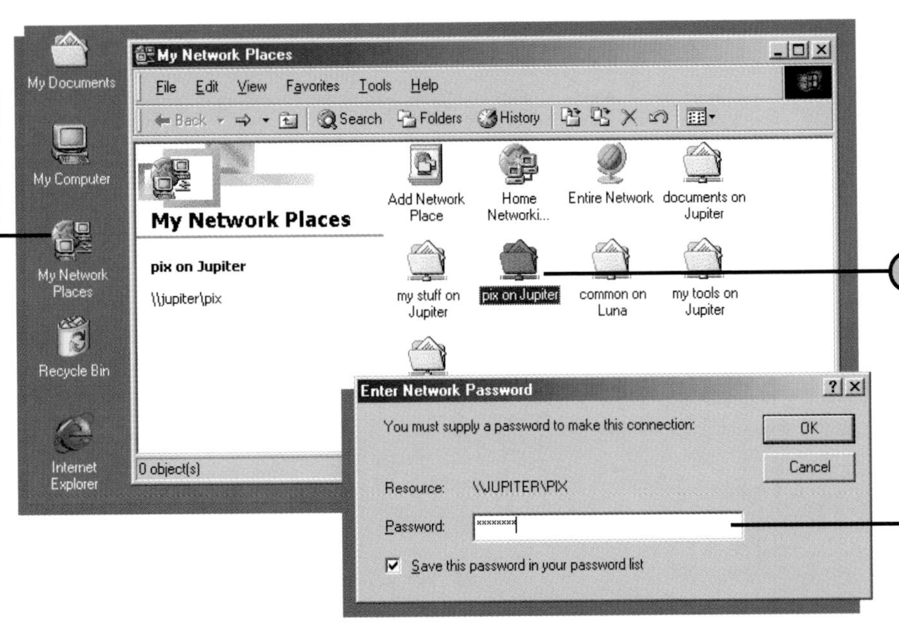

2. Double-click the shared folder to access its contents.
3. If prompted, enter the password you've been given to access that folder, and click OK. (Each shared folder can require a unique password, no password, or a different password for read-only or full-control access.)

TIP: My Network Places automatically displays the shared resources for the computers in your workgroup, and, if you're connected to a client-server domain, the shared resources on the domain. Double-click Entire Network to see the shared resources in other workgroups or on other domains.

TIP: If Windows Me doesn't automatically search the network for shared resources, choose Folder Options from the Tools menu in any folder window, and, on the View tab, turn on the option to search for network folders and printers.

Connect to a Shared Computer

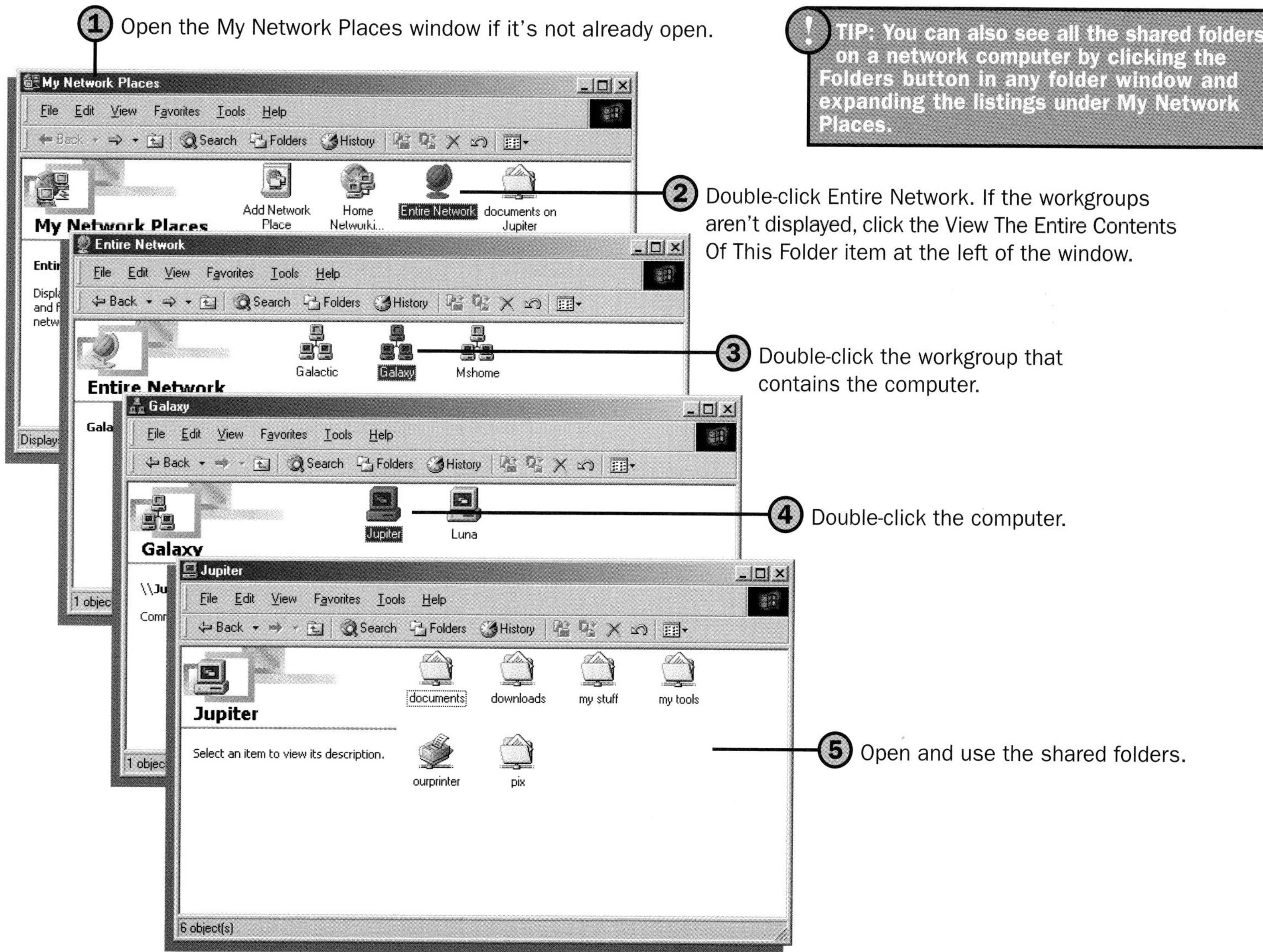

1. Open the My Network Places window if it's not already open.
2. Double-click Entire Network. If the workgroups aren't displayed, click the View The Entire Contents Of This Folder item at the left of the window.
3. Double-click the workgroup that contains the computer.
4. Double-click the computer.
5. Open and use the shared folders.

TIP: You can also see all the shared folders on a network computer by clicking the Folders button in any folder window and expanding the listings under My Network Places.

Sharing Files and Folders on the Network

When you run the Home Networking Wizard, you have the option of sharing your My Documents folder. If you do share the folder, it can be a convenient place to store any files you want to share with others on the network. You can also create your own structure of folders to be shared over the network, and you can specify the type of access other people have to the contents of each folder.

Share a File

1. Use My Computer to locate the file you want to share.

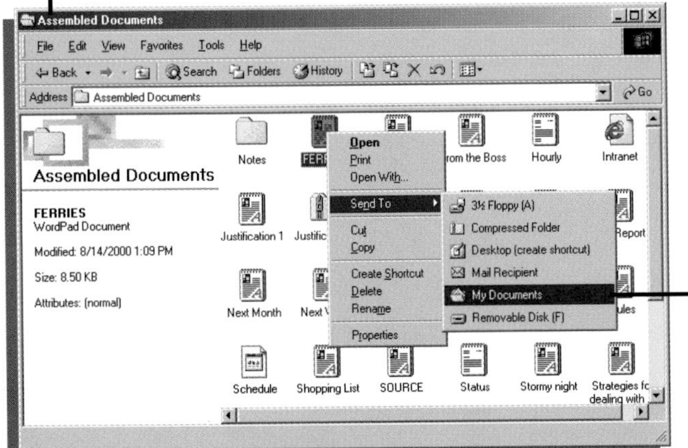

2. Right-click the file, point to Send To, and choose My Documents from the submenu.

SEE ALSO: For information about determining which folders are shared on your computer, as well as information about removing the sharing of a folder, see "Restricting Access to Files" on page 161.

TIP: If the Sharing command isn't on the folder's shortcut menu, your computer isn't properly set up to share folders on the network, so you'll need to rerun the Home Networking Wizard.

TIP: Use the Read-Only option if you want no one but yourself to save files to this folder. Use the Depends On Password option if you'll allow people who have the correct password to add files or to modify existing files, while preventing others from making any changes to the folder.

TRY THIS: Create a new folder and set it to be shared. Use the Folder Options command on the Tools menu to display any hidden files and folders. Click the Folders button to display the folders on your computer. Use the right mouse button to drag the new folder onto the Send To folder (in the Windows folder), and choose Create Shortcut(s) Here from the shortcut menu. Right-click a file in any folder, point to Send To, and send a copy of the file to the new folder.

Share a Folder

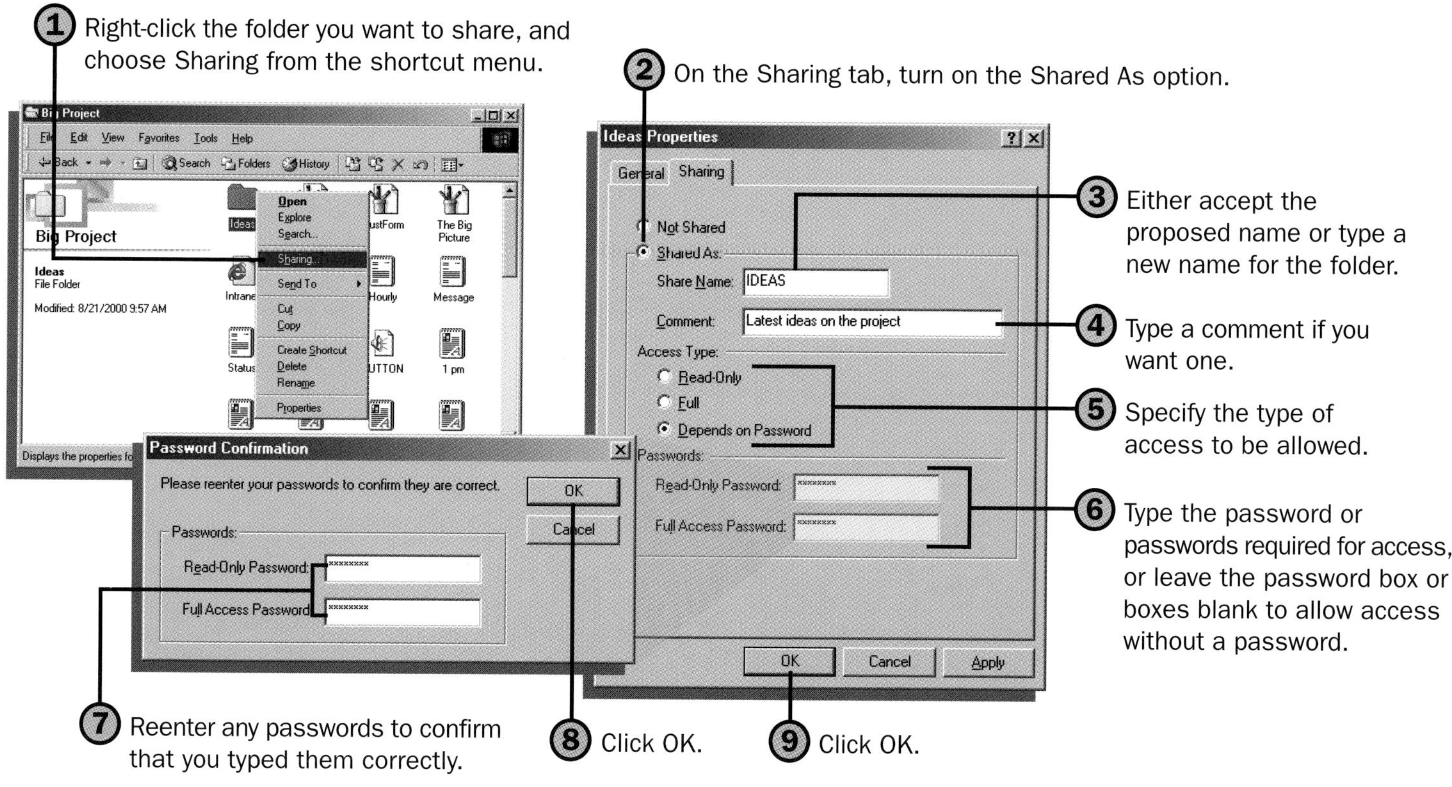

TIP: You can identify a shared folder on your computer by the hand attached to the folder's icon. A folder you've shared appears on the network with the name of your computer in its name.

TIP: If you didn't set up your printer for sharing over your network when you ran the Home Networking Wizard (or if you shared it and now want to stop sharing it), open the Printers folder from the Settings submenu of the Start menu, right-click the printer, choose Sharing from the shortcut menu, and specify whether you want to share the printer.

About Networks

A network, whether it's large or small, gives you the ability to connect computers so that they can communicate with each other. In a small network (a *peer-to-peer network*), all the computers communicate directly with each other. In a larger network (a *client-server network*), communication between computers is routed through a server. Windows Me offers a slight modification of these roles. You can exchange information among computers on a home network—sharing files, for example—using the traditional peer-to-peer network. However, if you share an Internet connection over your network, the computer with the connection becomes a server for that shared connection, and the other computers become its clients.

Computers can be connected to a network in a variety of ways: by direct connections with cables, with wires that go through network hubs, with connections through your power or phone lines, or even without any wires at all. With so many options, setting up a network can be a simple job or a truly miserable experience. Some connections use "standard" network software and settings; others require special software and configurations. If you're installing a network from a network installation kit, the kit should include all the instructions and software you'll need to get the network set up. If you're installing a network card in each computer without an accompanying setup program, you'll need to make sure that Windows Me knows the cards are installed. If Windows Me doesn't detect and set up each newly installed network card, run the Add New Hardware Wizard from the Control Panel. If the card (or cards) still isn't detected, select the device (the network card) from the list by specifying the manufacturer and model, and complete the wizard. For more information, see "Adding Hardware" on page 174. Note the information on the interrupt (IRQ) and memory settings that Windows Me will use for the card, and then read the documentation for information about making any required changes to the settings on the network card. Windows Me will automatically shut down your computer so that you can make the changes to your network card.

When Windows Me is installed, network software (called the *TCP/IP protocol*) is installed too. This software enables you to communicate over the Internet and on your own network. You can also add other network protocols (IPX/SPX and/or NetBEUI, for example) to your computer if you need them to communicate with other computers. With standard network configurations, and on special networks where the software drivers are already installed, Windows Me is almost ready to run. Before you use the network, though, you'll need to run the Home Networking Wizard to identify your computer to the network and to specify the types of access you want over the network. You'll also need to specify whether you want to share your Internet connection or any of your files. If you're creating a new network, you'll need to run the wizard on each computer so that the proper settings and software are installed on each machine. Once the network is set up, you'll find that sharing resources is easy and convenient.

Creating a Connection to a Network Folder

If you frequently use one particular folder on the network, you can access that folder quickly by assigning a drive letter to it. By doing so, you'll not only gain quick access to the folder from My Computer but you'll also be able to access the folder in programs that don't let you browse My Network Places to find a file.

Assign a Drive

1. Open My Network Places, double-click Entire Network, and navigate to the computer that contains the shared folder.

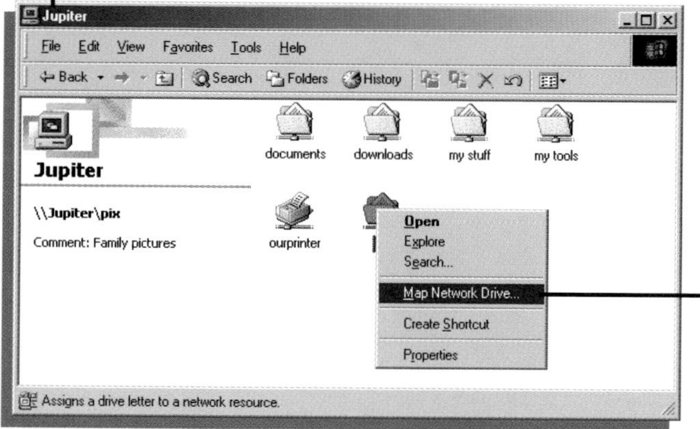

2. Right-click the folder, and click Map Network Drive.

3. Note the drive letter to be assigned, or select a different unused drive letter if you want.

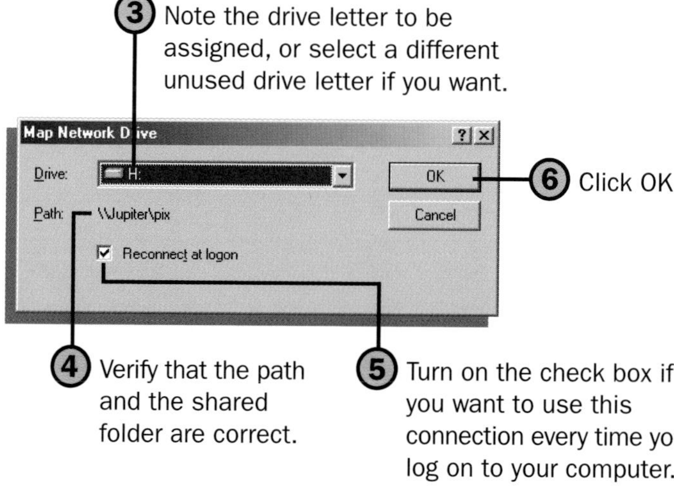

4. Verify that the path and the shared folder are correct.
5. Turn on the check box if you want to use this connection every time you log on to your computer.
6. Click OK.

SEE ALSO: For information about creating a shortcut to a network folder, see "Creating a Shortcut to a File or Folder" on page 140.

For information about connecting to a computer, see "Connect to a Shared Computer" on page 39.

TRY THIS: Create a network drive. Open My Computer and verify that the drive is listed in that window. Start a program, use the drive to open or save a file, and then close the program. Right-click My Computer, and choose Disconnect Network Drive to delete the drive assignment.

Sending Messages over the Network

Sending a short, instant message over your network is a great way to communicate from one computer to another. It's easy to do once you've set up the WinPopup program on all the computers you want to use. By placing WinPopup on the StartUp submenu of the Start menu, the program will start when each computer is started and will always be available.

Set Up WinPopup

1. On each computer that you want to communicate with over the network, use the Search command on the Start menu to find the winpopup.exe file.
2. Drag the file onto the Start button and, when the Start menu opens, onto the StartUp submenu.

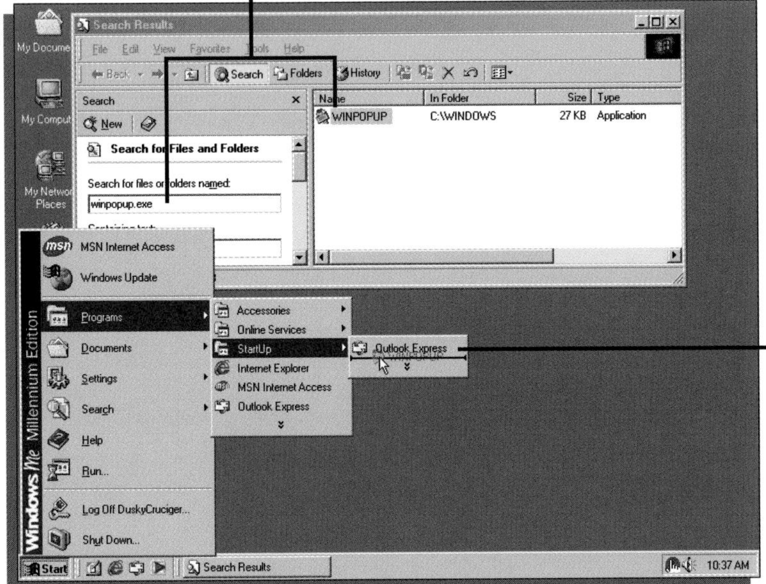

TIP: If you don't want WinPopup to start every time the computer starts, run it only when you want to. Click the Start button, choose Run, type *winpopup* in the Open box, and click OK.

SEE ALSO: For information about sending instant messages to other computers over the Internet, see "Sending and Receiving Instant Messages" on page 124.

For information about more complex communications over the network, including voice communications, see "Conferring on the Net" on page 128.

For information about adding programs to the Start menu, see "Reorganizing the Start Menu" on page 132.

For information about installing WinPopup if it isn't already installed, see "Adding or Removing Windows Me Components" on page 170.

Send a Message

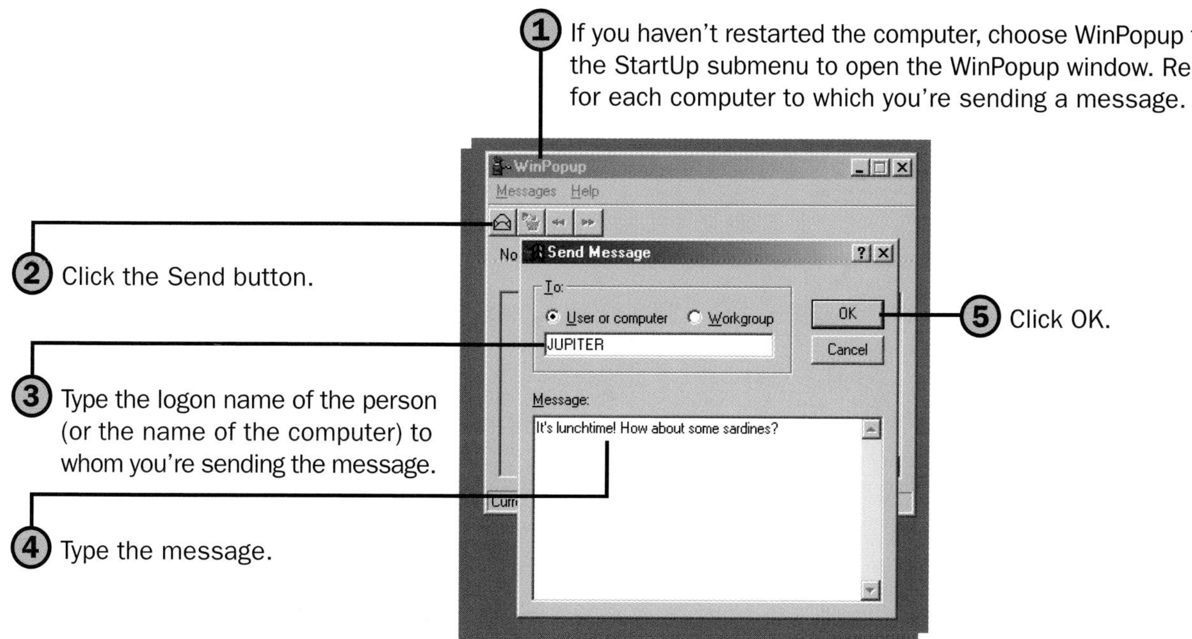

1. If you haven't restarted the computer, choose WinPopup from the StartUp submenu to open the WinPopup window. Repeat for each computer to which you're sending a message.
2. Click the Send button.
3. Type the logon name of the person (or the name of the computer) to whom you're sending the message.
4. Type the message.
5. Click OK.

TIP: WinPopup is available in most versions of Windows.

TIP: Choose the Workgroup option to send a message to all the computers in the workgroup that are running WinPopup.

TRY THIS: Choose Options from the Messages menu in WinPopup. Turn on the check box for the program to pop up on receipt of a message, and click OK. Minimize WinPopup so that it's out of your way. When a message is received, the WinPopup window will reappear.

Controlling Your Computer Remotely

Would you like to have full access to one computer from another over your network? By sharing a computer's Desktop using Microsoft NetMeeting, you can sit at one computer (a computer at your workplace, perhaps) and work on another computer (your home computer, for example). You can gain access to files, reorganize them, and run programs—all from the other computer's Desktop.

Share the Desktop

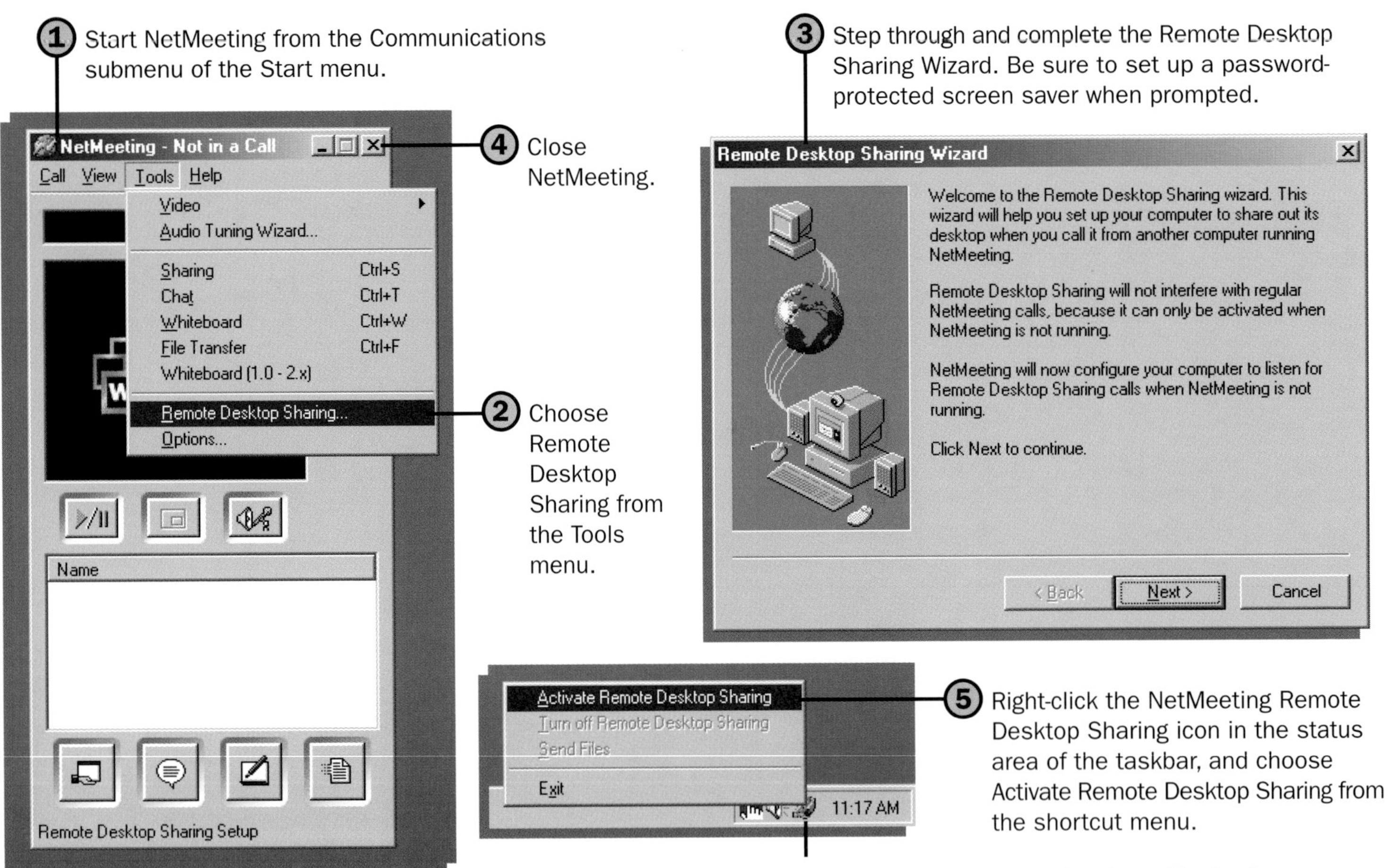

1. Start NetMeeting from the Communications submenu of the Start menu.
2. Choose Remote Desktop Sharing from the Tools menu.
3. Step through and complete the Remote Desktop Sharing Wizard. Be sure to set up a password-protected screen saver when prompted.
4. Close NetMeeting.
5. Right-click the NetMeeting Remote Desktop Sharing icon in the status area of the taskbar, and choose Activate Remote Desktop Sharing from the shortcut menu.

The NetMeeting Remote Desktop Sharing icon

Connect to the Computer

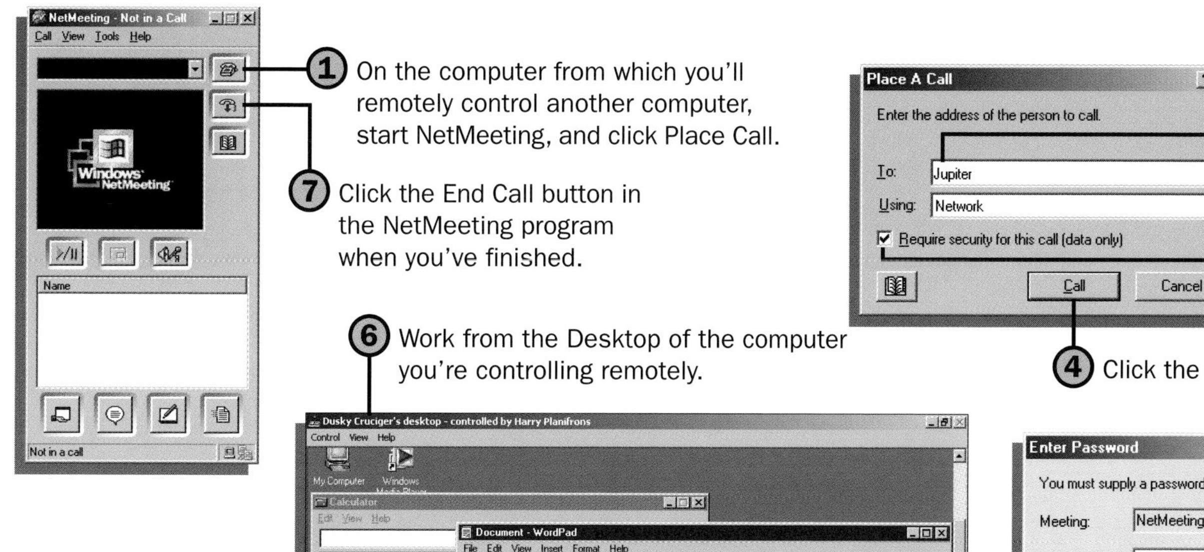

1. On the computer from which you'll remotely control another computer, start NetMeeting, and click Place Call.
2. Enter the name of the computer you're calling.
3. Turn on the check box to require security.
4. Click the Call button.
5. Enter your password, and click OK.
6. Work from the Desktop of the computer you're controlling remotely.
7. Click the End Call button in the NetMeeting program when you've finished.

Enter Password
You must supply a password to join this meeting
Meeting: NetMeeting Remote Desktop Sharing
Password: xxxxxxxx
OK Cancel

TIP: Using a password-protected screen saver prevents other people from using your computer while it's unattended.

SEE ALSO: For information about starting NetMeeting, see "Conferring on the Net" on page 128.

For information about using a password-protected screen saver, see "Displaying a Screen Saver" on page 149.

TIP: To deactivate Remote Desktop Sharing on your computer, right-click the NetMeeting Remote Desktop Sharing icon on the taskbar, and choose Turn Off Remote Sharing from the shortcut menu to temporarily deactivate the feature. To permanently remove Remote Desktop Sharing, start NetMeeting, choose Remote Desktop Sharing from the Tools menu, and turn off the Enable Remote Desktop Sharing On This Computer check box.

Connecting to a Network Using Your Modem

If you want to connect to a business network over a phone line, you can use Dial-Up Networking to make the connection and log on to the company's network. You'll be required to establish an account that lets you access resources on the network, and you'll need the proper permissions to connect. Be sure to get all the information you need from the company's network administrator before you connect. Every company has its own security settings and policies, so you'll need those details for the proper configuration.

Create the Connection

1. Choose Dial-Up Networking from the Settings submenu of the Start menu to open the Dial-Up Networking window.
2. Double-click Make New Connection.
3. Step through the wizard, completing the connection information.

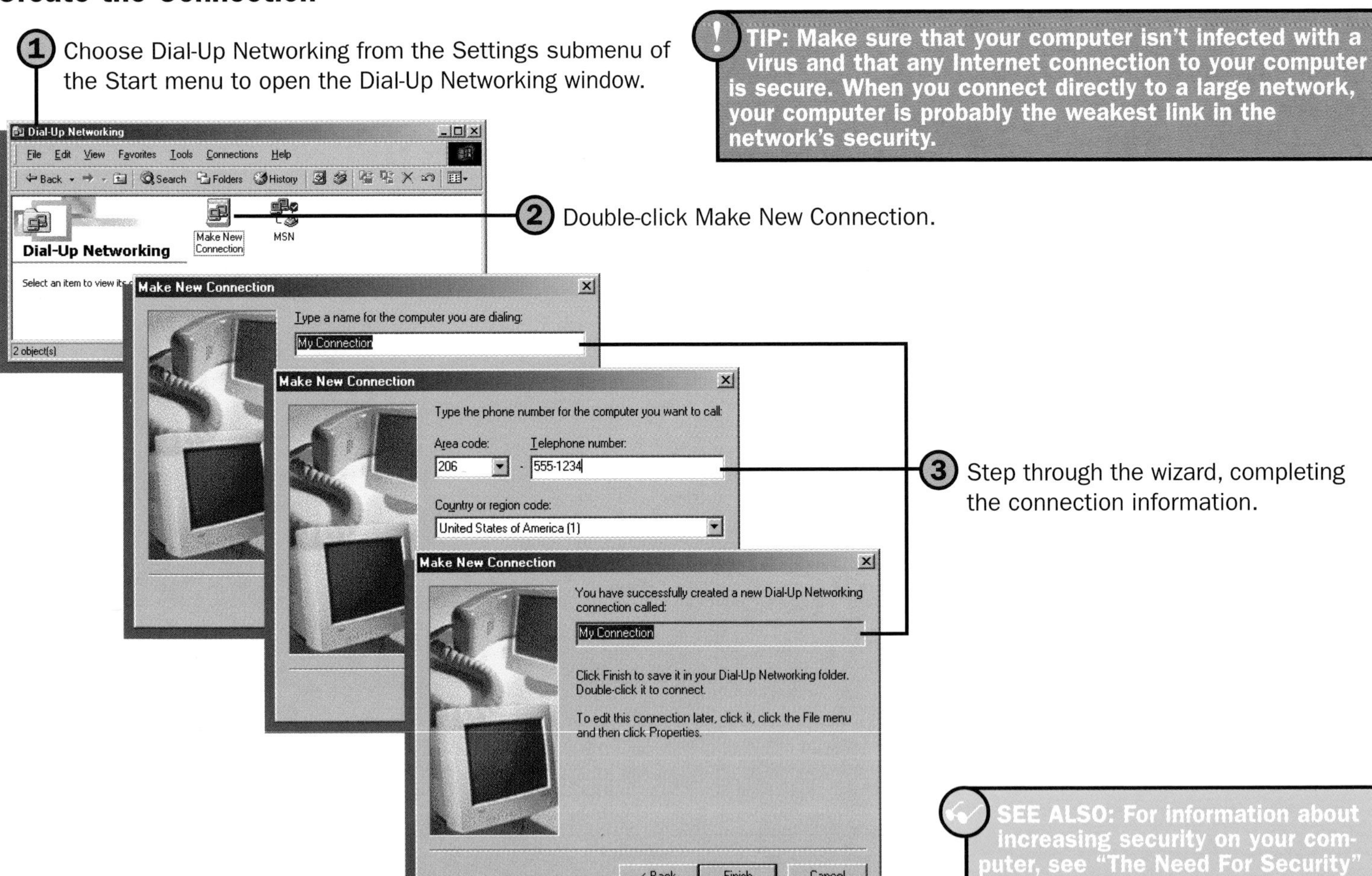

TIP: Make sure that your computer isn't infected with a virus and that any Internet connection to your computer is secure. When you connect directly to a large network, your computer is probably the weakest link in the network's security.

SEE ALSO: For information about increasing security on your computer, see "The Need For Security" on page 159.

Connect

1. Double-click the new connection to display the Connect To dialog box.

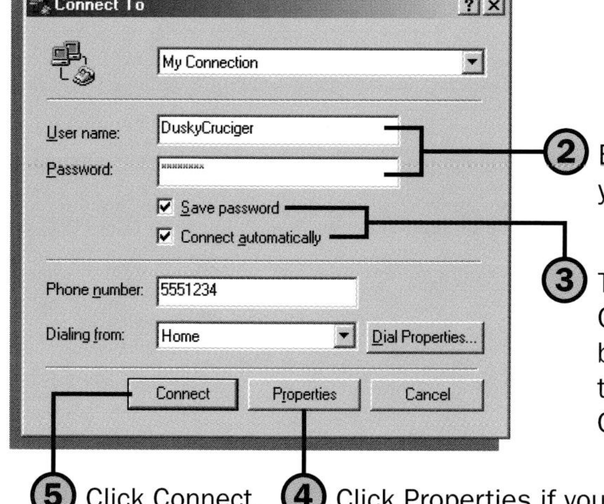

2. Enter the name and password you've been assigned.
3. Turn on the Save Password and Connect Automatically check boxes if, in the future, you want to connect without displaying the Connect To dialog box.
4. Click Properties if you need to make changes to the connection or to the network settings.
5. Click Connect.
6. Wait for the connection to be made, and click Close. Use the connection as you would any network connection.
7. When you've finished, double-click the connection icon on the taskbar (or the connection in the Dial-Up Networking window), and click Disconnect.

TIP: You can also disconnect by double-clicking the modem icon on the taskbar.

TIP: Dialing up a network sometimes requires a user name and password to connect to the server, and then a different user name and password (as well as the domain name) to access the network. Click the Properties button in the Connect To dialog box to specify different logon information, or complete the information when prompted after connecting.

TIP: If you turn on the Connect Automatically check box but later want to make changes in the Connect To dialog box, right-click the connection, choose Properties, and, on the Security tab, turn off the Connect Automatically check box. The Connect To dialog box will appear the next time you double-click the connection.

Connecting to a Network over the Internet

To connect over the Internet, you can use a virtual private network (VPN) that provides a secure connection between your computer and the network. The computer you connect to must be configured as a VPN server and must be a member of a domain that's connected to the Internet. Before you connect, verify that you have the correct name of the host computer and the correct user name and password that have been assigned to you.

Create the VPN Connection

1. Point to Settings on the Start menu, choose Dial-Up Networking from the submenu, and double-click the Make New Connection icon to start the wizard.

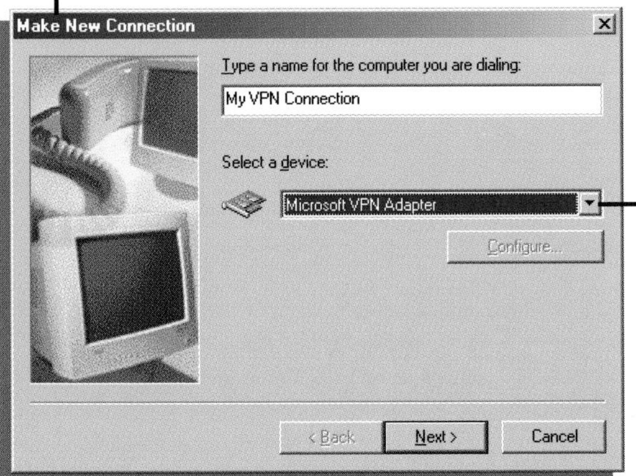

TIP: Sometimes the configuration used by an Internet Service Provider (ISP) can interfere when you're creating a VPN connection. If you have problems, check with your ISP to see whether you need to change some of your settings.

2. Select Microsoft VPN Adapter from the list of devices, and click Next.

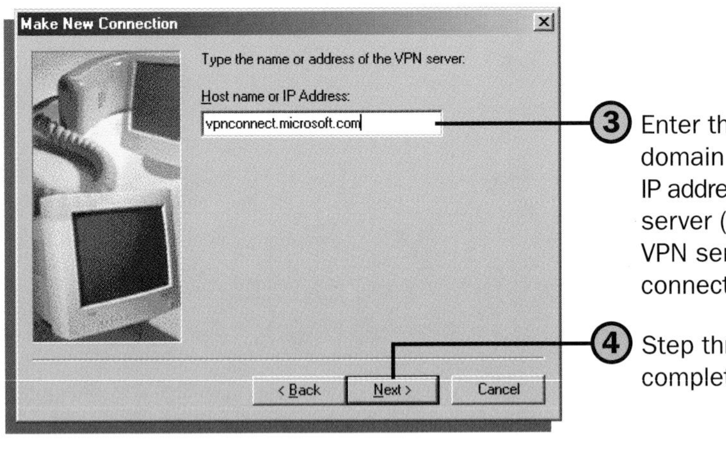

3. Enter the Internet domain name or the IP address of the host server (that is, the VPN server you're connecting to).
4. Step through and complete the wizard.

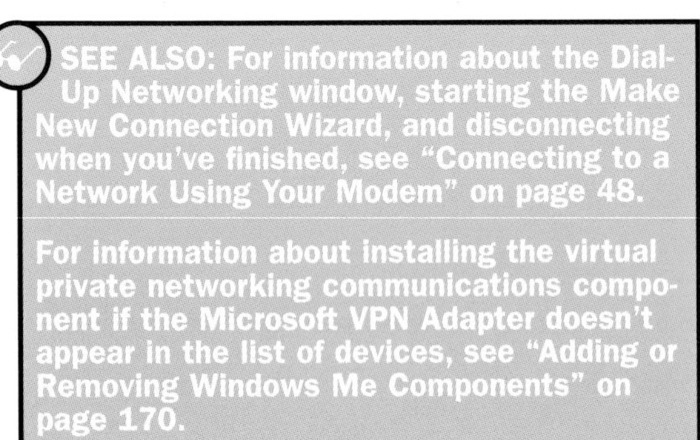

SEE ALSO: For information about the Dial-Up Networking window, starting the Make New Connection Wizard, and disconnecting when you've finished, see "Connecting to a Network Using Your Modem" on page 48.

For information about installing the virtual private networking communications component if the Microsoft VPN Adapter doesn't appear in the list of devices, see "Adding or Removing Windows Me Components" on page 170.

Connect

1. If you're not already connected, connect to the Internet.
2. Double-click the new VPN connection you created.

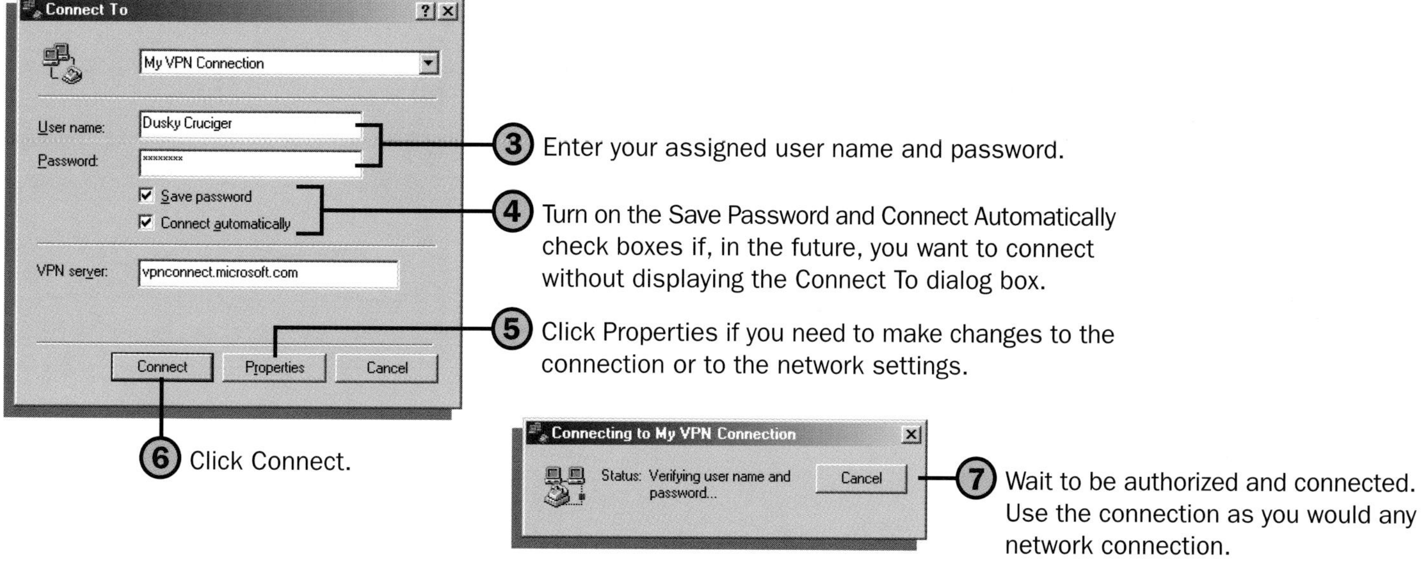

3. Enter your assigned user name and password.
4. Turn on the Save Password and Connect Automatically check boxes if, in the future, you want to connect without displaying the Connect To dialog box.
5. Click Properties if you need to make changes to the connection or to the network settings.
6. Click Connect.
7. Wait to be authorized and connected. Use the connection as you would any network connection.

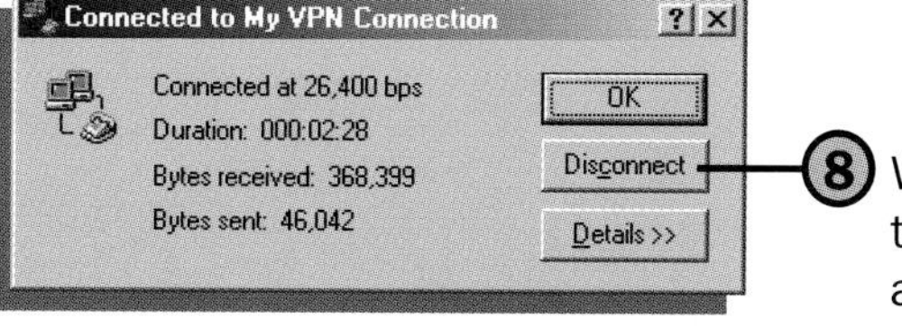

8. When you've finished, double-click the connection icon on the taskbar (or the connection in the Dial-Up Networking window), and click Disconnect.

TIP: Although a VPN connection provides a direct and secure connection to the network, you're still subject to all the slowdowns that you can experience whenever you use the Internet, including a slow connection to your service provider, slow performance by your service provider, a general slowdown of the Internet, and poor performance from the VPN server. If you're planning to transfer large files, be prepared to wait!

Connecting to Your Computer from Another Location

If you want to create a network connection over a phone line between your computer and another computer, you can turn your computer into a dial-up network server. You can specify who can gain access to your computer using a password, and you can disable the server at any time. When someone gains access to your computer, he or she also has access to any shared folders on your network.

Create a Dial-Up Server

1. Choose Dial-Up Networking from the Settings submenu of the Start menu.
2. Choose Dial-Up Server from the Connections menu.

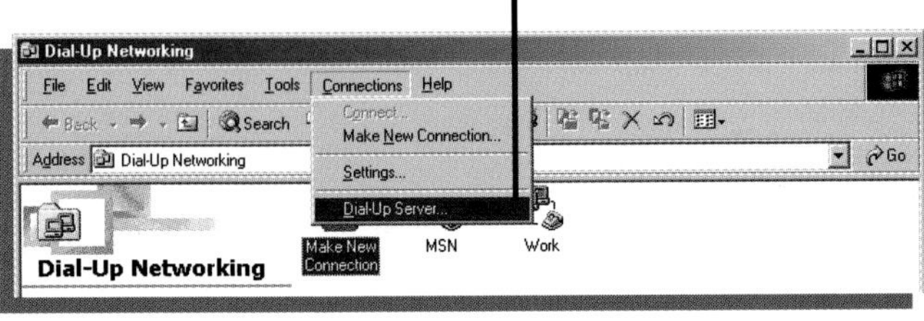

TIP: Once the dial-up server is configured, double-click the Dial-Up Server icon on the taskbar to display the Dial-Up Server dialog box, from which you can monitor the connections, terminate any connections you don't want, or completely disable the server so that no one can connect.

3. Turn on the Allow Caller Access option.
4. Click Change Password, type a new password, confirm it, and click OK.

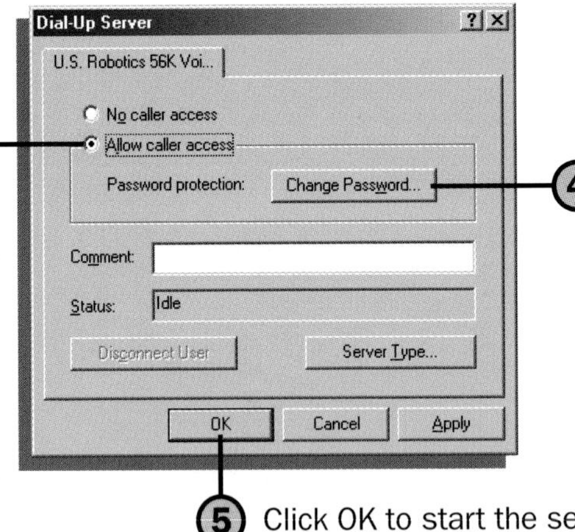

5. Click OK to start the server, and provide the access number, server type, and password to the people who need the information.

SEE ALSO: For information about connecting to your server, see "Connecting to a Network Using Your Modem" on page 48.

For information about installing Dial-Up Server if it isn't listed on the Connections menu, see "Adding or Removing Windows Me Components" on page 170.

Running Programs

In this section

Getting to know the programs that come with Microsoft Windows Millennium Edition is a bit like moving into new living quarters. Just as your new abode has the basics—stove, refrigerator, and (dare we say it?) windows—the Windows Me operating system comes with many basic accessories and tools. Just as you'll add all the accoutrements that transform empty rooms into a cozy home, you'll add programs to Windows Me to utilize its full potential as you work (and play).

But let's cover the basics first. There's WordPad, a handy little word processor; Paint, an easy-to-use graphics program; and Calculator, for scientific calculations as well as quick basic arithmetic. Windows Me provides other goodies: a web browser, mail and newsgroup capabilities, multimedia, and many accessory programs.

Right now, though, we'll concentrate on everyday tasks: composing, saving, and printing a document; creating and editing text; copying items between documents that were created in different programs; and inserting characters such as © and é that don't exist on your keyboard. We'll also take a look at the Calculator and try out some different types of calculations. Finally, we'll discuss working at the command prompt, running MS-DOS programs, and what you can do to get out of trouble when a program isn't working properly.

Composing a Document

WordPad is a powerful little word processor with which you can create documents in Microsoft Word format or Rich Text format, or as plain text or Unicode text documents. In most cases you'll want to create a document with formatting for a well-designed, professional look. Save the document as you create it, and print it when you've finished.

TIP: WordPad is a useful program for writing short documents and letters and for viewing text, WordPad, and Word documents. For more complex or extensive word processing, you'll need a more powerful program such as Microsoft Word.

Create a Document

1. Start WordPad from the Accessories submenu of the Start menu.
2. Click the New button on the toolbar.
3. Select Word 6 Document to create a document in which you can format the text and the paragraphs.
4. Click OK.

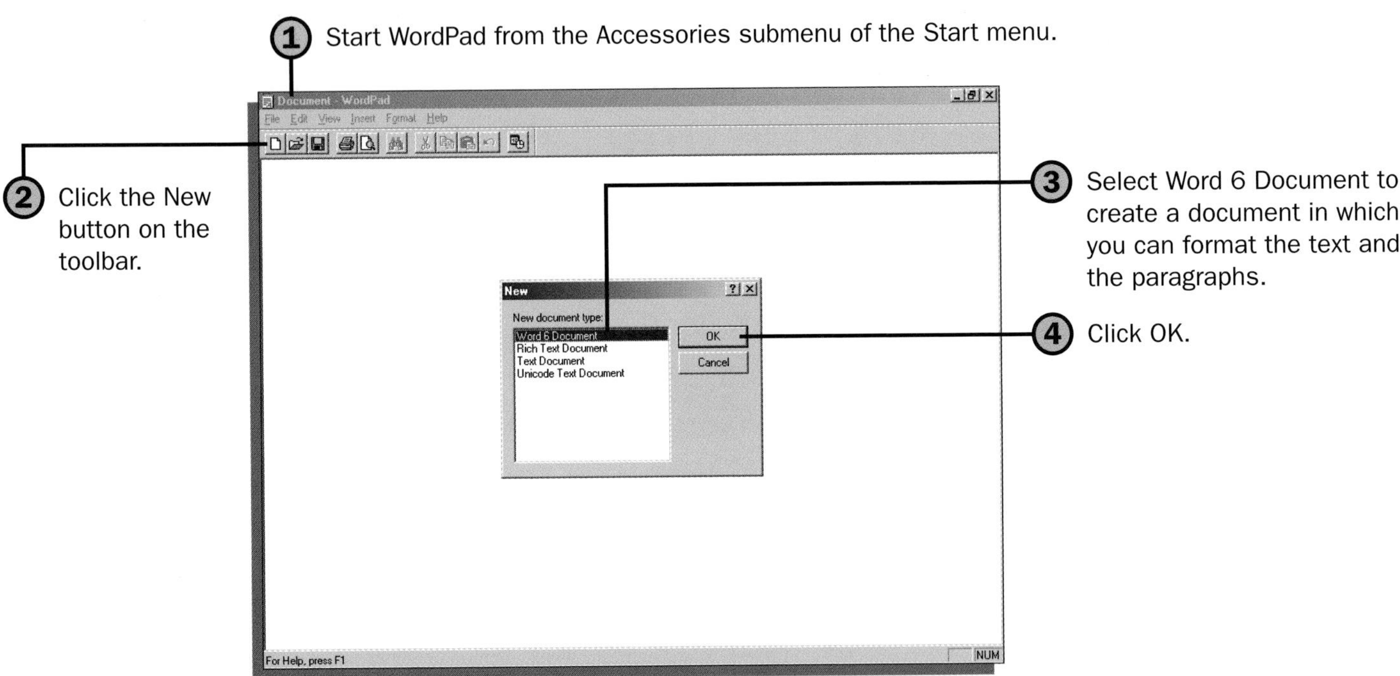

TIP: Use the Word 6 Document or Rich Text Document options for formatted text, and the Text Document option for documents associated with programs that don't use formatted text or for maximum compatibility with other programs. Use the Unicode Text Document option to display the necessary characters if the file is to be used in a language that uses a Unicode character set, or for system files that require a Unicode character set.

Enter and Format Text

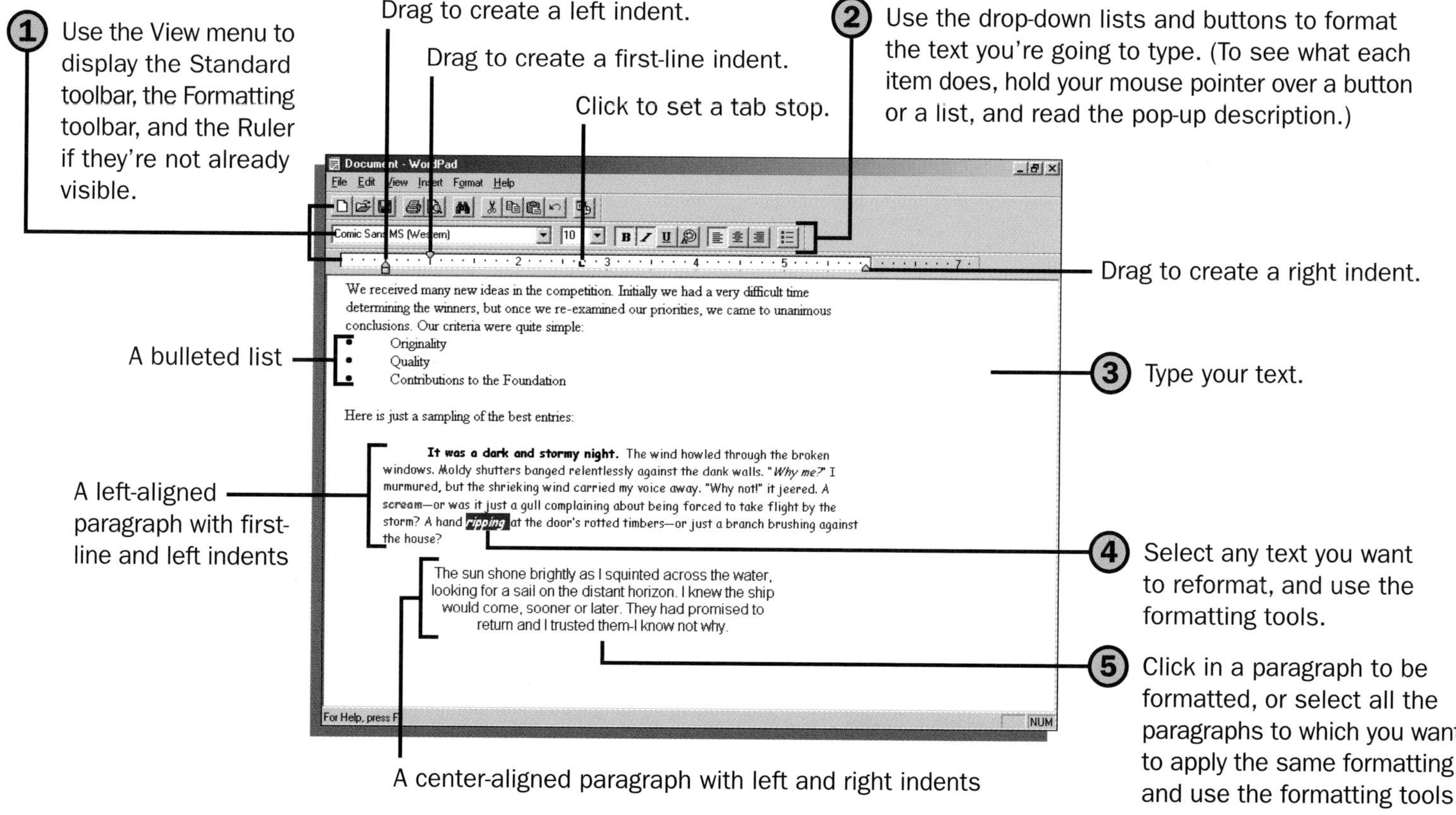

Saving a Document

When you create a document, you should save it frequently to your computer's hard disk. Once you've saved your document, you can reopen it to edit it or continue composing it. Another reason to save your documents frequently is that if you (or a misbehaving program) inadvertently shut down the computer, you won't lose all your work.

> ! TIP: In many programs, pressing Ctrl+S (hold down the Ctrl key, press the S key, and then release the Ctrl key) is a quick way to save a document.

Save It

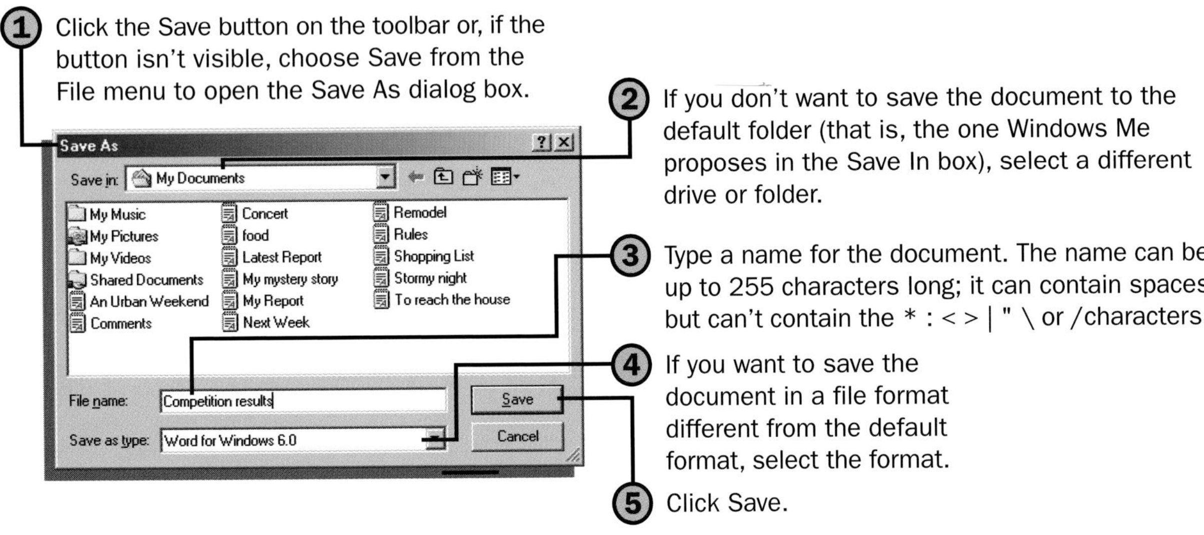

1. Click the Save button on the toolbar or, if the button isn't visible, choose Save from the File menu to open the Save As dialog box.
2. If you don't want to save the document to the default folder (that is, the one Windows Me proposes in the Save In box), select a different drive or folder.
3. Type a name for the document. The name can be up to 255 characters long; it can contain spaces but can't contain the * : < > | " \ or /characters.
4. If you want to save the document in a file format different from the default format, select the format.
5. Click Save.

> ! TIP: Long filenames are often truncated by programs, so a descriptive short name is more useful than a long one. For the greatest compatibility with other programs and operating systems, limit the filename to eight characters and don't use any spaces.

> ! TIP: As you work with the document, click the Save button frequently. Windows Me will save the file without displaying the Save As dialog box.

Printing a Document

In most programs, you can print a document on any printer that's installed on the computer or shared on the network. By using the Print dialog box, you can select which printer to use and can customize the way the document is printed.

> TIP: Some programs don't support all the printing features listed in the Print dialog box. In those cases, the option is either not listed or is grayed and unavailable. In the situation illustrated here, WordPad does not support collating, so the Collate check box is grayed.

Print It

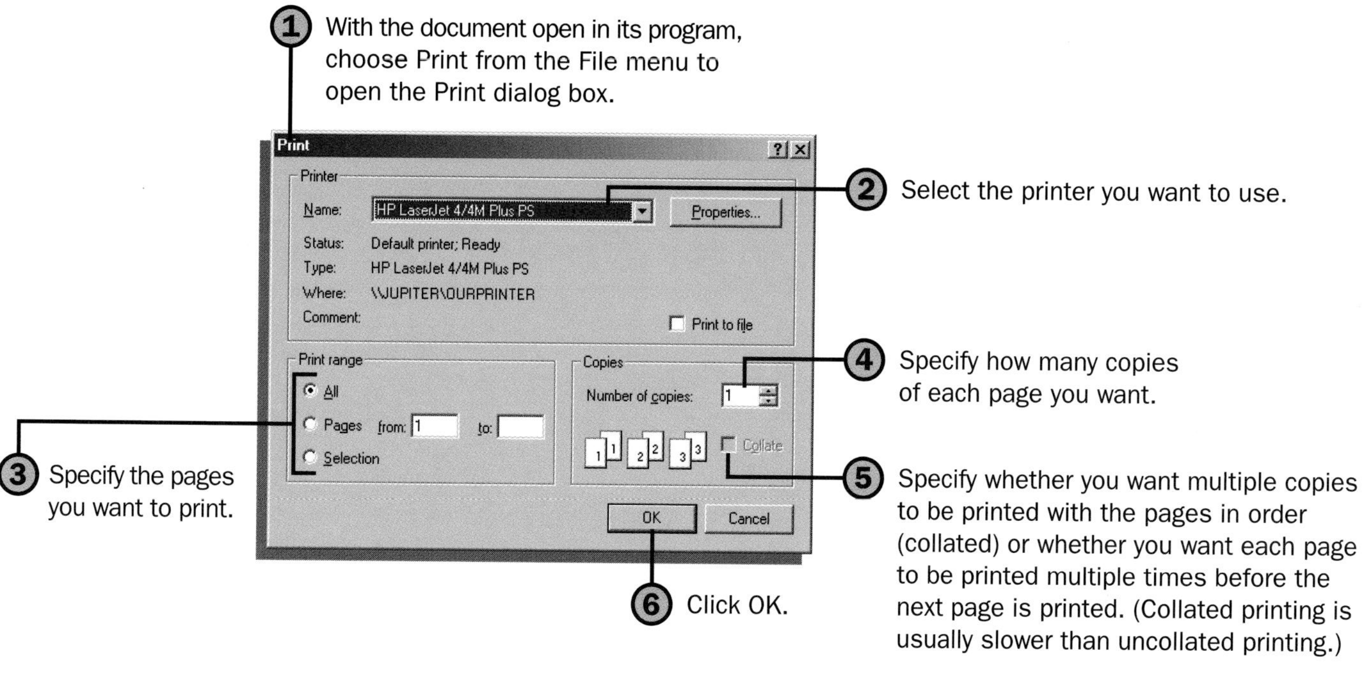

> TIP: If the Print command isn't followed by an ellipsis (...), the Print dialog box won't be displayed, and the document will be printed to the default printer using the default settings. In many programs, when you click the Print button on the toolbar, your document will be printed either to the default printer or to the last printer you specified in the Print dialog box. In some programs, clicking the Print button displays the Print dialog box.

Opening a Document in a Program

When a program is running, or if you want to make sure a document will open in a particular program, you can easily find and open a document from the program.

Open It

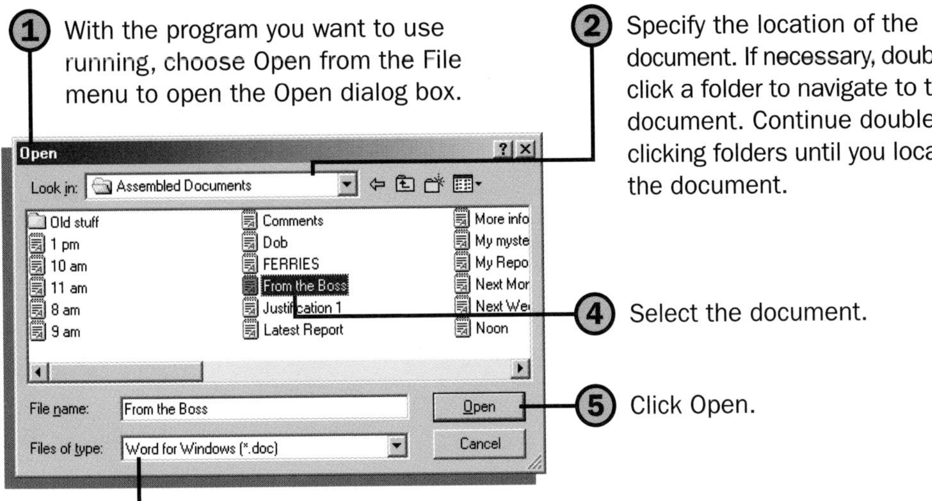

1. With the program you want to use running, choose Open from the File menu to open the Open dialog box.
2. Specify the location of the document. If necessary, double-click a folder to navigate to the document. Continue double-clicking folders until you locate the document.
3. If necessary, select the type of document you want to open. (Many programs specify the default type of document used by the program, and such programs display only documents of the specified file type in the list of files.)
4. Select the document.
5. Click Open.

TIP: Many programs list at the bottom of the File menu the documents you used most recently. If you choose one of these files, you don't need to use the Open dialog box.

TIP: To see the date a document was last modified, click the View button in the Open dialog box, and select Details.

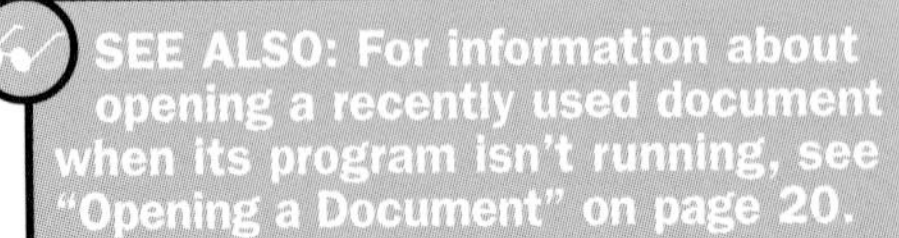
SEE ALSO: For information about opening a recently used document when its program isn't running, see "Opening a Document" on page 20.

Editing a Word Processed Document

You can use WordPad to edit Word, Microsoft Write, Rich Text Format (RTF), text (ANSI), MS-DOS text (ASCII), or Unicode text documents. When you use WordPad to edit a document that was created in Word, however, you'll lose any special formatting that WordPad doesn't support.

TIP: To avoid the possible loss of all your efforts, don't forget to save a document frequently as you edit it. If you want to keep a copy of the original unedited document in addition to your edited version, use the Save As command on the File menu to save the edited document under a different filename.

TIP: To replace repetitive words or phrases throughout a document, use the Replace command on the Edit menu.

Insert and Delete Text

1 Start WordPad and open the document you want to edit.

Click where you want to insert the text.

> It was a dark night. The wind nearly howled through the broken windows. Moldy shutters banged relentlessly against the wet walls. "Why me?" I murmured, but the

Type the text.

> It was a dark and stormy night. The wind nearly howled through the broken windows. Moldy shutters banged relentlessly against the wet walls. "Why me?" I

Select the text you want to delete by dragging the mouse pointer over it.

> It was a dark and stormy night. The wind nearly howled through the broken windows. Moldy shutters banged relentlessly against the wet walls. "Why me?" I

Press the Delete key to delete the text.

> It was a dark and stormy night. The wind howled through the broken windows. Moldy shutters banged relentlessly against the wet walls. "Why me?" I murmured, but the

Replace Text

Select the text you want to replace by dragging the mouse pointer over it.

> It was a dark and stormy night. The wind howled through the broken windows. Moldy shutters banged relentlessly against the wet walls. "Why me?" I murmured, but the

Type the new text. The selected text is replaced.

> It was a dark and stormy night. The wind howled through the broken windows. Moldy shutters banged relentlessly against the dank walls. "Why me?" I murmured, but the

Move Text

Select the text you want to move by dragging the mouse pointer over it.

> It was a dark and stormy night. The wind howled through the broken windows. Moldy shutters banged relentlessly against the dank walls. "Why me?" I murmured, but the wind shrieking carried my voice away. "Why not!" it jeered. A scream—or was it just a gull complaining about being forced to take flight by the storm? A hand ripping at

Drag the selected text to a new location.

TIP: WordPad can open Word 6, Word 97, and Word 2000 documents, but it can save Word documents only in the Word 6 format.

SEE ALSO: For information about different ways to open a document, see "Opening a Document" on page 20 and "Opening a Document in a Program" on the facing page.

Copying Material Between Documents

It's usually easy to copy material from a document that was created in one program to a document that was created in another program. How you insert the material depends on what it is. If it's similar to and compatible with the receiving document—text that's being copied into a Word document, for example—it's usually inserted as is and can be edited in the receiving document's program. If the item is dissimilar—a sound clip, say, inserted into a Word document—it's either *encapsulated,* or isolated, as an object and can be edited in the originating program only, or you simply are not able to paste that item into your document.

Copy and Insert Material

1. In the source document, select the material you want to copy.

2. Choose Copy from the Edit menu. Windows Me places the copied item on the Clipboard.

3. Switch to the destination document.

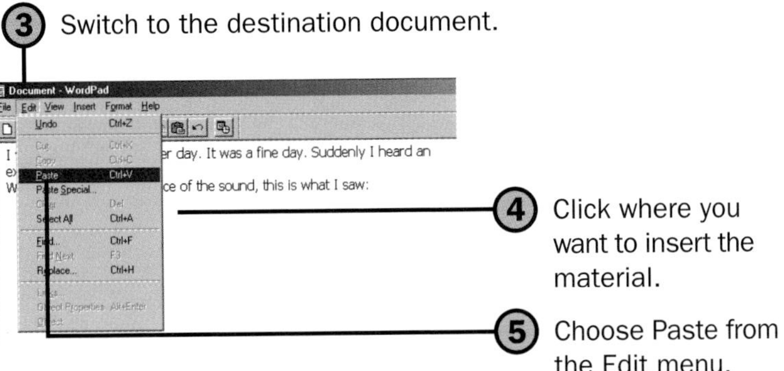

4. Click where you want to insert the material.
5. Choose Paste from the Edit menu.

6. Confirm that the inserted item looks the way you want. If necessary, use the program's formatting or editing tools to modify the item, or delete the inserted item, return to the source document, and modify the item before you copy and insert it again.

TIP: To insert an item using a different format, to insert the item showing an icon instead of the contents, or to link the item to the original file, choose Paste Special instead of Paste. To insert an entire document as an icon, drag the item from its folder into the document.

Inserting Special Characters

Windows Me provides a special accessory program called Character Map that lets you insert into your programs the characters and symbols that aren't available on your keyboard. Character Map displays all the characters that are available for each of the fonts on your computer.

SEE ALSO: For information about installing Character Map if it's not already installed on your system, see "Adding or Removing Windows Me Components" on page 170.

TIP: The Windows Me Clipboard is a temporary "holding area" for items you want to copy and paste. The Clipboard can hold only one item at a time, so do your pasting immediately after you've done your copying.

Find and Insert a Character

1. Start Character Map from the System Tools submenu of the Start menu.
2. Select a font.
3. Double-click the character you want to insert to select it. (If you want, you can select additional characters and insert all of them into your document at one time.)
4. Click Copy to place the character or characters on the Clipboard.
5. Switch to your program, click where you want to insert the character or characters, and press Ctrl+V (or choose Paste from the Edit menu) to paste the character or characters from the Clipboard.

Displays the character you've selected to be copied to the Clipboard

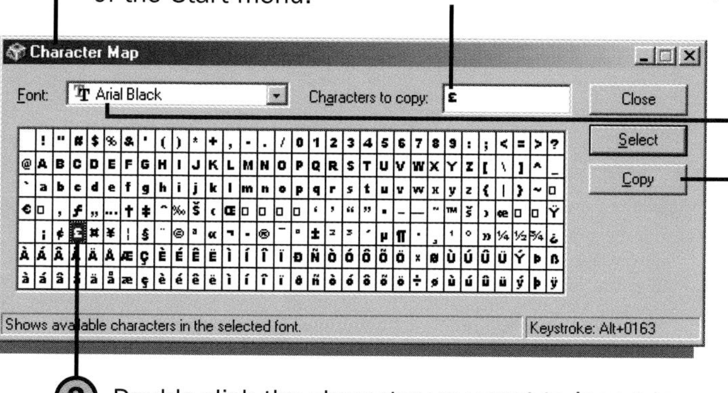

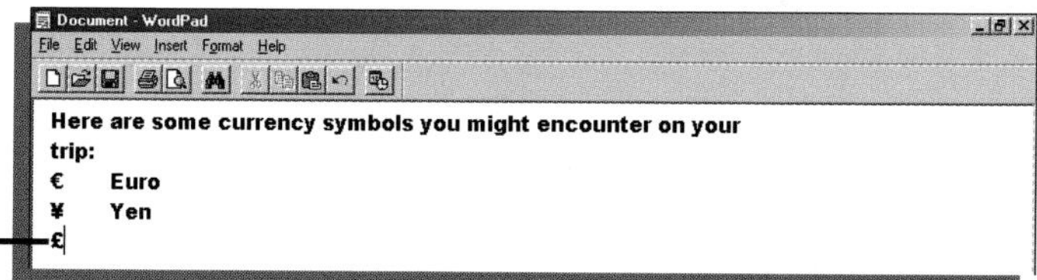

TRY THIS: In Character Map, select a character you insert frequently, and note the keystroke for the character in the bottom right corner. Switch to the program in which you want to insert the character, hold down the Alt key, and use your numeric keypad to enter the numbers. Format the inserted character with a different font or font size if desired.

TIP: To see an enlarged view of a character, click it without releasing the mouse button.

Crunching Numbers

Need to do a quick calculation but don't have enough fingers? Want to convert a decimal number into a hexadecimal or binary number? You can do these procedures, and even a few complex geometric and statistical calculations, with the Calculator.

Calculate a Value

1. Start the Calculator from the Accessories submenu of the Start menu.

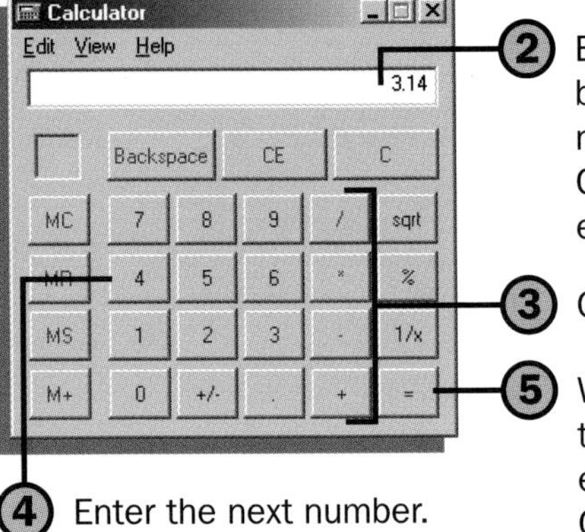

2. Either click the number buttons or type the numerals you want. Continue until you've entered the entire number.
3. Click a function.
4. Enter the next number.
5. When you've entered all the numbers, click the equal (=) button. Press Ctlr+C to copy the result if you want to paste it into your document.

TIP: When you choose Digit Grouping from the View menu, the Calculator makes large numbers easier for you to read by inserting a separator character between groups of numbers (a comma, for example, between the third and fourth digits). The separators and the decimal character are determined by your regional settings.

TRY THIS: With the Calculator in Scientific view, enter the number *699050*. Click the Hex button, then the Oct button, and then the Bin button to view the number in the different numbering systems.

Make Complex Calculations

1. Choose Scientific from the View menu.
2. Choose a numbering system if you don't want to calculate using the standard decimal system.

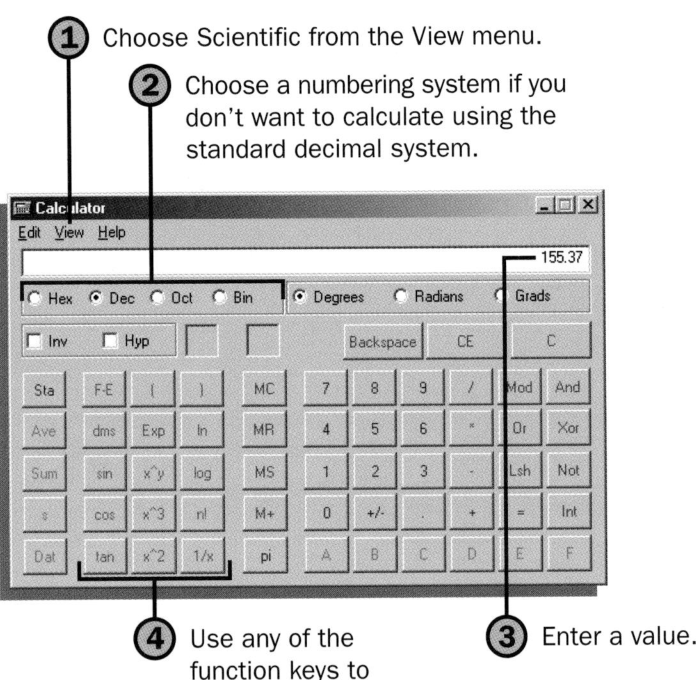

3. Enter a value.
4. Use any of the function keys to calculate a new value.

Make Statistical Calculations

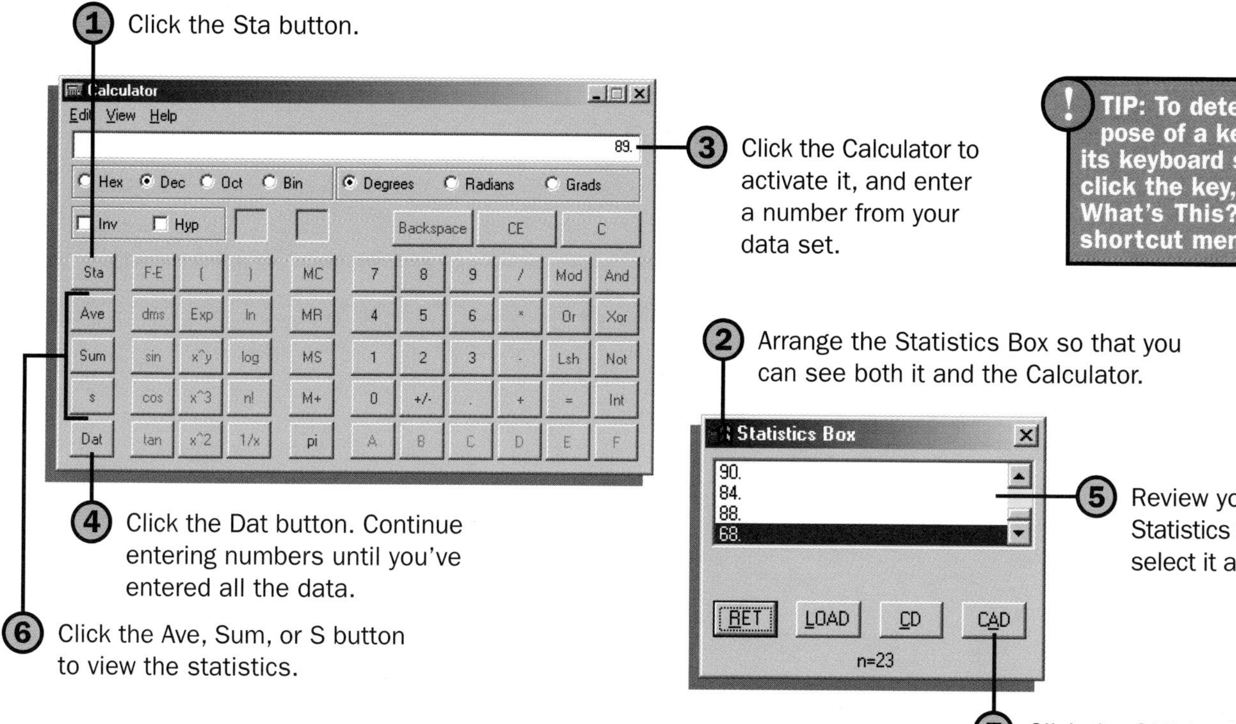

1. Click the Sta button.
2. Arrange the Statistics Box so that you can see both it and the Calculator.
3. Click the Calculator to activate it, and enter a number from your data set.
4. Click the Dat button. Continue entering numbers until you've entered all the data.
5. Review your data set in the Statistics Box. To delete an entry, select it and click the CD button.
6. Click the Ave, Sum, or S button to view the statistics.
7. Click the CAD button to clear the data and enter a new data set, or close the Statistics Box when you've finished.

! TIP: To determine the purpose of a key and to view its keyboard shortcut, right-click the key, and choose What's This? from the shortcut menu.

! TIP: To speed up your calculations, use the numeric keypad, pressing the + - * / and Enter keys instead of clicking the corresponding buttons. When you're entering statistical data, press the Insert key instead of clicking the Dat button. Make sure, however, that the Num Lock key is turned on.

Using MS-DOS Commands

In Windows Me, the MS-DOS prompt is the place where you can execute command-line instructions. Most of the commands are the old standard MS-DOS commands, some are enhancements of the MS-DOS commands, and others are commands that are unique to Windows Me. When you want or need to work from the MS-DOS prompt, you can open an MS-DOS Prompt window and execute all your tasks there, including using the basic commands, starting a program, and even starting a program in a new window.

Run a Command

1. Start an MS-DOS window by choosing MS-DOS Prompt from the Start menu.
2. At the prompt, type a command, including any switches and extra parameters, and press Enter.
3. Enter any additional commands you want to run.

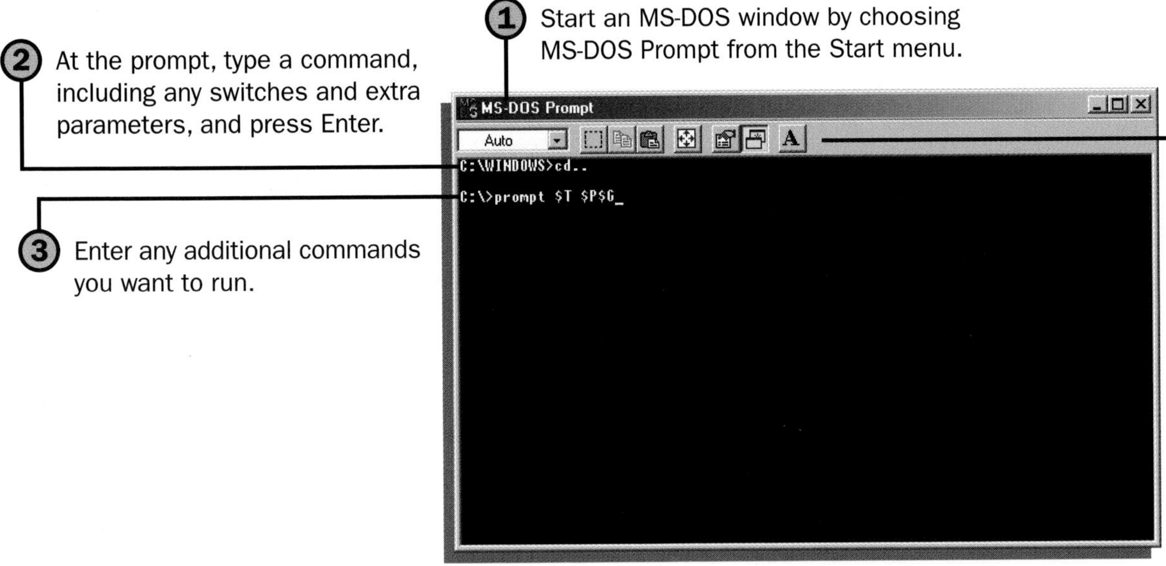

Use the toolbar buttons to select text for copying, to copy or paste text, to switch to full screen view, to show the properties for the MS-DOS program, to have the window run in the background while other programs are being run, or to change the font you're using. If you change the font, the window will automatically resize to accommodate the new font size.

TIP: Any changes you make to the current environment with commands such as *path* and *prompt* affect the current session only. To make the changes permanent, edit the Autoexec.bat file to include those settings.

TIP: Many commands have switches that allow the use of extra parameters, giving you greater control of the command. A switch is the part of the command with the forward slash (/) followed by a letter, a number, or another instruction. A parameter is an additional instruction you provide, such as the filename or drive letter.

Get Information About a Command

1 Type a command followed by a space and /? and press Enter to get information about the command.

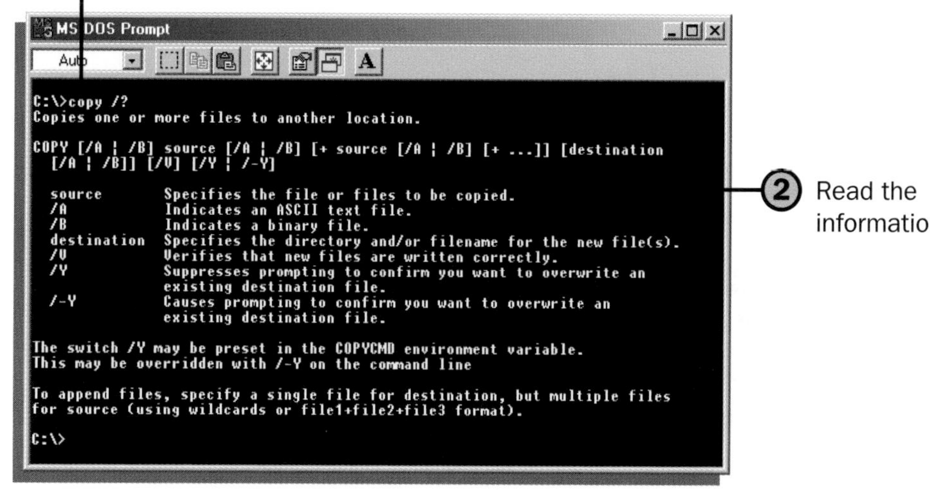

2 Read the information.

TIP: The "|" used before the word "more" is known as a *pipe*, and is usually typed by pressing Shift+\. This tells the system to send (or pipe) the output of the command through the More program, which displays the information one screenful at a time.

The Top 10 MS-DOS Commands

Command	Use
cd	Changes to the specified folder (or directory).
cls	Clears the screen.
copy	Copies the specified files or folders.
dir	Shows the contents of the current directory.
drive:	Changes to the specified drive (type the drive letter and a colon).
exit	Ends the session.
mem	Displays memory configuration.
path	Displays or sets the path the command searches.
prompt	Changes the information displayed at the prompt.
rename	Renames the specified file or files if the wildcard characters ? or * are used.

TRY THIS: Try typing the following commands to see how the switches after each command affect the results. Use the Up arrow key to repeat previous commands, and then edit them to include the correct switches.

Type *dir* and press Enter.

Type *dir /w* and press Enter.

Type *dir /?* and press Enter.

Type *dir /? |more* and press Enter to see the different ways to run a command.

Quitting When You're Stuck

If a program isn't working properly and doesn't respond when you try to close it, Windows Me gives you the option of forcing the program to close. When you use this option, you'll lose any unsaved work in the program, and, if the problem persists, you might need to reinstall the offending program.

Force a Program to Close

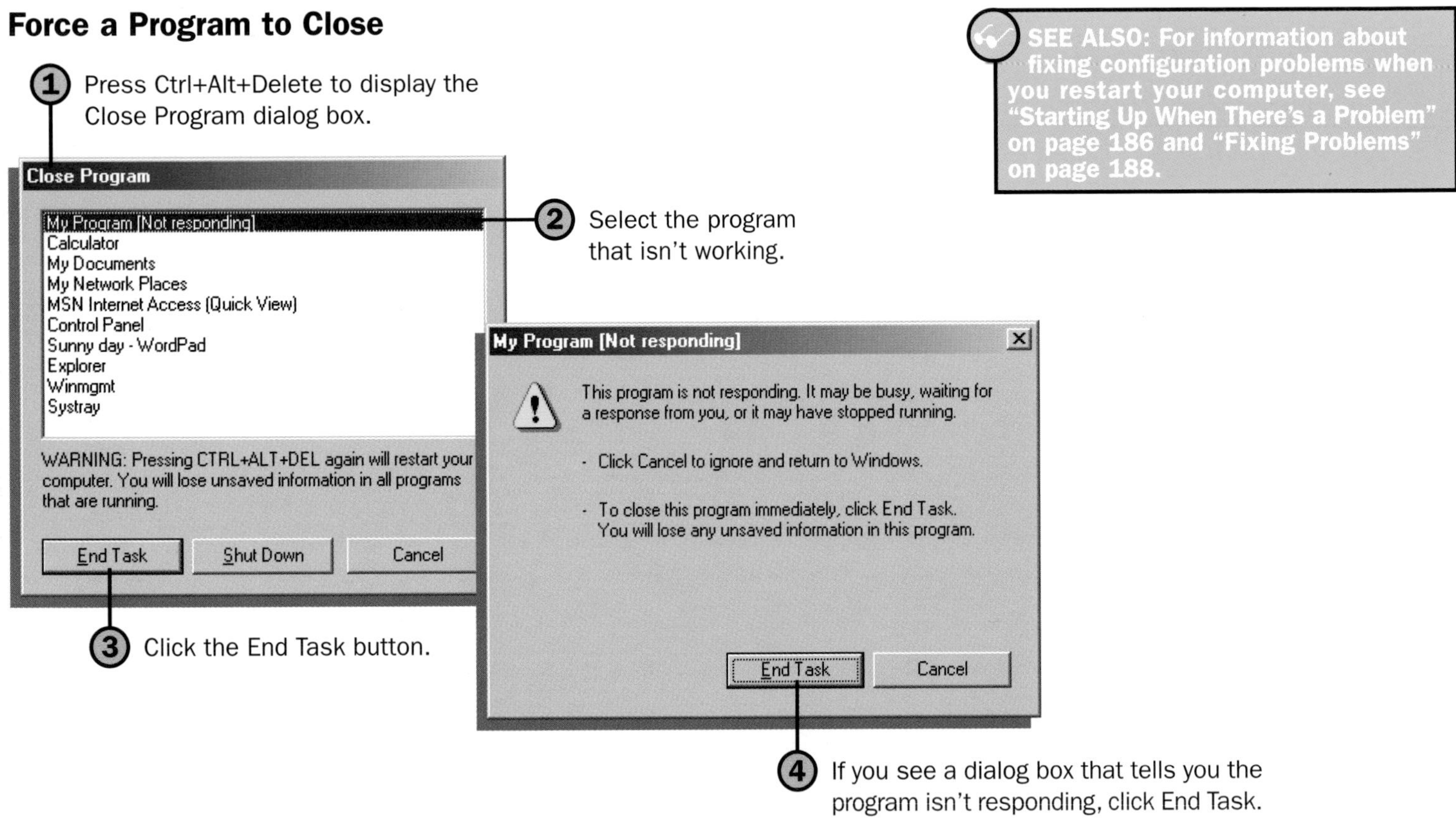

SEE ALSO: For information about fixing configuration problems when you restart your computer, see "Starting Up When There's a Problem" on page 186 and "Fixing Problems" on page 188.

TIP: If you can't end a specific program, close all your other programs and shut down Windows Me from the Start menu. If Windows Me is really misbehaving and still doesn't respond, your last resort is to turn off the computer's power.

Playing Games

In this section

Microsoft Windows Millennium Edition is a game-player's paradise. Whether you want to take a few minutes to work off some energy with a quick game of pinball or lose yourself for an hour in a game of Solitaire, Windows Me is ready. If you'd rather play games that involve several players, you can spend an evening competing with others over your network in an intense game of Hearts, or you can go farther afield and seek out players from around the world to join you in an international game of Backgammon or Checkers.

We're assuming that you know most of the basics about the games that come with Windows Me, but if you're unsure about the stratcgy or the rules, check out each game's Help menu for more complete information than we can provide here.

Windows Me is also an excellent platform for playing advanced computer games that you install yourself. With Windows Me's built-in support for advanced gaming technology, you'll find that gaming can be as intense and exciting as you want. Also, if your Internet game supports it, you can conduct a voice chat with your opponent while you're playing. These features, however, depend on the abilities of your game and the requirements it demands of your computer system. To set up and optimize the games you install yourself, see the documentation that came with the game.

Have fun!

Playing Classic Hearts

You can play Hearts either by yourself or over a network with up to three other players. The objective is to score the *fewest* points. For each trick you win, you're awarded one point for each heart and 13 points for the Queen of Spades. You must use the same suit that's played first unless you're void of that suit. You take the trick if you've played the highest card of the suit played.

TIP: Another scoring option is to "shoot the moon," where you collect all the points in one hand. If you succeed, each of the other players receives 26 points, and you receive zero points for the hand.

Play Classic Hearts

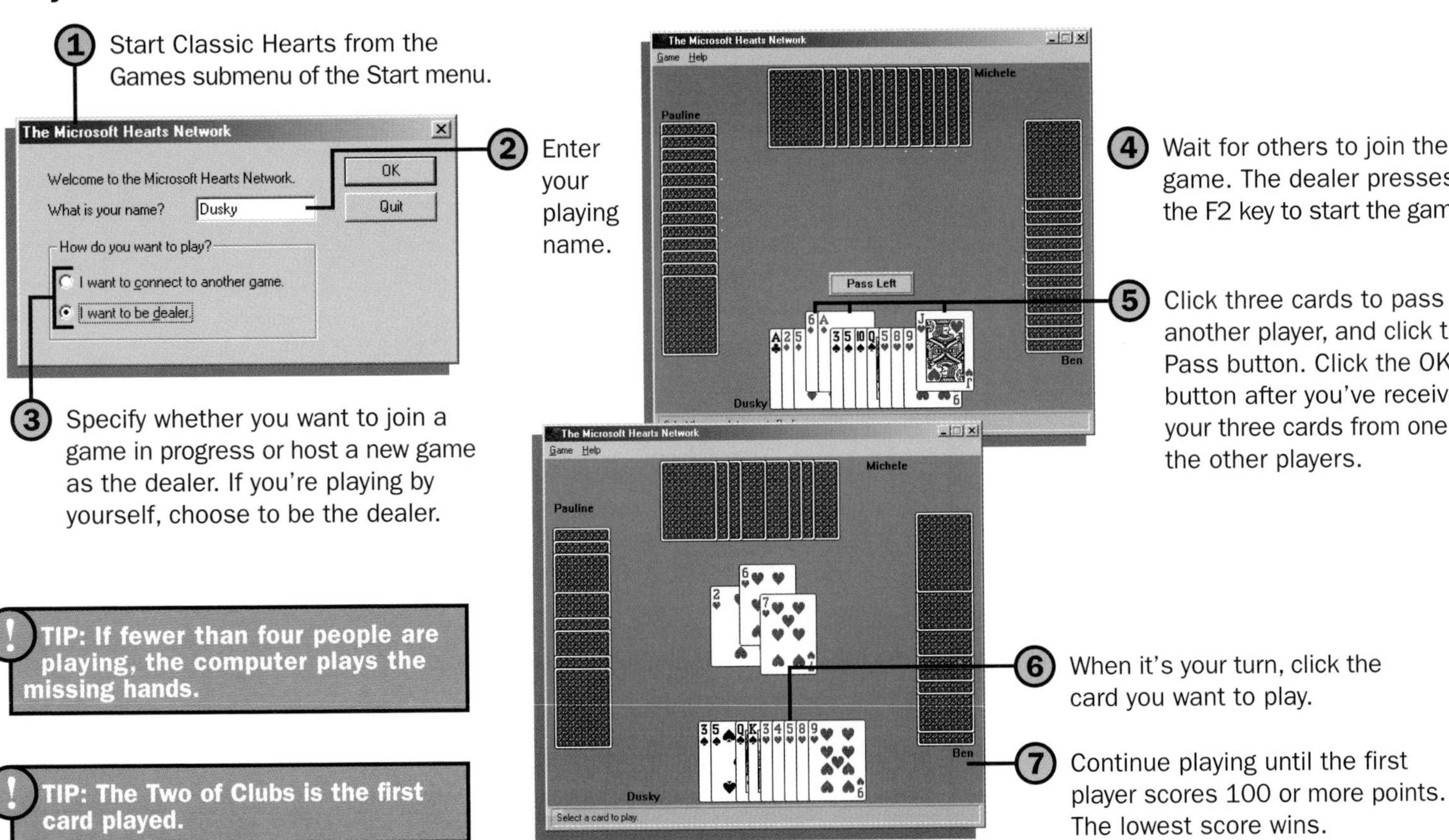

1. Start Classic Hearts from the Games submenu of the Start menu.
2. Enter your playing name.
3. Specify whether you want to join a game in progress or host a new game as the dealer. If you're playing by yourself, choose to be the dealer.
4. Wait for others to join the game. The dealer presses the F2 key to start the game.
5. Click three cards to pass to another player, and click the Pass button. Click the OK button after you've received your three cards from one of the other players.
6. When it's your turn, click the card you want to play.
7. Continue playing until the first player scores 100 or more points. The lowest score wins.

TIP: If fewer than four people are playing, the computer plays the missing hands.

TIP: The Two of Clubs is the first card played.

Playing Classic Solitaire

Solitaire is a classic card game that, as its name implies, you play by yourself. The object is to reveal all the cards that are turned face down and eventually to arrange all the cards in four piles, with each pile being a single suit stacked in ascending order from Ace through King.

TIP: To change the way a game is played, choose Options from the Game menu. To change the pattern of the card backs, choose Deck from the Game menu.

Play Classic Solitaire

1. Start Classic Solitaire from the Games submenu of the Start menu.
2. Use the mouse to drag one card on top of another card. (The cards must be stacked in descending numeric order, alternating the red and black cards.)

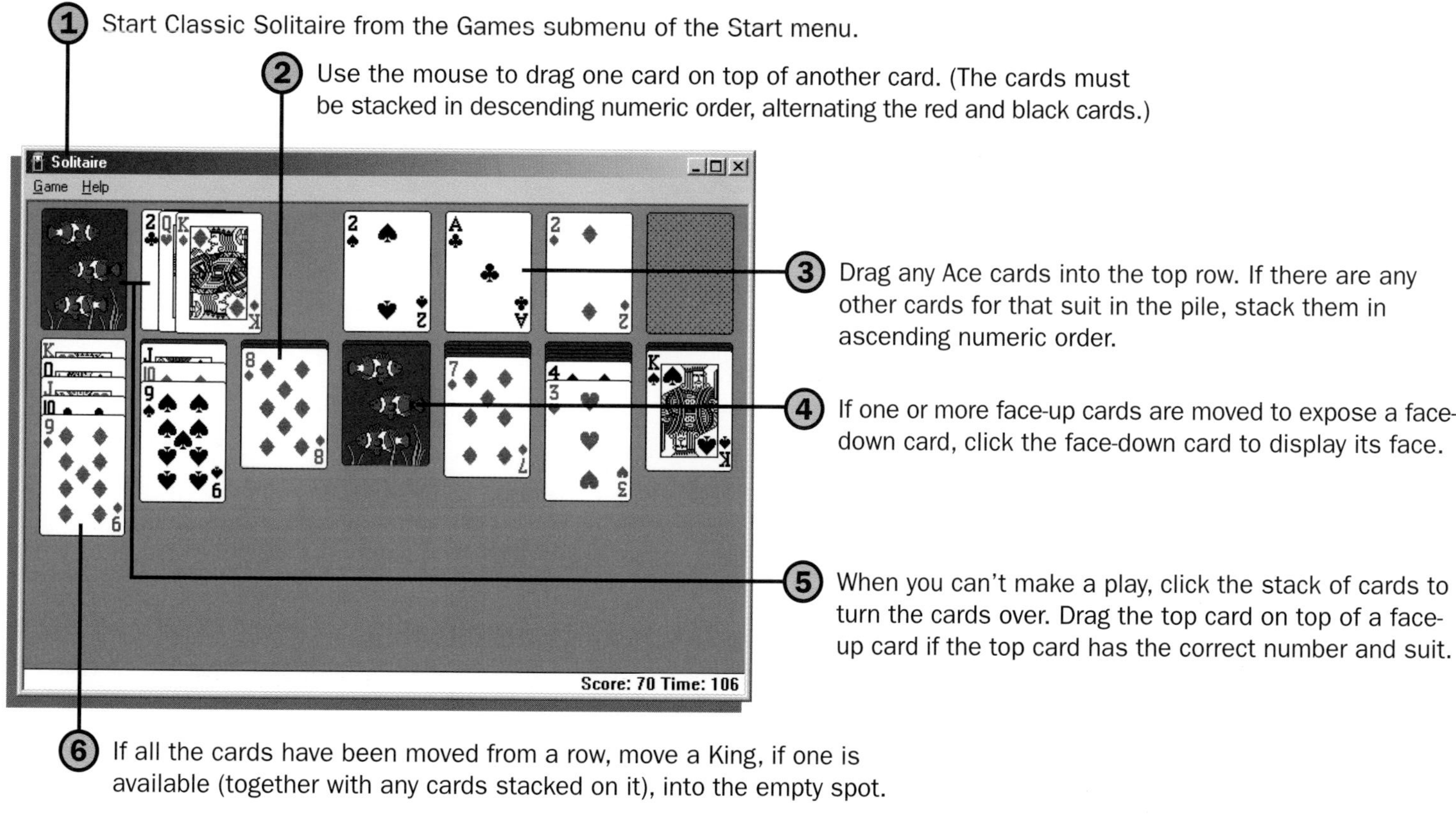

3. Drag any Ace cards into the top row. If there are any other cards for that suit in the pile, stack them in ascending numeric order.
4. If one or more face-up cards are moved to expose a face-down card, click the face-down card to display its face.
5. When you can't make a play, click the stack of cards to turn the cards over. Drag the top card on top of a face-up card if the top card has the correct number and suit.
6. If all the cards have been moved from a row, move a King, if one is available (together with any cards stacked on it), into the empty spot.

Playing FreeCell

FreeCell—a modified version of Solitaire—is another game that you play by yourself. The entire deck is dealt, and, as in Solitaire, you arrange the cards by stacking them in descending order, alternating the red and black cards. Unlike Solitaire, the sequence of cards can begin anywhere in the stack. You can move a single card on top of another card to add to the sequence of cards, or into one of the free cells at the top, or into a blank column after the column has been emptied of cards. You win by stacking all the cards by suit in ascending order.

> **TIP: If there are adequate free cells, you can move an entire series of cards from one column into another.**

> **TIP: Try to free the Ace cards early in the game and to keep as many free cells and empty columns as possible.**

Play FreeCell

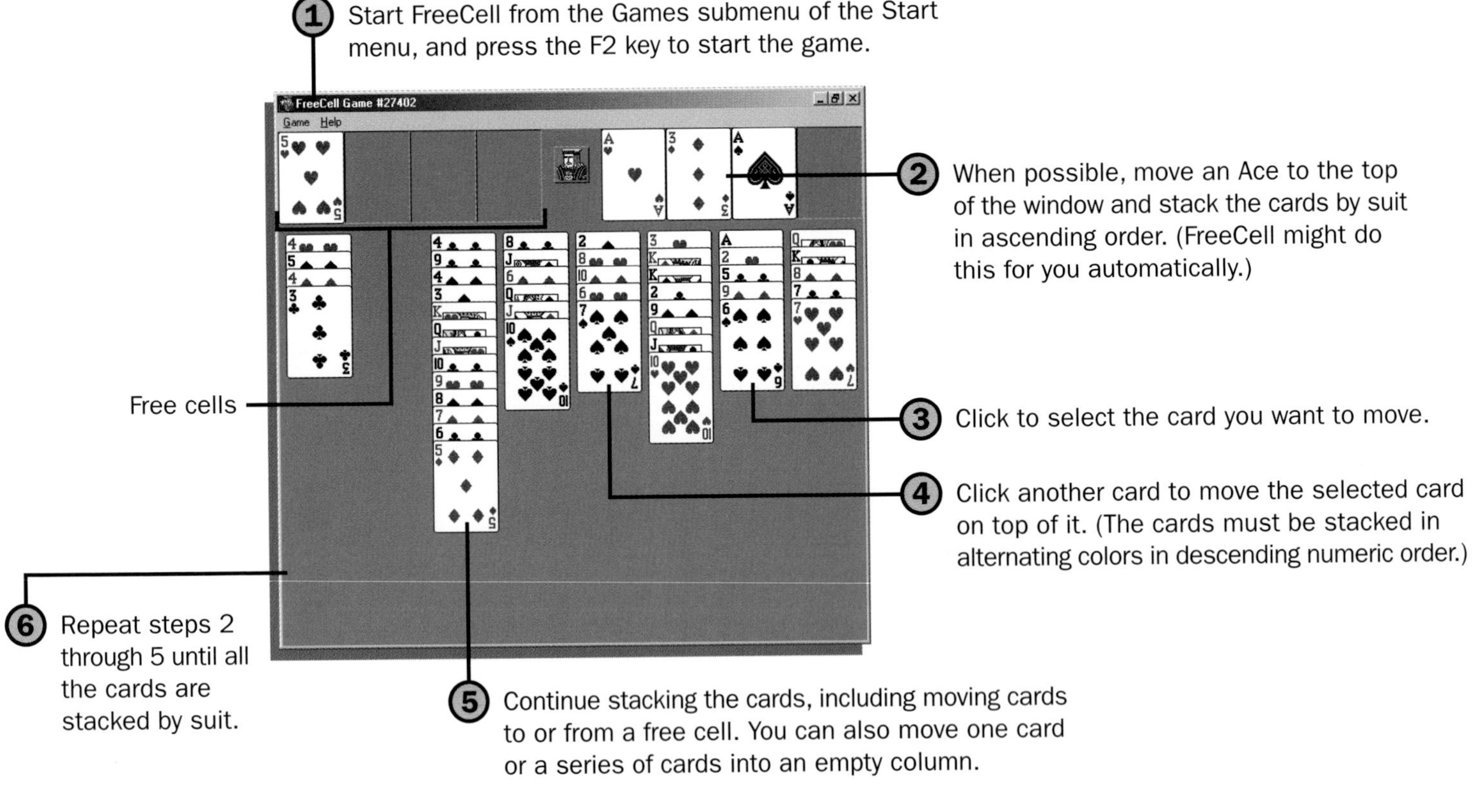

Playing Minesweeper

Minesweeper is a game that you play against the computer. The goal is to uncover, in the shortest possible time, all the squares that don't contain mines. If you uncover a square that contains a mine, you lose. The key is to use the numbers in the uncovered squares to determine which adjacent squares contain the mines.

TIP: The number in a square represents the total number of mines in adjacent squares—directly above, below, diagonal to, or to the left or right of the numbered square. Use several exposed numbers to figure out where the mines are.

Play Minesweeper

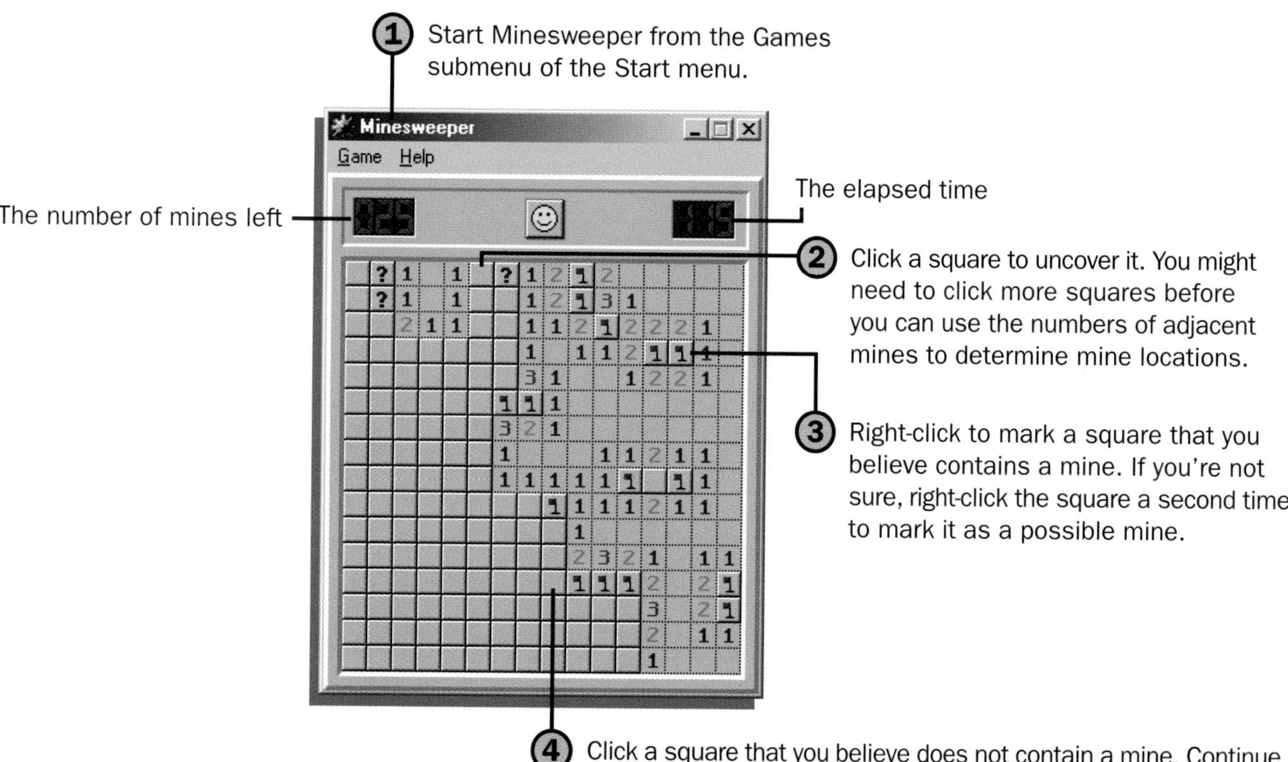

1. Start Minesweeper from the Games submenu of the Start menu.
2. Click a square to uncover it. You might need to click more squares before you can use the numbers of adjacent mines to determine mine locations.
3. Right-click to mark a square that you believe contains a mine. If you're not sure, right-click the square a second time to mark it as a possible mine.
4. Click a square that you believe does not contain a mine. Continue finding unmined squares and marking squares that contain mines until you've revealed all the unmined squares.

TIP: If the game is too easy or too difficult, select a different level of difficulty for the game. The greater the level of difficulty, the more squares and mines the game contains.

Playing Pinball

Pinball is a dazzling game with extensive sound effects. The object of the game is to keep each ball in play as long as possible while scoring the greatest number of points. Unlike most computer games, Pinball is played using the keyboard exclusively. You have three balls for the game unless you win extra balls, and you can advance through nine steps, or ranks, with each rank being more difficult to achieve and awarding a greater number of points.

TIP: Use the Nudge keys sparingly and cautiously—it's quite easy to tilt the game.

TIP: Press the F8 key to change which keys you use to control the game.

Play Pinball

1. Start Pinball from the Games submenu of the Start menu.

2. From the Options menu, specify how many players are in the game.
3. Hold down the Spacebar and then release it to shoot the ball into play.
4. Use the keys as shown in the table to control the play.

Key	Function
Z	Left flipper
/ (forward slash)	Right flipper
X	Nudge from the left
. (period)	Nudge from the right
Up arrow key	Nudge from the bottom
F2	New game
F3	Pause/resume
F4	Full screen/window

TIP: Pressing either flipper button changes which reentry lanes are lit.

Playing Spider Solitaire

Spider Solitaire is yet another version of Solitaire. Unlike other Solitaire games, the object is to stack the cards by suit in one column in descending order. When a series from King to Ace is complete, the cards are removed. The level of difficulty is determined by the number of suits used (one, two, or four).

TIP: To display possible moves, press the M key. Press it again to see another possible move.

TIP: Choose the Save This Game command from the Game menu to save the game for later play.

Play Spider Solitaire

1. Start Spider Solitaire from the Games submenu of the Start menu.
2. Specify how many suits you want to use.
3. Use the mouse to drag one card on top of another card. You can stack the cards in descending numeric order regardless of suit, but it's best to stack by suit. 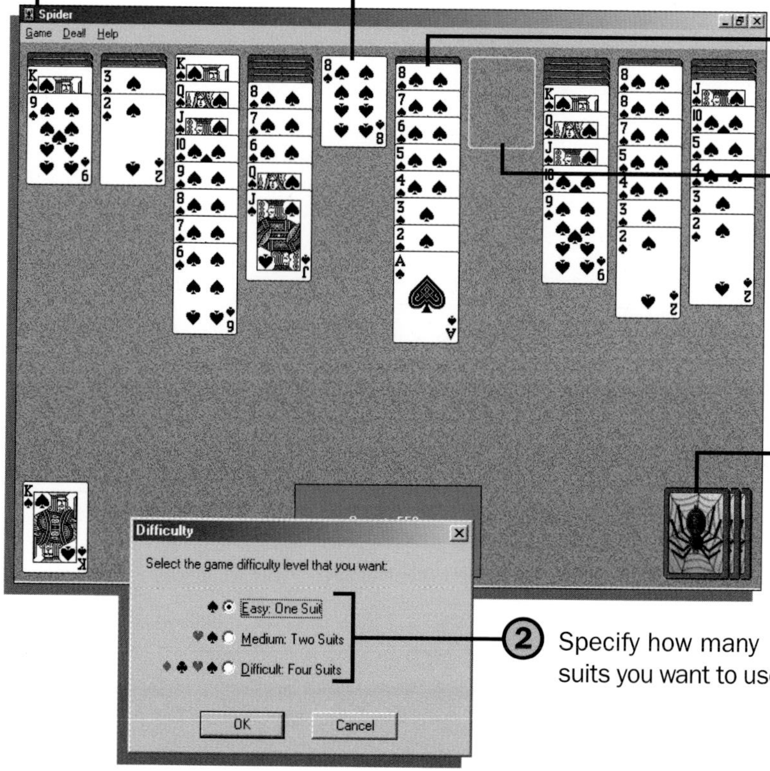
4. Drag a group of sequential cards of the same suit onto another card. (Only cards of the same suit can be moved as a group.)
5. If there's an empty column, move a card or a sequence of cards into the column.
6. If no moves are available, click the stacked cards to deal another round. (You can't deal if there's an empty column.) Continue playing until all the cards have been removed or until all the cards have been dealt and there are no longer any moves available.

Playing Games over the Internet

Windows Me provides five games that are designed to be played against other players over the Internet. When you start a game and connect to the Internet, the game server will try to find players matched to your skill level and language. (You can't select the players or the locations of your opponents.) You can communicate with the other player(s) by using the Chat feature.

TIP: To play additional types of games and to select specific individuals to be your opponents, connect to the Gaming Zone. You'll see the MSN Gaming Zone item on the Contents tab of the game's Help program.

Play a Game

1. Start an Internet game from the Games submenu of the Start menu.

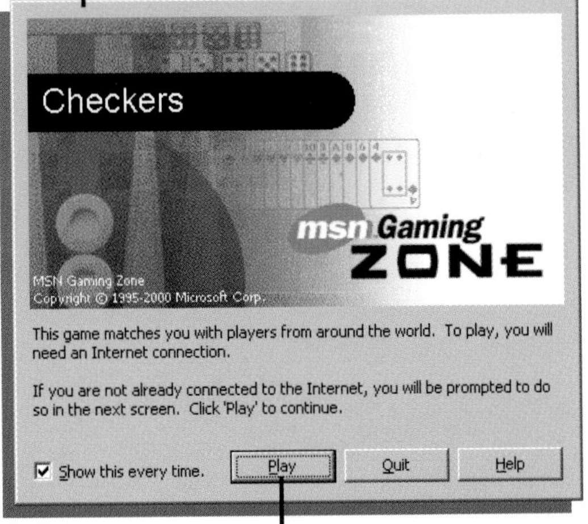

2. Click Play. If you're not already connected to the Internet, connect when prompted.

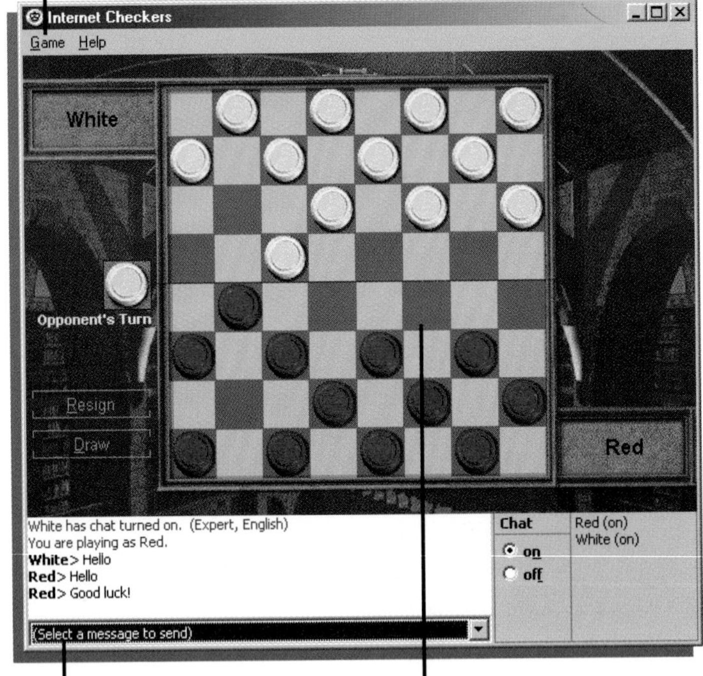

3. Select a message to send to your opponent.
4. Play the game and make your moves as prompted.
5. At the conclusion of the game, use the Game menu to start a new game with the same players, to start a game with different players, or to quit playing.

7 Working with Pictures

In this section

- Drawing a Picture
- Editing a Picture
- Scanning a Picture
- Downloading Digital Camera Pictures
- Customizing a Folder for Pictures
- Viewing and Printing Pictures

Drawings and paintings, illustrations in magazines, photographs of people, pets, or places…we all love pictures. Whether you want to enliven your documents with original drawings or add family photographs to your e-mail or your web page, Microsoft Windows Millennium Edition provides the tools that will help you achieve professional-looking results.

You can create your own drawings or edit existing ones in the Paint program, using Paint's tools to create the effects you want. Even if you're not a great artist, it can be a lot of fun! You might even want to use your creation as your Desktop wallpaper.

However, you're not limited to Paint's bitmap images. Windows Me was designed to enable you to work confidently with digital images as well. With help from the Scanner And Camera Wizard, you can easily scan images directly into your computer or into any graphics program that's designed to accept scanned images. With a couple of mouse-clicks, you can also review, select, and download photographs from your digital camera into your computer.

You can organize your pictures in the special pictures-friendly My Pictures folder that Windows Me provides, or you can create your own customized folders to house the picture-storage system that works best for you. You can then preview your pictures, rotate them if they're not correctly oriented, print them in the sizes you require, or view all the pictures in an automated slide show.

Drawing a Picture

If you're feeling artistic, you can create a picture in Paint. The Paint program comes with Windows Me and was designed to create and edit bitmap (BMP) pictures. Although you can print your picture if you want to, Paint pictures are often inserted into other documents. You can also create a Paint picture and use it as the wallpaper for your Desktop.

TIP: A bitmap is just that: a map created from small dots, or bits. It's a lot like a piece of graph paper with some squares filled in and others left blank to create a picture.

Create a Picture

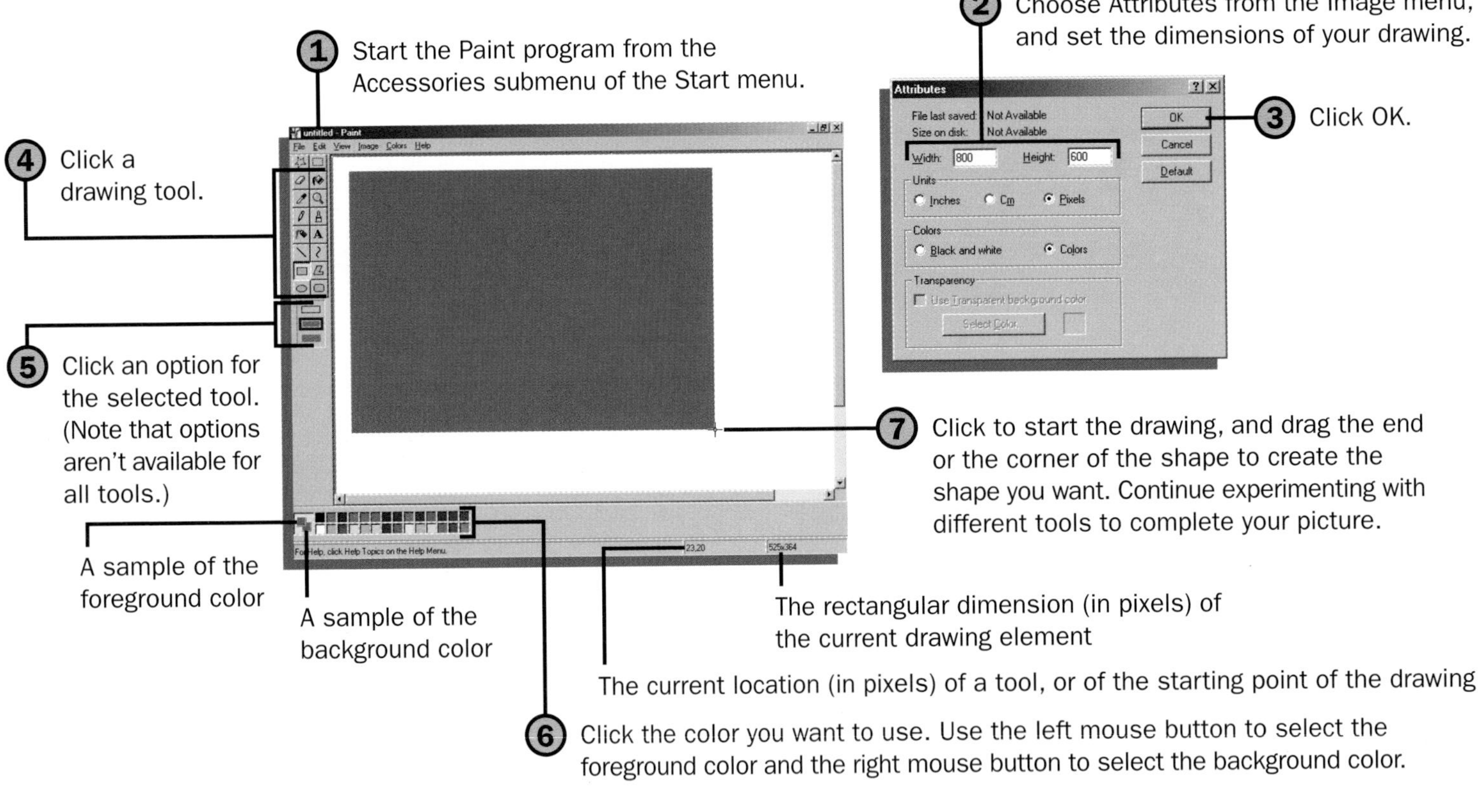

TIP: A bitmap picture can create a very large file, depending on the resolution and color depth of your screen and the size and color depth at which you save the picture. You can substantially reduce the file size of a bitmap file (sometimes by more than 90 percent) by storing it in a compressed folder.

Use the Tools

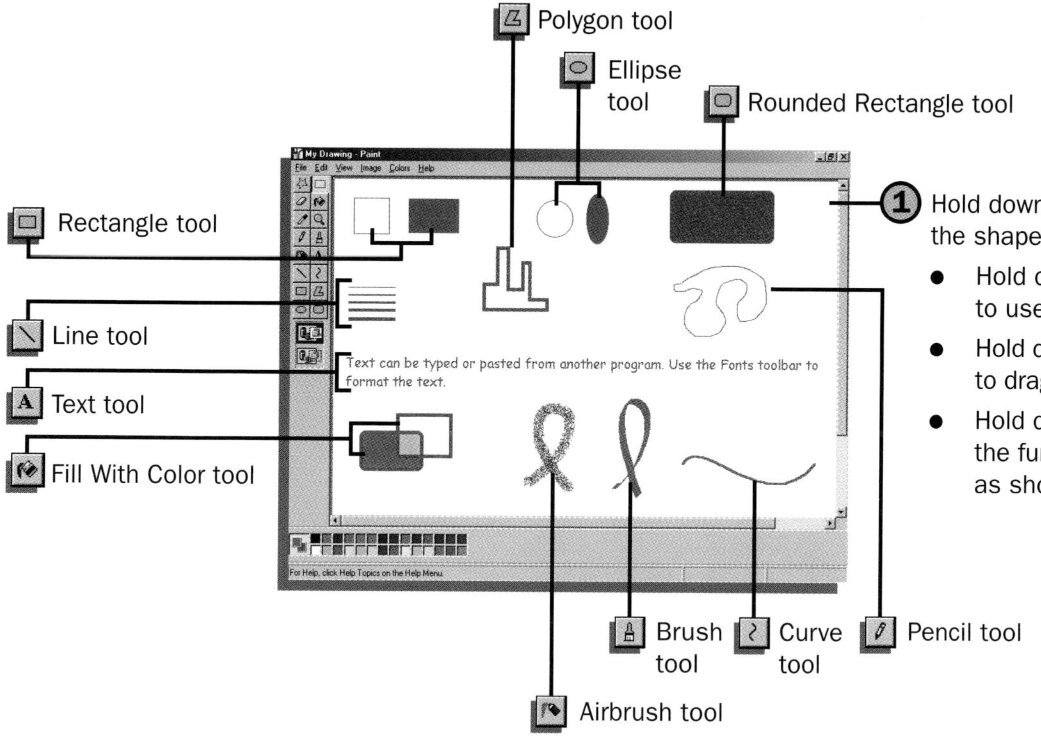

1. Hold down a mouse button and drag the shapes you want:
   - Hold down the left mouse button to use the foreground color.
   - Hold down the right mouse button to drag with the background color.
   - Hold down the Shift key to modify the function of some of the tools, as shown in the table.

TIP: Choose the Undo command from the Edit menu to remove your last drawing; use the Undo command again to remove the previous drawing.

Change a Tool's Function with the Shift Key

Hold down the Shift key and	Result
The Ellipse tool	Creates a circle.
The Rectangle tool	Creates a square.
The Rounded Rectangle tool	Creates a square with rounded corners.
The Line tool	Draws a horizontal, vertical, or diagonal line.

TRY THIS: Start a new Paint picture, and set the picture's Width and Height to the dimensions of your screen in pixels (800 x 600, for example). Create and save your picture, and then choose Set As Wallpaper (Centered) from the File menu.

TIP: To add text to a picture, use the Text tool to draw a text box, and just start typing. As long as the text box is active, you can edit the text, change the font, and resize the text box. When you click outside the text box, the text is turned into a bitmap image that can be edited just like any other picture element.

SEE ALSO: For information about compressed folders, see "Compressing Files" on page 27.

Editing a Picture

It's easy and fun to modify an existing bitmap picture to customize it, or to create a new picture using only part of the original picture. You can also modify the size or shape of part of the picture and can even create some special effects.

> **TIP:** If you have a scanner or a digital camera attached to your computer, you can scan an image directly into Paint from the File menu. You'll have more options, however, if you use the Scanner And Camera Wizard on the Accessories submenu of the Start menu to scan the picture and save it as a bitmap file.

Crop a Picture

1. Start Paint if it isn't already running. Use the drawing tools to create a picture, scan or download an image into Paint, or choose the Open command from the File menu to open an existing bitmap file.
2. Click the Select tool.
3. Drag a selection rectangle around the area you want to keep, and choose Copy To from the Edit menu.
4. Specify a name for the new image.
5. Click Save.

> **TIP:** To tweak your picture, click the Magnifier tool, select a magnification level, and use the Pencil tool to edit individual pixels, clicking the left mouse button for the foreground color and the right mouse button for the background color.

6. Open the cropped picture and modify it if you want.

TRY THIS: Create a cropped picture. Open another picture in Paint, choose Paste From from the Edit menu, locate the cropped picture, and paste it into the second picture. Drag the inserted picture into the location you want, and click outside the selection. Save the edited picture.

TIP: To replace a large area with the background color, use the Select tool to select the area, and then press the Delete key.

Modify a Picture's Size, Shape, or Color

1. Use the Select tool to select the part of the picture you want to work on.

Drag a handle...

...to resize the selection.

Hold down the Shift key and drag the selection to create a series of copies.

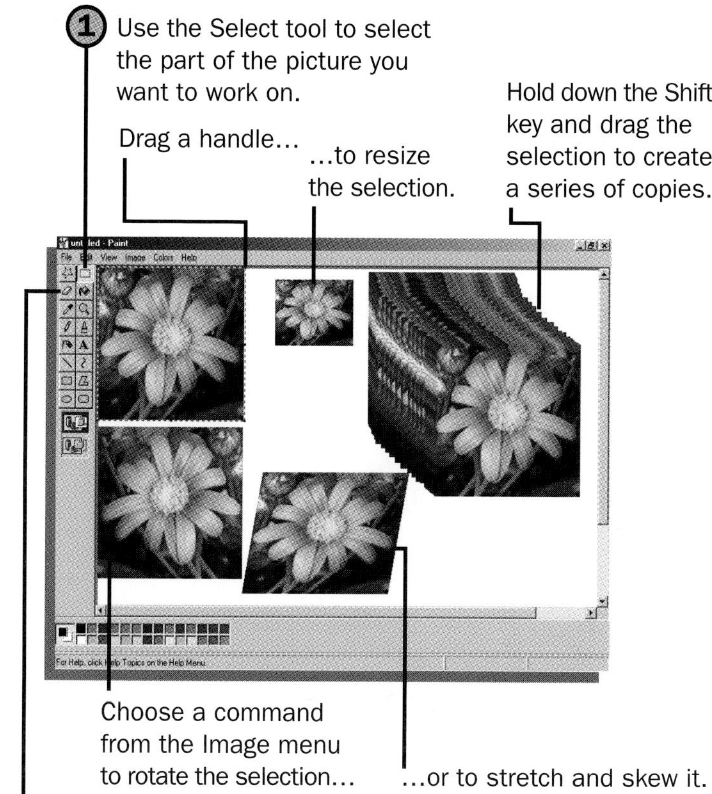

Choose a command from the Image menu to rotate the selection...

...or to stretch and skew it.

2. Use the Eraser tool to replace any color with the background color. To replace one color with another, set the foreground color to the color to be replaced and the background color to the replacement color, and then hold down the right mouse button and drag the Eraser over the area whose color you want to replace.

Scanning a Picture

A scanner is a great tool to digitize images and make them available on your computer. Windows Me provides access to your scanner with the Scanner And Camera Wizard, which steps you through the process. The wizard adapts to the specific features of your scanner, so the options you see in the wizard might be different from those described here. If you want to scan using a specific program, you can tell Windows Me to bypass the wizard and to automatically start that program when you press the scanner button.

Scan a Picture

1. Choose Scanner And Camera Wizard from the Accessories submenu of the Start menu, and, if the Select Device dialog box appears, double-click the scanner.

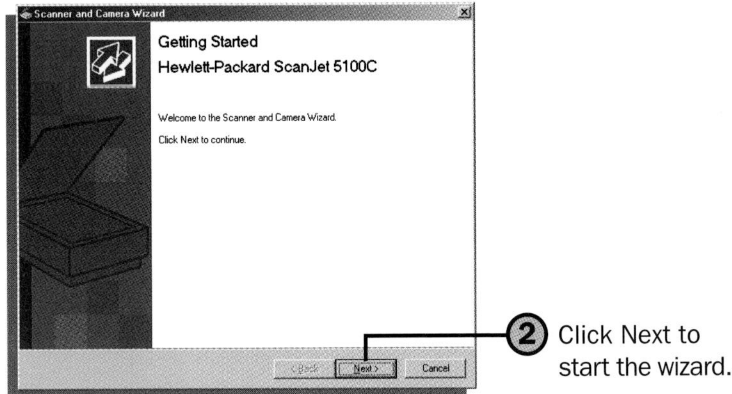

2. Click Next to start the wizard.

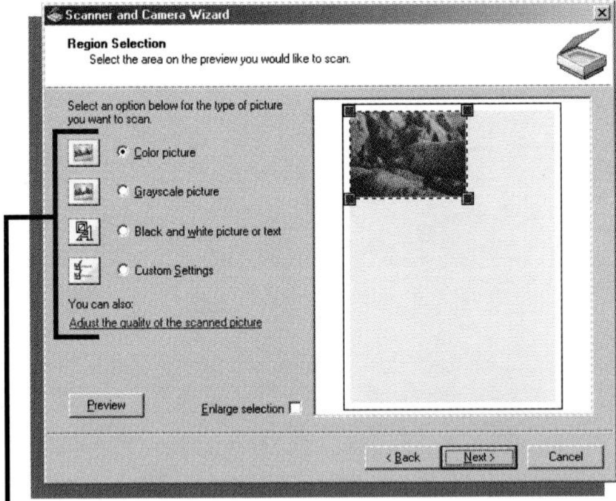

3. Make your settings for the scan. (Some of the options depend on the features of your scanner.) Click Next.

TIP: If your scanner is connected to your computer but isn't set up in Windows Me, use the manufacturer's setup disk to install it. Neither the Scanners And Cameras item in the Control Panel nor the Scanner And Camera Wizard on the Start menu will be present until you've installed one imaging device (a scanner or a camera).

4. Specify a name for the picture, where you want it to be stored, and the appropriate file format.

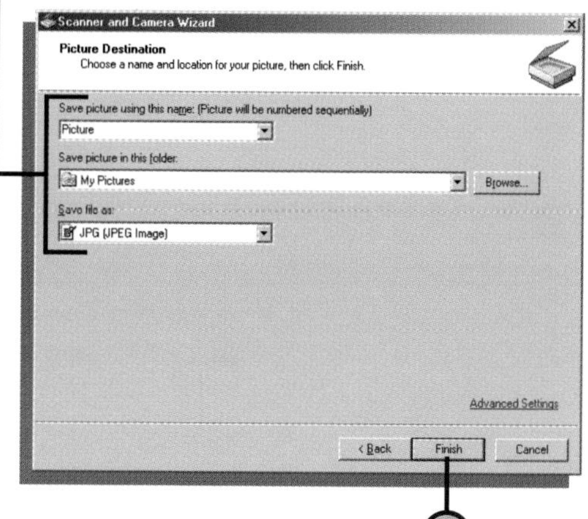

5. Click Finish to scan the picture and create the file.

> **!** TIP: You can also run the Scanner And Camera Wizard from the My Pictures folder, provided the folder is set to display web content.

SEE ALSO: For information about installing your scanner if Windows Me doesn't install it automatically, see "Adding Hardware" on page 174.

Use a Specific Program

1. From the Settings submenu of the Start menu, choose Control Panel, double-click the Scanners And Cameras item, and double-click the scanner to display its Properties dialog box.

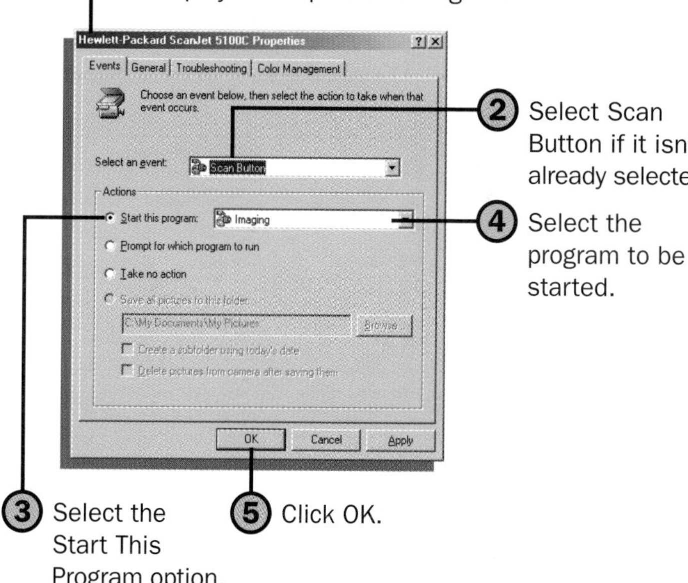

2. Select Scan Button if it isn't already selected.
3. Select the Start This Program option.
4. Select the program to be started.
5. Click OK.

> **!** TIP: If you want to use different programs for different scans, select the Prompt For Which Program To Run option. In most imaging programs, you can also access and control the scanner directly from the program.

Downloading Digital Camera Pictures

Once your digital camera is set up in Windows Me, the Scanner And Camera Wizard makes it simple to preview the pictures on your digital camera and to select the ones you want to download. You can also specify where you want the pictures to be stored, how they're to be named, and whether you want them to be deleted from your camera after they've been downloaded.

Download Pictures

1. Choose Scanner And Camera Wizard from the Accessories submenu of the Start menu, double-click your camera in the Select Device dialog box, and click Next to start the wizard.

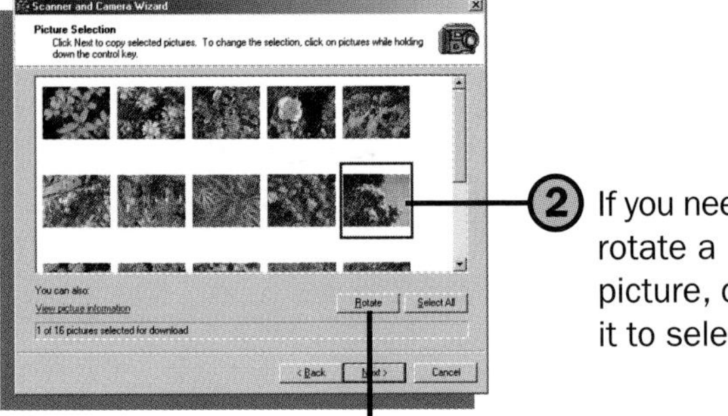

2. If you need to rotate a picture, click it to select it.
3. Click Rotate to rotate the picture 90 degrees. If necessary, click Rotate again to rotate the picture an additional 90 degrees.

4. Select the picture or pictures you want to download. Hold down the Ctrl key and click individual pictures to select multiple pictures, or click Select All to download all the pictures. Click Next.
5. Type a name or select an existing name for the series of pictures.

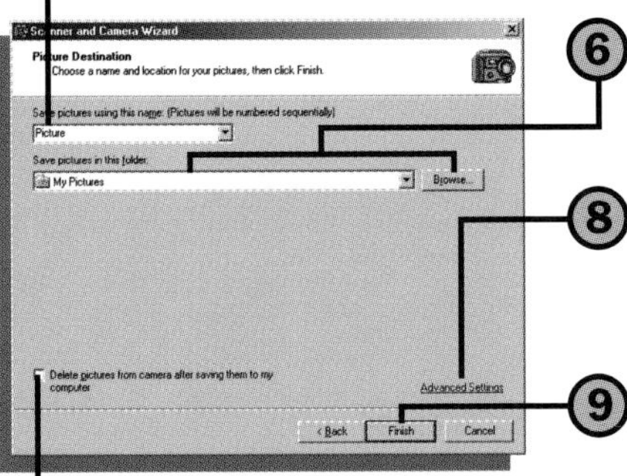

6. Specify the folder in which to store the pictures, or click Browse to specify a different folder.
7. Turn on the check box if you want the pictures to be deleted from the camera.
8. Click to automatically place the pictures in a subfolder labeled by date or by the picture name you chose.
9. Click Finish, and wait for the pictures to be downloaded.

TIP: Until you've completed the wizard, only small thumbnail images of your pictures have been sent to your computer; the pictures themselves still reside only in your camera.

Manage Individual Pictures

1. In My Computer, double-click your camera.

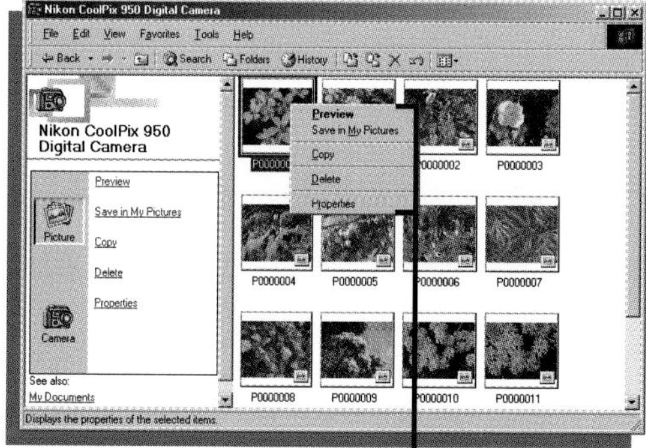

2. Right-click a picture, and choose
   - Preview to view the entire picture.
   - Save In My Pictures to download the picture.
   - Copy to download the picture to a different folder by switching to that folder and choosing Paste from its Edit menu.
   - Delete to delete the picture from the camera.
   - Properties to see details about the picture.

Manage the Camera

1. Click Camera.

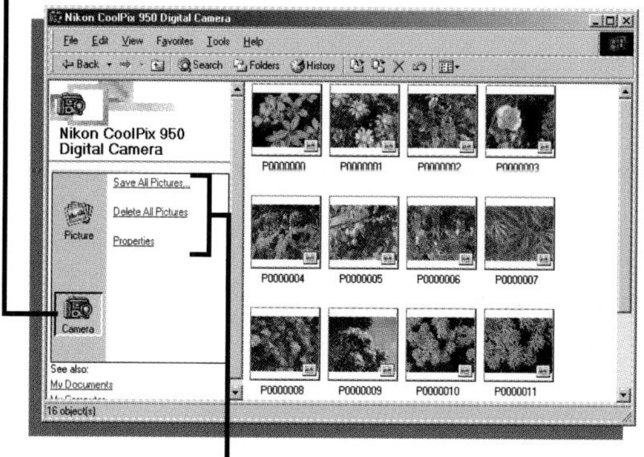

2. Select
   - Save All Pictures to start the Scanner And Camera Wizard for the camera.
   - Delete All Pictures to delete all the pictures in the camera.
   - Properties to see and modify camera settings and to conduct a diagnostic test of the camera.

TIP: If Windows Me doesn't automatically set up the camera when it's first connected, you'll need to use the manufacturer's setup disk to install it.

TIP: If you download pictures from a camera using infrared ports, the camera initiates and controls the downloading. See your camera's documentation for details.

Customizing a Folder for Pictures

Windows Me provides a useful folder, appropriately named My Pictures, for storing, managing, and viewing your pictures. However, if you want to use a different filing structure to store your pictures, you can modify a folder so that it will be customized to hold and work with pictures.

Customize the Folder

1. Open the folder you want to customize, choose Customize This Folder from the View menu, and click Next to start the Customize This Folder Wizard.

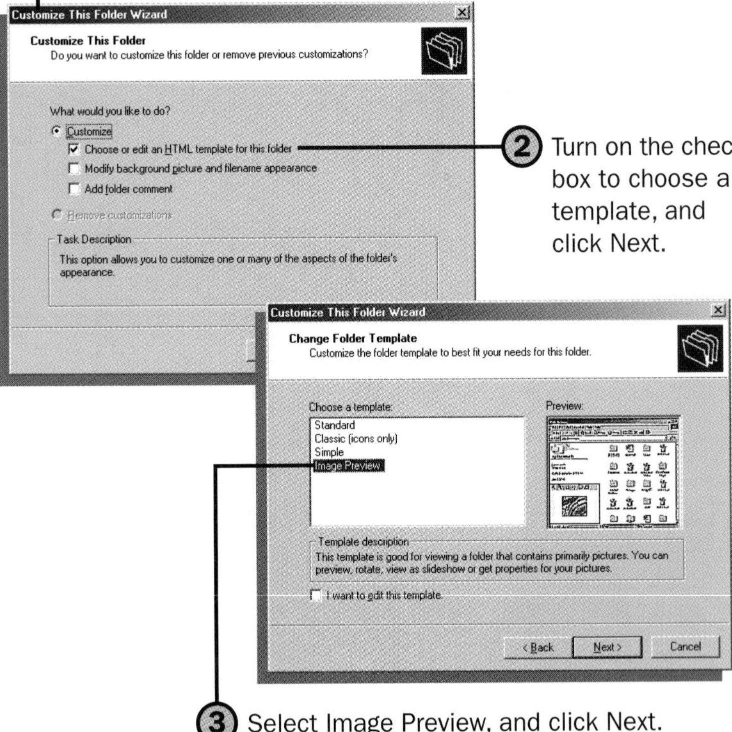

2. Turn on the check box to choose a template, and click Next.

3. Select Image Preview, and click Next. Click Finish to complete the wizard.

4. Copy or download the images into the folder, and then use the tools in the folder just as you would in the My Pictures folder.

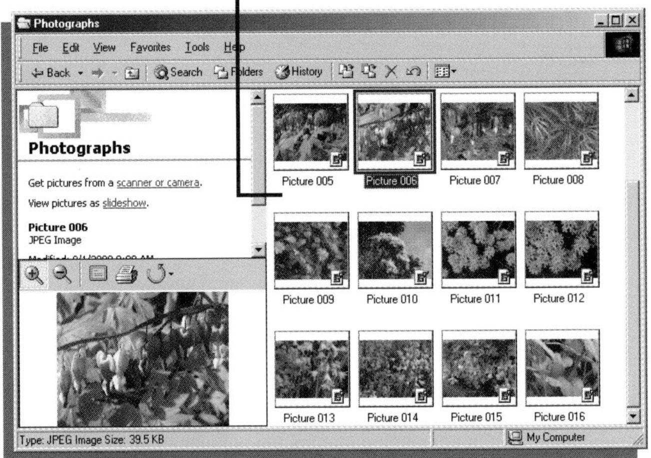

TIP: To remove the customization, rerun the Customize This Folder Wizard, and select the Remove Customizations option.

Viewing and Printing Pictures

Windows Me provides a variety of ways to view your pictures, depending on whether you want to view a group of pictures as a slide show or simply print a single image. Before you print a picture, you can preview it, change its size, and correct its orientation if necessary.

View Your Pictures as a Slide Show

1. Open the folder that contains the pictures, and click Slideshow.

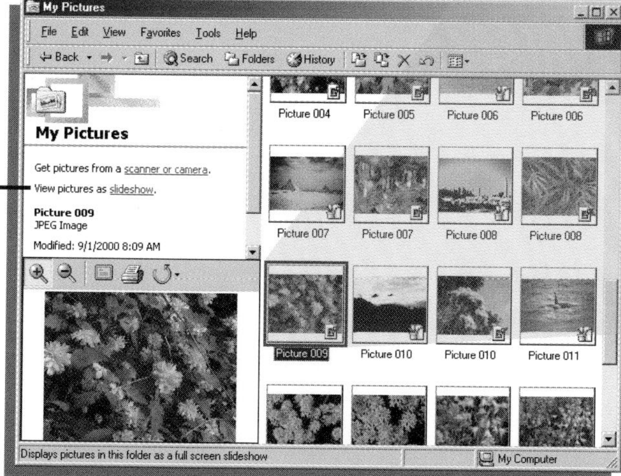

The slide show controls

2. Do either of the following:
   - Click anywhere to advance to the next picture.
   - Move the mouse to display the controls, and use them to pause, advance, repeat, or end the slide show.

TIP: You'll have more control over sizing and printing a picture if you insert it into a program such as Microsoft Word, or if you use a graphics-editing program before you print the picture.

SEE ALSO: For information about setting a folder to display slide shows and image previews, see "Customizing a Folder for Pictures" on the facing page.

For information about displaying a series of pictures as a screen saver, see "Displaying a Screen Saver" on page 149.

Preview and Print a Picture

1. Select the picture you want.
2. View the image.
3. Use the tools to zoom in or out, to rotate the picture, or to print it.
4. Click the Image Preview button.

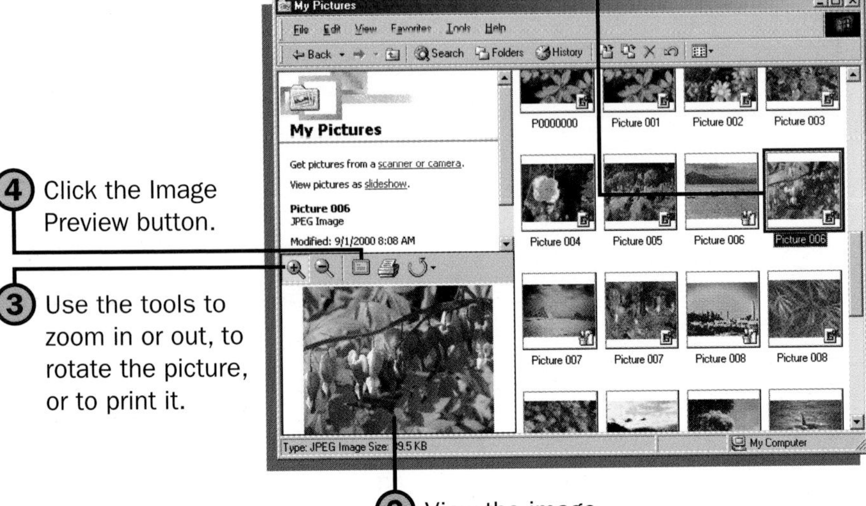

5. Use the tools to zoom in or out, or rotate or print the picture.
6. Close the Image Preview window when you've finished.

TIP: To zoom in or out, click a Zoom control, and then click in the picture.

TIP: If you haven't yet set up your printer for printing graphics, when you click the Print button, you'll need to click the Properties button in the Print dialog box and make any necessary changes on the Graphics tab.

8 Multimedia

In this section

If you like music and videos, you'll *love* Windows Media Player because of the freedom it gives you to control and customize your music and videos. You can use Media Player to download information about albums from the Internet; to play streaming media—videos, live broadcasts, or music tracks; or to copy individual pieces of music or entire CDs to your computer. You can also create your own "jukebox" by arranging the media you want to play, regardless of the format—songs, video clips, and so on—in the order you want in your own customized playlist. And it's a lot of fun to give Media Player a new "skin" to change its appearance!

Another exciting tool that comes with Microsoft Windows Millennium Edition is Windows Movie Maker, which enables you to make great little movies from a variety of sources—you can use a digital video camera, a digital web camera, existing video clips, material from an analog video camera or from videotape or television, or even still pictures. You can edit your clips, create fade-in/fade-out transitions between clips for a professional look, and add an audio track, a musical soundtrack, background sounds, or narration. There's a convenient storyboard where you assemble your clips to create the visual and auditory sequence of your movie, and Movie Maker compresses the files into a size small enough that you can send your movie via e-mail.

Playing a Music CD

Playing a CD is as simple as putting the CD into the drive and waiting for Windows Media Player to start playing the music. However, Windows Media Player can also provide additional information from the Internet about the music and the performer. With or without this additional information, you can control and customize the way the music is played.

Play a CD

1. Insert the CD into the disc drive and wait for Windows Media Player to start playing the CD. If you want to download the album information but aren't connected to the Internet, connect when prompted.
2. Click the Show Equalizer & Settings button if the Equalizer isn't displayed.
3. Click the Show Playlist button if the playlist isn't displayed.
4. Double-click a track to jump to that track.
5. Drag the Equalizer bars to modify the playback.

6. Drag to change the volume.
7. Use the buttons to control the play just as you would on any CD player.

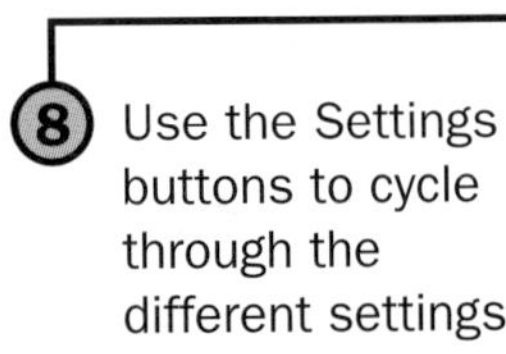

8. Use the Settings buttons to cycle through the different settings you can make.

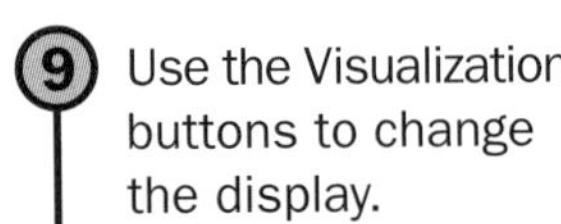

9. Use the Visualization buttons to change the display.

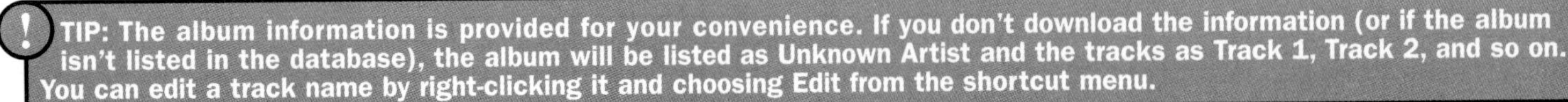

TIP: If the CD doesn't start Media Player, either click the Windows Media Player button on the Quick Launch toolbar or double-click the shortcut on the Desktop.

TIP: The album information is provided for your convenience. If you don't download the information (or if the album isn't listed in the database), the album will be listed as Unknown Artist and the tracks as Track 1, Track 2, and so on. You can edit a track name by right-clicking it and choosing Edit from the shortcut menu.

Copying CD Music

Instead of playing a different CD every time you want to hear a particular song or piece of music, you can create your own "jukebox" by copying individual tunes (or entire CDs) onto your computer's hard disk; then you can play the saved music in any order you want. When you copy the music, it's saved in Windows Media Format, which takes about half as much space as the original CD format and which allows you to transfer the music to another device—a portable player or handheld computer, for example.

Copy the Music

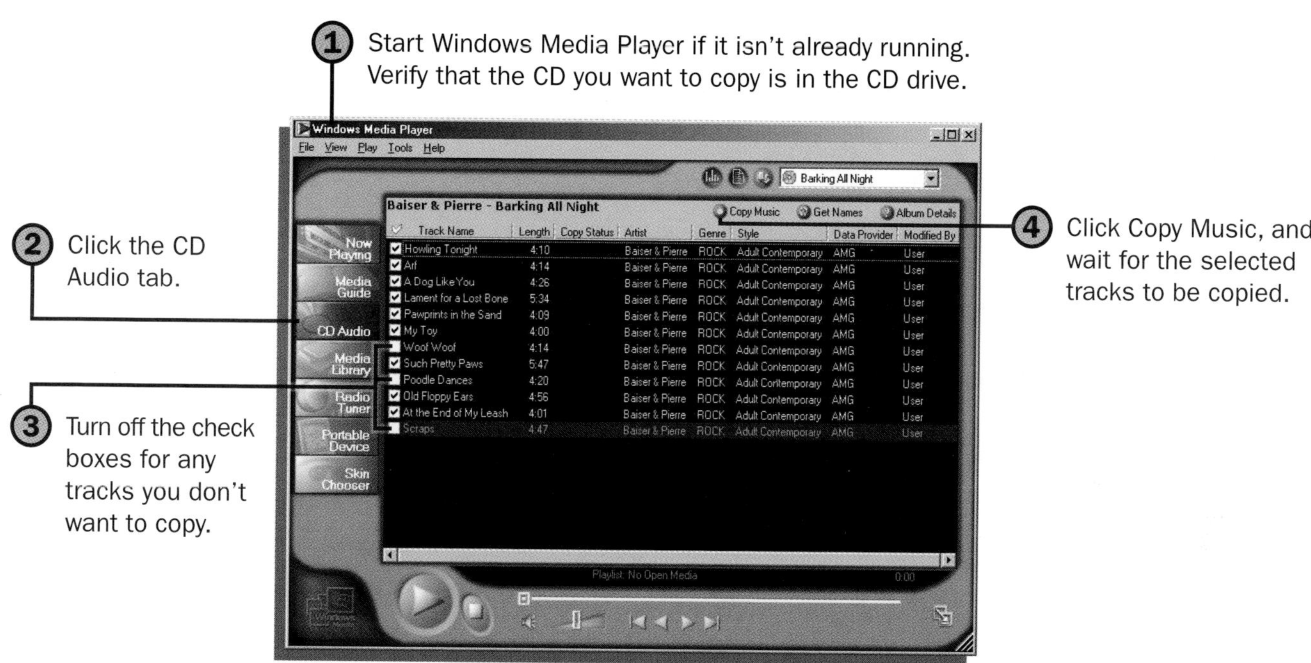

SEE ALSO: For information about playing saved music, see "Playing a Saved Media File" on page 90 and "Playing Media Using Your Own Playlist" on page 94.

TIP: When you copy a CD track, a license that allows you to play that track on your computer is created automatically. You can copy the file from your computer to a portable device or another computer only if the license (as specified by the CD manufacturer) permits it.

Playing a Saved Media File

Windows Media Player makes it easy to play audio or video files that you've saved on your computer. The files are listed by category for easy access, whether they're stored on your computer, on a network, or on the Internet.

Start Playing

1. Start Windows Media Player from the Quick Launch toolbar or the Desktop shortcut. To play items from the Internet or to obtain album information, connect to the Internet if you're not already connected.
2. Click the Media Library tab.
3. Select a category and a subcategory to locate the file you want to play. If the file isn't on the list, you can locate it by pressing the F3 key and searching your computer for all media files.
4. Double-click the file to play it. If you want, you can switch to the Now Playing tab to watch the file being played.

SEE ALSO: For information about creating a personal playlist that preprograms the items to be played, see "Playing Media Using Your Own Playlist" on page 94.

Add an Item to the Media Library

1. Select the category to which you want to add a file.
2. Click the Add To Library button.
3. Select the type of item you want to add. If you chose to add a file or a URL (an Internet address), specify the file or the URL in the Open dialog box that appears.

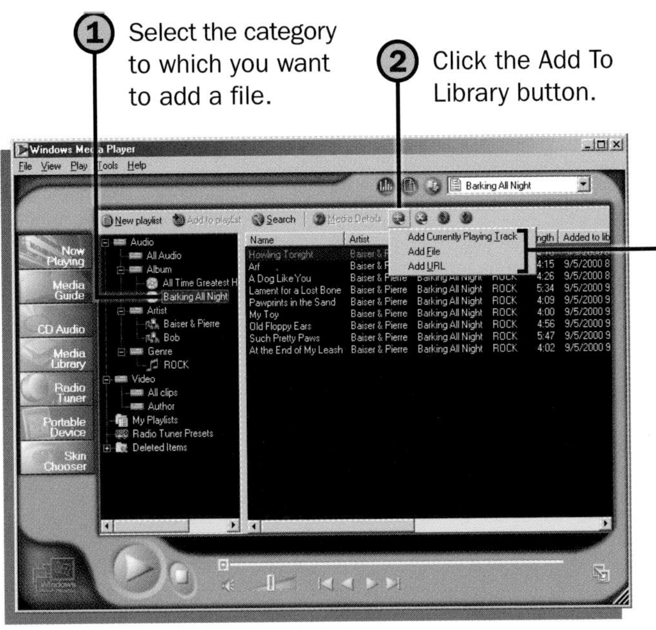

Playing Media from the Internet

You can play media that's available from the Internet—videos, live broadcasts, or music tracks, for example—either by playing the media directly from the web site (*streaming media*) or by downloading the file. When you use streaming media, the video or music starts playing while the file is being sent to you, but the material isn't stored on your computer. When you download a file, you wait for the entire file to be downloaded, and it stays on your computer so that you can play it at any time. These downloaded items often require a license, which is usually downloaded automatically with the file and stored and managed by Windows Media Player.

Start Playing

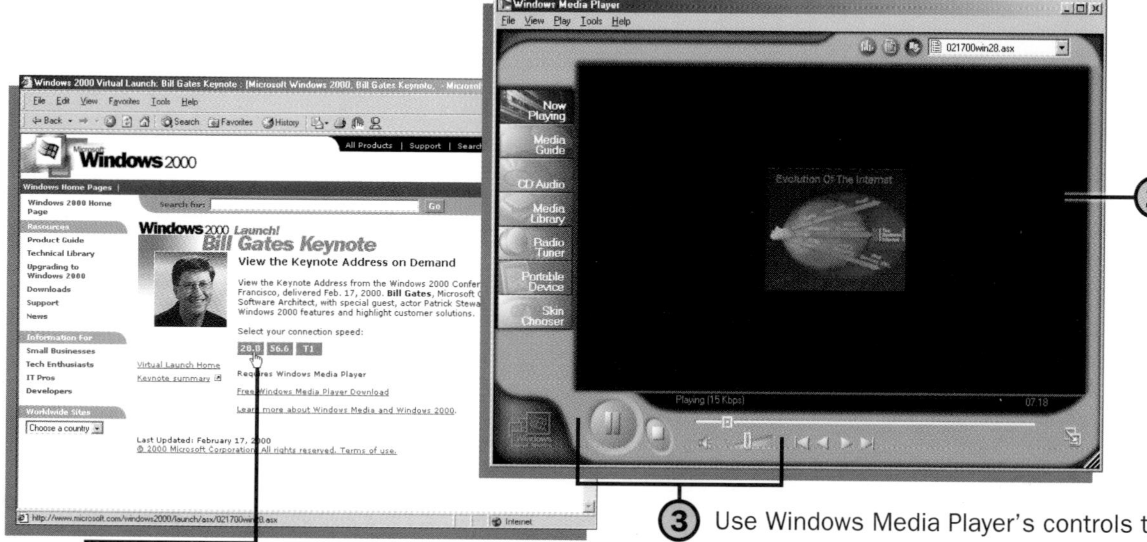

1. Locate the web site that contains the media you want to play, click the link to the media, and, if it's available on the web site, select the best-suited speed (bandwidth) for your net connection.
2. Wait for the connection to be made, for Windows Media Player to start if it isn't already running, and for the first data to be transmitted and buffered. Listen to and/or watch the multimedia.
3. Use Windows Media Player's controls to monitor and modify the show.

TIP: Whenever you download a file, use a virus-scanning program to scan the file before you open it for the first time.

Download a File

1. Start Windows Media Player if it isn't already running. Use either the Media Guide tab or a web browser to locate the video or the music you want to download from the Internet, and follow the instructions on the page to download the file.

2. Select the option to save the file to a folder on your computer.

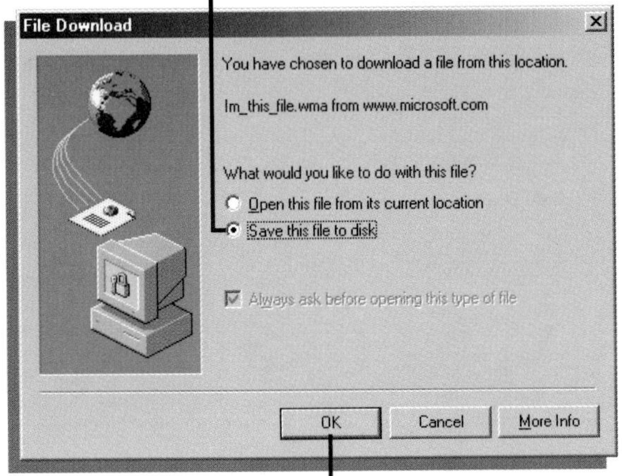

3. Click OK, and specify the location in which you want to save the file.

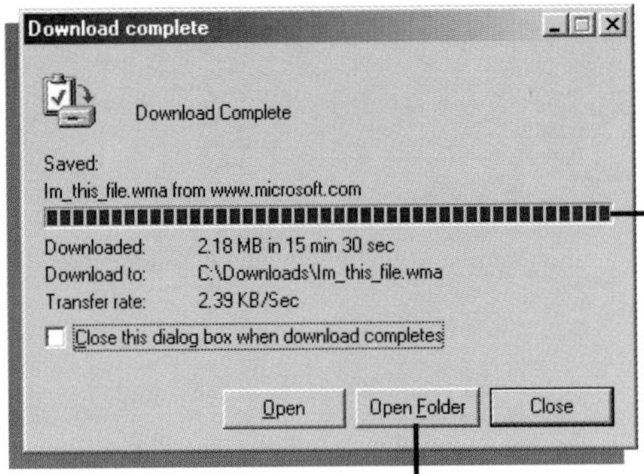

4. Wait for the file to be downloaded. Depending on the speed of your Internet connection and the size of the file, this could take a while.

5. Click Open Folder to go to the folder that contains the downloaded file, and double-click the file to play it.

File Download

You have chosen to download a file from this location.

Im_this_file.wma from www.microsoft.com

What would you like to do with this file?

Open this file from its current location

Save this file to disk

Always ask before opening this type of file

OK Cancel More Info

Download complete

Download Complete

Saved:

Im_this_file.wma from www.microsoft.com

Downloaded: 2.18 MB in 15 min 30 sec

Download to: C:\Downloads\Im_this_file.wma

Transfer rate: 2.39 KB/Sec

Close this dialog box when download completes

Open Open Folder Close

TIP: The Media Guide tab takes you to the WindowsMedia.com web site, which provides multimedia downloads and links.

TIP: Windows Media Player has a license management feature that stores and coordinates any licenses you obtained to play music or video on your computer. Use the License Management command on the Tools menu to back up and restore your licenses.

SEE ALSO: For information about adding a downloaded file to your media library in Windows Media Player, see "Playing a Saved Media File" on page 90.

For information about adding a downloaded file to your personal playlist, see "Playing Media Using Your Own Playlist" on page 94.

Customizing Windows Media Player

You can change the appearance of Windows Media Player by viewing it in Full Mode or Compact Mode, and by changing its "skin." Skins are designs that alter the appearance—but not the functionality—of Windows Media Player. You can apply skins only to the compact form of Windows Media Player, and it's quick and easy to switch between the two modes whenever you want.

Change the Skin

1. Start Windows Media Player from the Quick Launch toolbar or the Desktop shortcut.

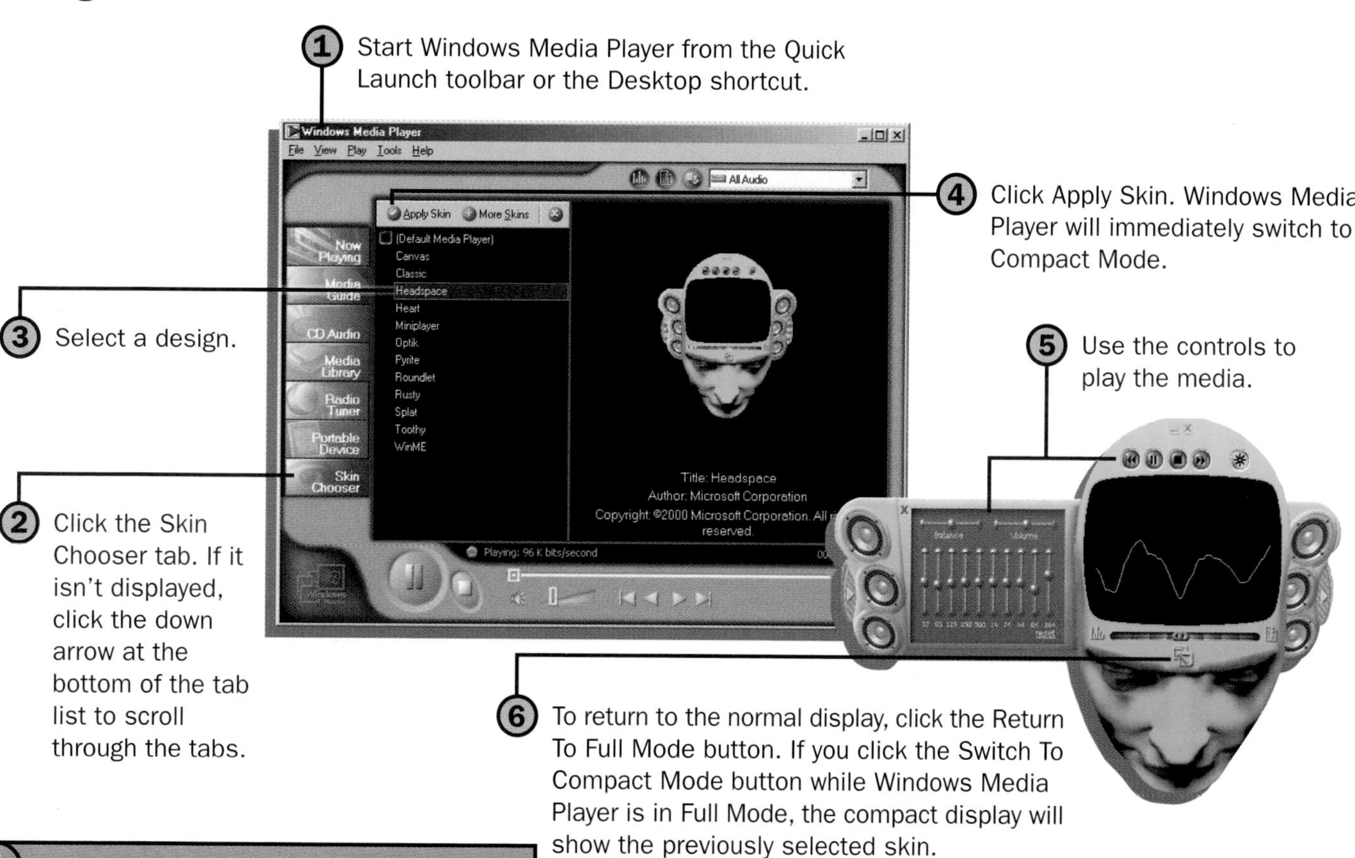

2. Click the Skin Chooser tab. If it isn't displayed, click the down arrow at the bottom of the tab list to scroll through the tabs.
3. Select a design.
4. Click Apply Skin. Windows Media Player will immediately switch to Compact Mode.
5. Use the controls to play the media.
6. To return to the normal display, click the Return To Full Mode button. If you click the Switch To Compact Mode button while Windows Media Player is in Full Mode, the compact display will show the previously selected skin.

TIP: You can download additional skins by clicking the More Skins button on the Skin Chooser tab. Custom skins are also available from many music web sites, as well as other sites.

Playing Media Using Your Own Playlist

A playlist is a list of media files and their locations that you can use to organize your music, your videos, and any other multimedia files and locations for easy access and play. When you use your playlist, the items on it, regardless of their format and location, are played in the order you specify.

Create a Playlist

1. Start Windows Media Player from the Quick Launch toolbar or the Desktop shortcut, and click the Media Library tab.
2. Click New Playlist.
3. Type a name for the playlist, and click OK.
4. Select an item or multiple items in any Media Library category.
5. Click Add To Playlist, and select the newly created playlist to add the selected item or items to the list. Repeat to add other items to the playlist.
6. Select the playlist to play the items on the list. Switch to the Now Playing tab to see all the items on the playlist.

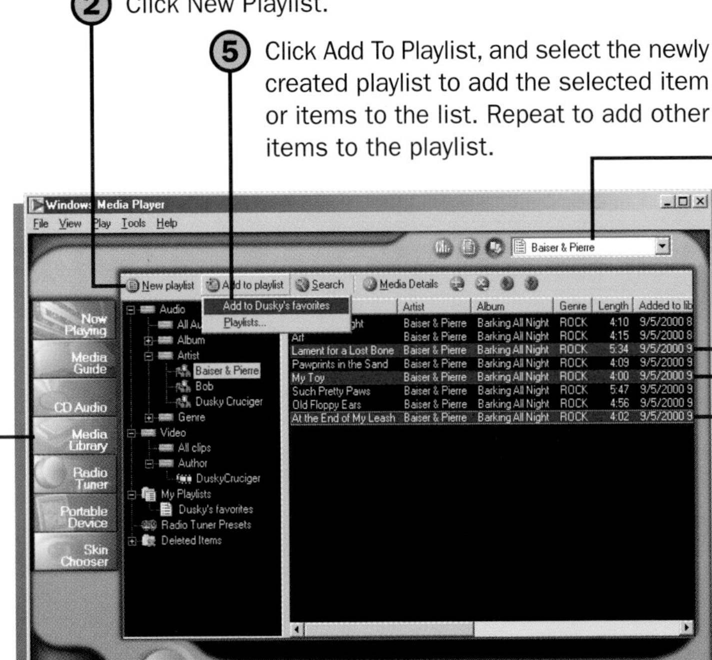

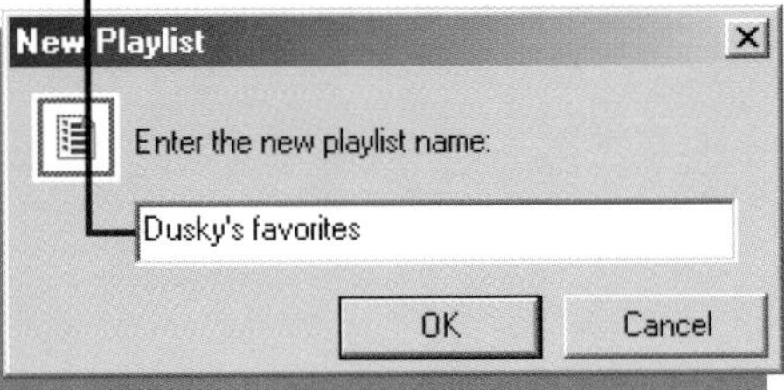

TIP: To change the order of the items in your playlist or to delete items from it, go to the Media Library, click your playlist, right-click an item in the playlist, and choose an action from the shortcut menu.

SEE ALSO: For information about adding items to the Media Library, see "Playing a Saved Media File" on page 90.

Recording a Video Clip

With Windows Movie Maker, you can create a digital video clip from a digital video camera or from a digital web camera. If neither of these is available, you can use a video capture card or other device to convert images from an analog camera or from videotape or television. Once you've created the video clip, you can play it as is or combine it with other video and audio clips to make a movie.

TIP: To record a movie, your computer should have at least a 300-MHz Pentium II processor, 64 MB of RAM, and 2 GB of free disk space.

Record a Video Clip

1. Start Windows Movie Maker from the Accessories submenu of the Start menu, and click the Record button.
2. Specify the type and quality of the recording. The higher the quality, the larger the file that will be created.
3. If you have multiple video input devices and you want to change the device you'll be using, or if you want to change the audio source, click Change Device, and select the device or the audio source.
4. If you're recording from a digital video camera, click Play.
5. Click Record. Use your video device to capture the video you want, and then click Stop. If you're using a digital video camera, click the Stop button. In the Save Windows Media File dialog box that appears, type a name for the file, and click Save.
6. Close the Record dialog box when you've finished.

TIP: When you record a video clip, a digital movie is created in Windows Media Format, and you can play that file as is. Use Windows Movie Maker to refine the video, to add special effects or soundtracks, or to combine video from different clips to create a new movie.

Making a Movie

You can create and edit digital movies with Windows Movie Maker, and, because Movie Maker compresses the files, your movies can be small enough to include with your e-mail. You can record video clips while you're assembling your movie or you can import existing video clips or pictures. By storing your clips in a specific Collection, you can keep them organized for use in different movie projects.

Organize Your Resources

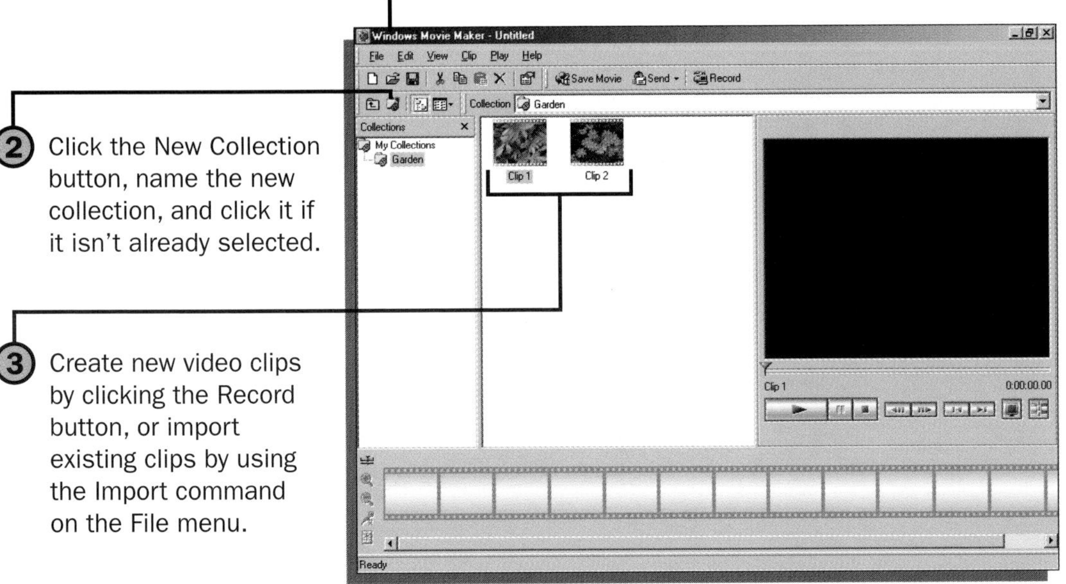

1. Start Windows Movie Maker from the Accessories submenu of the Start menu.
2. Click the New Collection button, name the new collection, and click it if it isn't already selected.
3. Create new video clips by clicking the Record button, or import existing clips by using the Import command on the File menu.

TIP: To send a movie directly to an e-mail recipient or to a web server, point to Send Movie To on the File menu, and choose a destination from the shortcut menu.

SEE ALSO: For information about recording video clips, see "Recording a Video Clip" on page 95.

For information about editing clips or adding transition effects between clips, see "Editing Your Movie" on page 98.

For information about adding narration or a soundtrack to your movie, see "Adding Audio to Your Movie" on page 100.

For information about including digital still pictures in your movie, see "Creating a Slide Show" on page 102.

Create a Movie

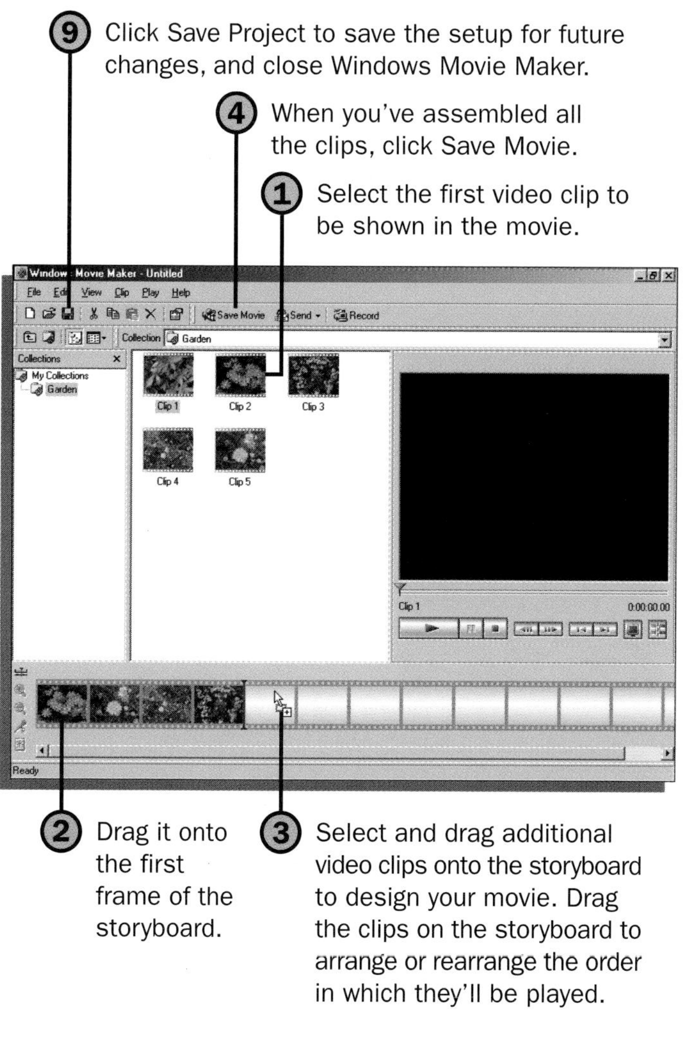

9. Click Save Project to save the setup for future changes, and close Windows Movie Maker.
4. When you've assembled all the clips, click Save Movie.
1. Select the first video clip to be shown in the movie.
2. Drag it onto the first frame of the storyboard.
3. Select and drag additional video clips onto the storyboard to design your movie. Drag the clips on the storyboard to arrange or rearrange the order in which they'll be played.

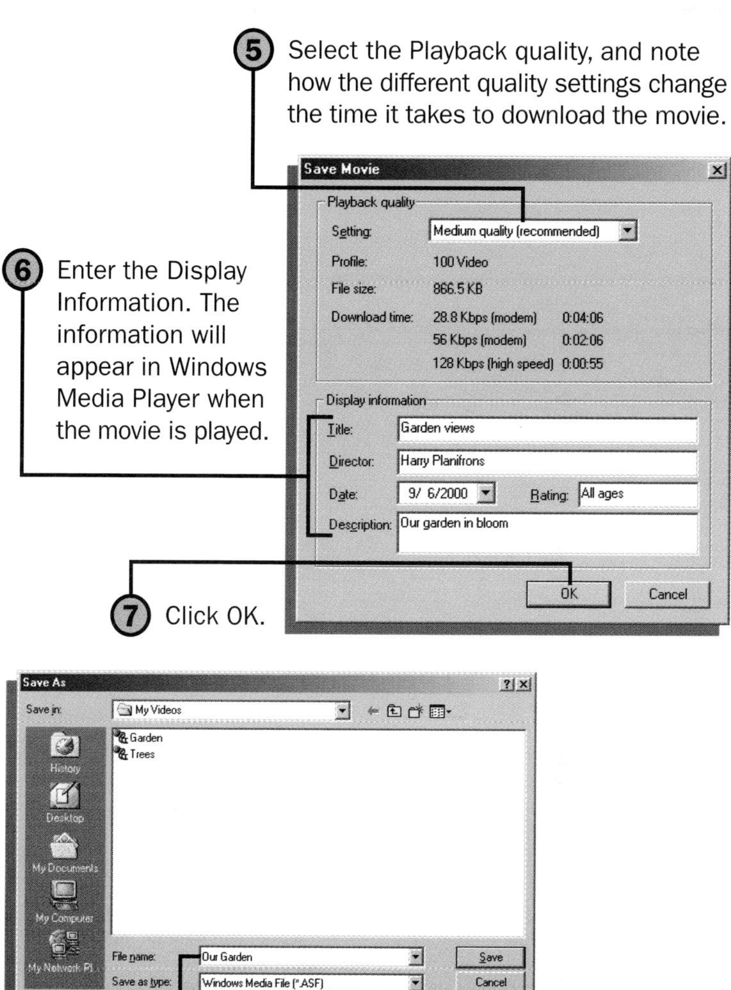

5. Select the Playback quality, and note how the different quality settings change the time it takes to download the movie.
6. Enter the Display Information. The information will appear in Windows Media Player when the movie is played.
7. Click OK.
8. Type a name for the movie, and click Save.

Editing Your Movie

After you've created a movie using Windows Movie Maker, you can modify your movie by cropping to include only part of a clip, creating fade-in/fade-out transitions between clips, adding a background sound clip, or recording a narration.

> **!** TIP: The part of the clip that you trim away isn't deleted—it's just hidden. To restore the entire clip, select it, and choose Clear Trim Points from the Clip menu.

Crop the Clip

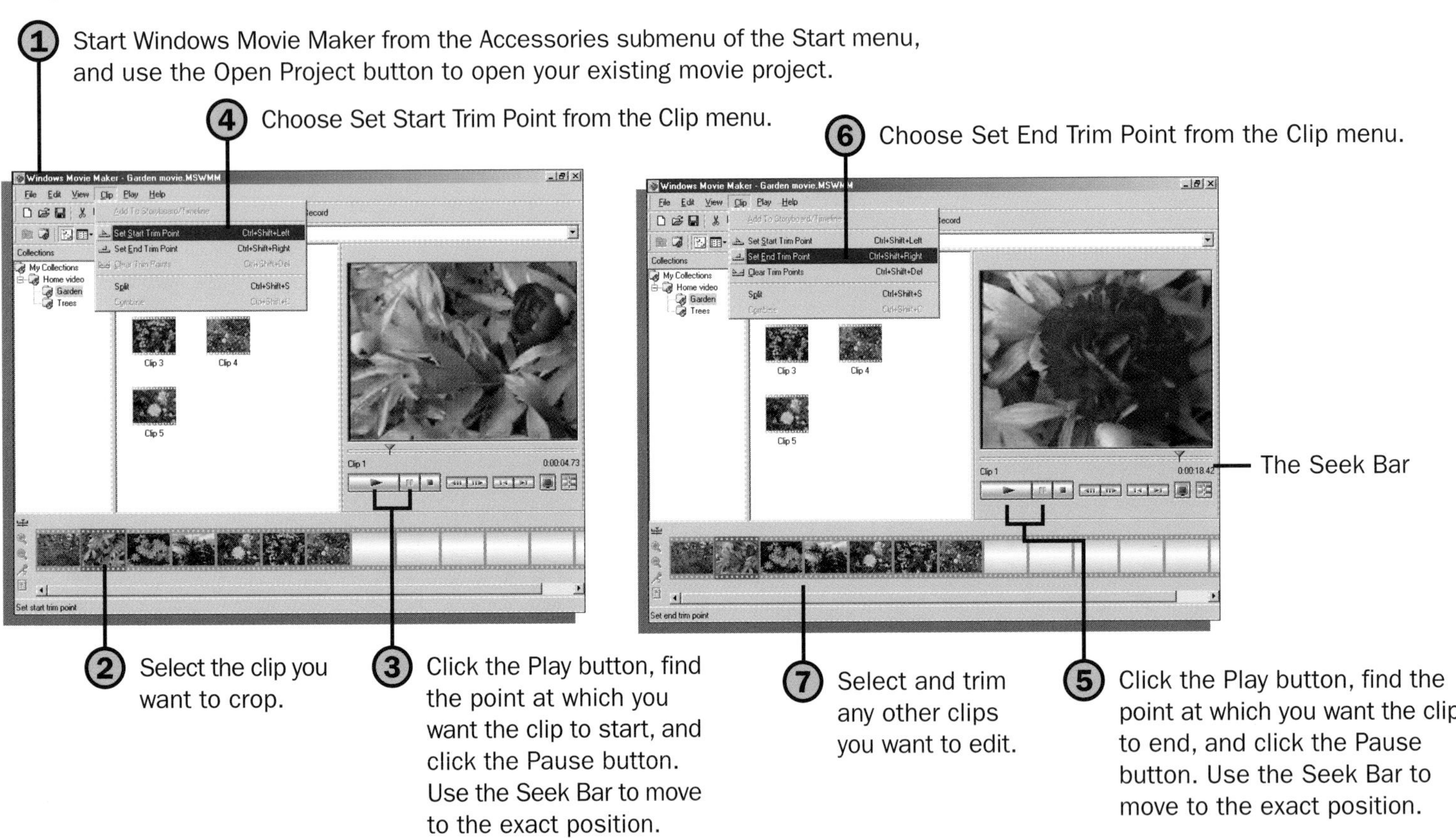

Create a Transition

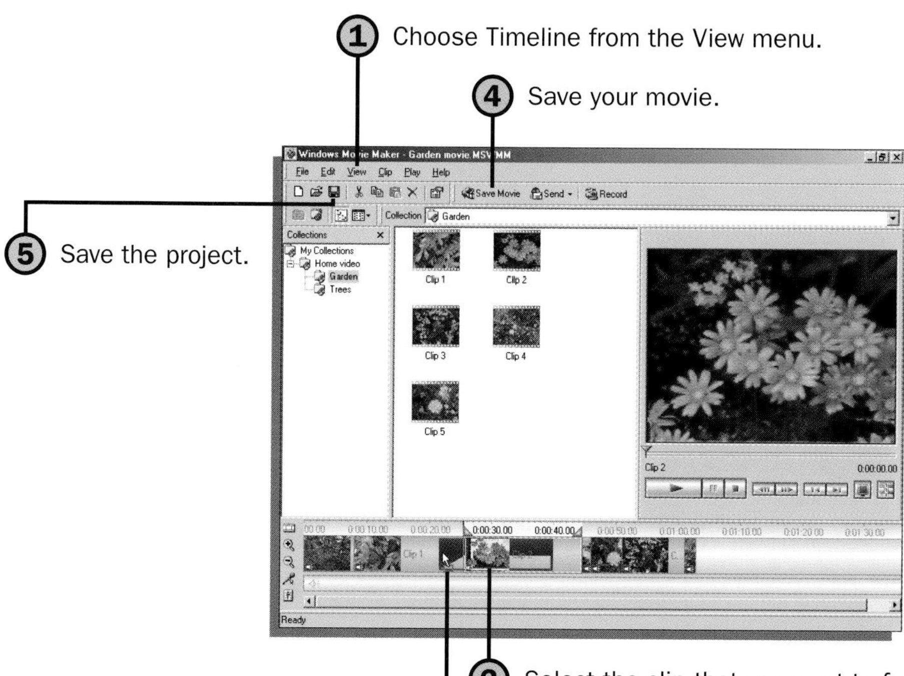

1. Choose Timeline from the View menu.
2. Select the clip that you want to fade into. (It's at the right of the clip that you want to fade out of.)
3. Drag the left border of the clip onto the clip at the left. The farther you drag the clip, the longer the transition. Repeat with any other clips between which you want to create transitions.
4. Save your movie.
5. Save the project.

TIP: Use the Zoom In or Zoom Out button on the timeline to change the scale of the timeline for easier manipulation of clip transitions or cropping.

TIP: You can modify the trim points of a clip in Timeline view by selecting the clip and dragging the triangular clip markers at the top of the timeline.

TIP: To quickly change between Storyboard and Timeline views, click the Timeline button at the left of the storyboard or the Storyboard button at the left of the timeline.

TRY THIS: Assemble your clips on the storyboard, and crop them as you want. Switch to Timeline view, and drag the left border of a clip onto the clip at the left. Create additional transitions. Click at the beginning of the timeline, and then click the Play button to preview the effects. Change any trim point or transition that's not to your liking.

Adding Audio to Your Movie

When you record a movie with Windows Movie Maker, you can include the audio that was recorded with an original video or you can record the audio while you're recording the movie in Movie Maker. If you didn't record an audio track and want to add one, or if you want to add a narration or a musical soundtrack to an existing project, you can easily do so. A narration can be merged with the existing audio for the video or can completely replace it; a soundtrack is always merged with any audio for the video.

Create a Narration

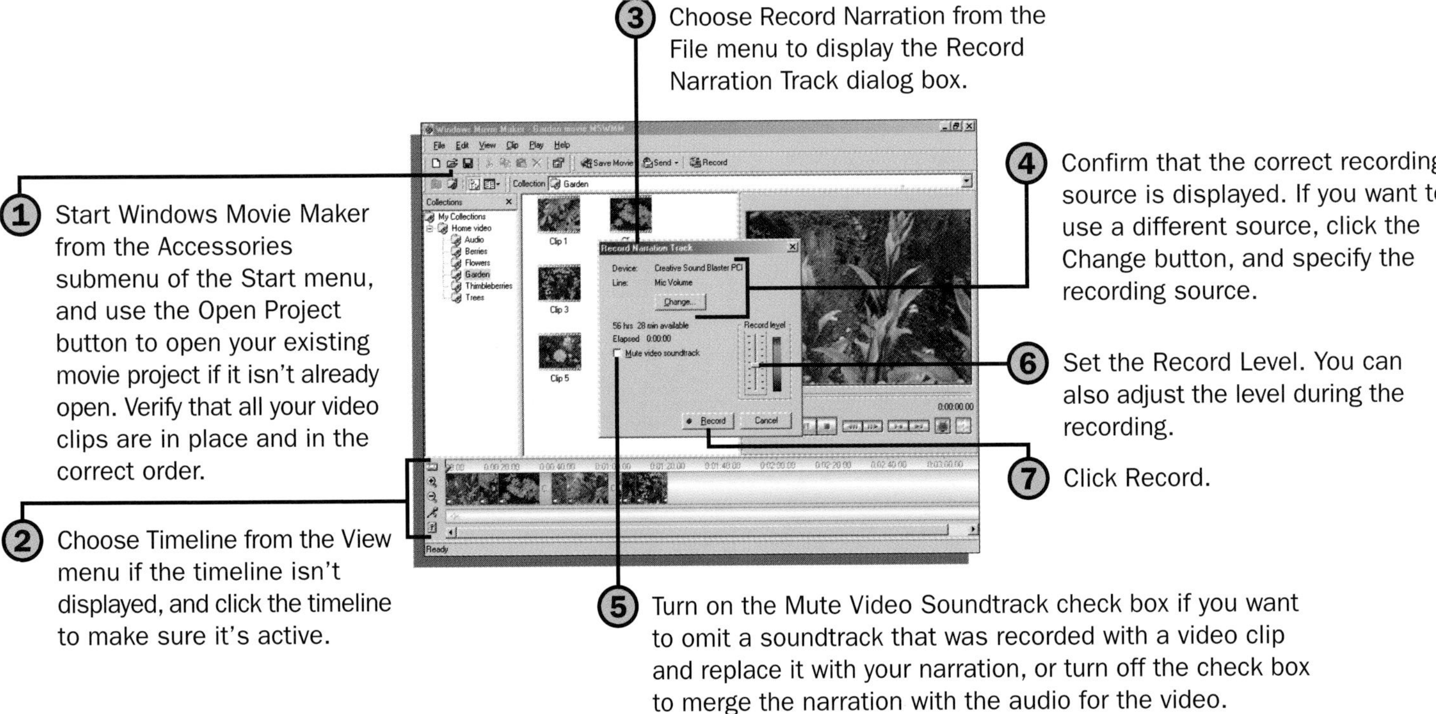

1. Start Windows Movie Maker from the Accessories submenu of the Start menu, and use the Open Project button to open your existing movie project if it isn't already open. Verify that all your video clips are in place and in the correct order.
2. Choose Timeline from the View menu if the timeline isn't displayed, and click the timeline to make sure it's active.
3. Choose Record Narration from the File menu to display the Record Narration Track dialog box.
4. Confirm that the correct recording source is displayed. If you want to use a different source, click the Change button, and specify the recording source.
5. Turn on the Mute Video Soundtrack check box if you want to omit a soundtrack that was recorded with a video clip and replace it with your narration, or turn off the check box to merge the narration with the audio for the video.
6. Set the Record Level. You can also adjust the level during the recording.
7. Click Record.

8 Watch the video in the preview window and on the timeline, and record your narration.

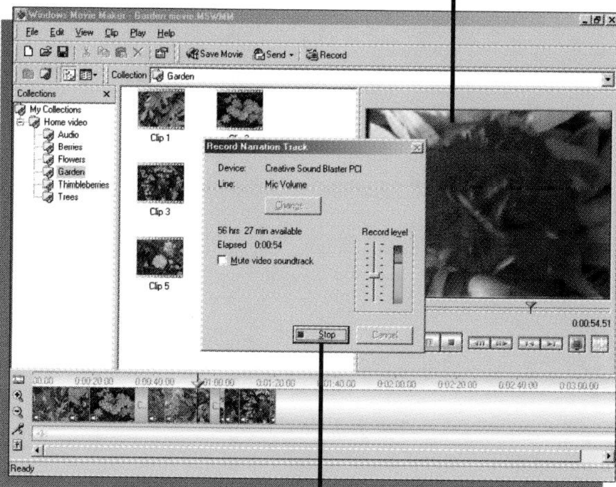

9 When you've finished, click Stop, save the narration file to a folder, and then save your movie.

TIP: A narration file is a WAV-type file, not a Windows Media Format file. When you add a narration file to a movie, its content is incorporated into the movie's Windows Media Format file.

SEE ALSO: For information about recording your own audio files, see "Creating a Sound File" on page 103 and "Creating an Audio Clip" on page 104.

Add a Soundtrack

1 Create or import the audio files that you want to use as your soundtrack. The files need not be in Windows Media Format.

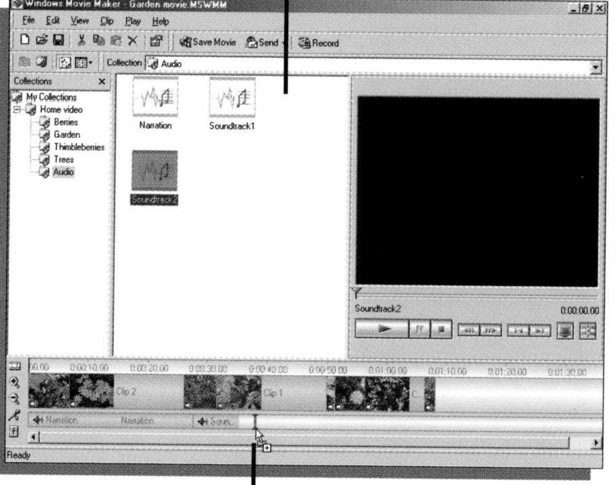

2 Drag a sound clip onto the audio bar at the location (that is, the time) where you want the clip to be played during the movie. Add and position any other sound clips. Save the movie and the project when you've finished.

Creating a Slide Show

When you use digital pictures—for example, photographs from a digital camera—instead of video clips when you're making a movie with Windows Movie Maker, you can create a slide show to display all your prized pictures. You can add a soundtrack to the slide show for additional drama.

> **TIP:** The pictures will probably lose some detail when they're incorporated into a movie. Still pictures work best in a video when they're used with video or audio clips.

Create the Slide Show

1. Start Movie Maker from the Accessories submenu of the Start menu.

> **TIP:** Click the New Collection button, name the collection, and select it before you import any pictures to create an effective filing system for your clips.

2. Choose Import from the File menu, locate and select the pictures you want to use, and click Open. (Hold down the Ctrl key and click individual pictures to select multiple pictures.)

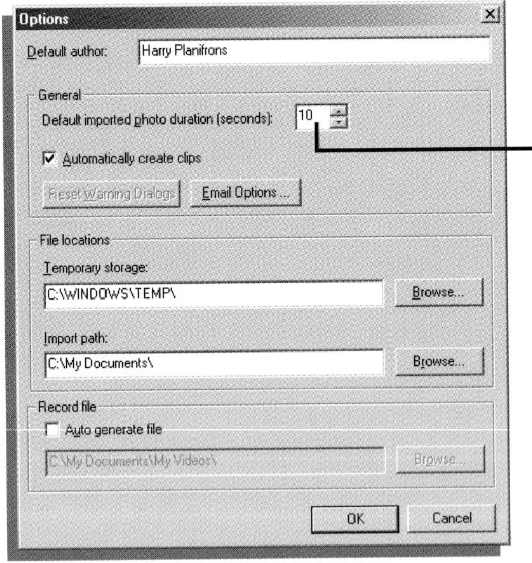

3. Choose Options from the View menu, and specify the length of time you want each picture to be displayed. Click OK.

> **SEE ALSO:** For information about adding transition effects and changing the length of time an item is displayed, see "Editing Your Movie" on page 98.
>
> For information about adding narration or a soundtrack, see "Adding Audio to Your Movie" on page 100.

5. Click Save Movie when you've finished.

4. Drag the pictures onto the storyboard in the sequence in which you want them to be displayed. Use Timeline view to add transition effects or audio, or to modify how long an individual picture is displayed.

Creating a Sound File

A sound file is generally used to record and play a short, simple sound—a beep, a bark, or even a couple of musical chords. You've heard sound files of this type (WAV files) when you start Windows Me or shut it down. Using a microphone and Sound Recorder, you can record and play your own sound files, which can be up to 60 seconds long.

Record Sounds

1. Open Sound Recorder from the Entertainment submenu of the Start menu.

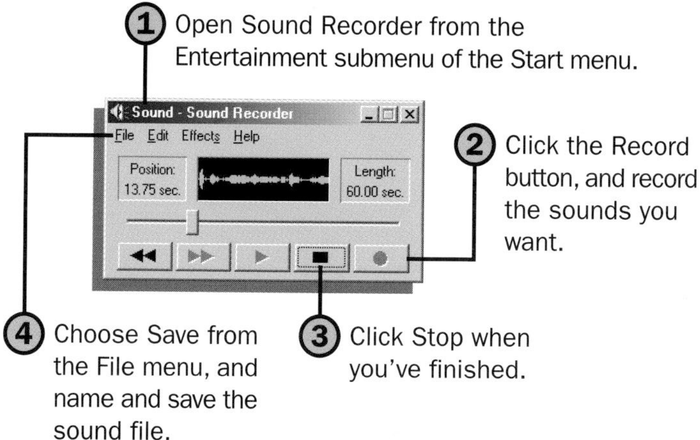

2. Click the Record button, and record the sounds you want.
3. Click Stop when you've finished.
4. Choose Save from the File menu, and name and save the sound file.

TIP: The Record button is grayed and inactive while you're recording.

TIP: Instead of using a microphone to record sounds, you can use a tape player or other playback device by hooking it up to the Line In port on your computer's sound system. To use the device, choose Audio Properties from the Edit menu, and select the device.

SEE ALSO: For information about recording audio files in Windows Media Format, which gives you greater control of the quality of the recording, see "Creating an Audio Clip" on page 104.

For information about assigning sound files to different Windows Me actions, see "Associating a Sound with an Event" on page 107.

Creating an Audio Clip

An audio clip is a file in Windows Media Format that contains audio only. You can record a single audio clip using a microphone or any other input device attached to your computer, or you can create a more complex clip by combining several audio clips into a single clip.

> **TIP:** You can record from different devices by attaching them to the Line In connection on your computer's sound card or sound system. You can also record from a CD playing on your computer's CD drive. You can't, however, import and use files that require licenses, such as some downloaded music or CD tracks you've saved on your computer using Windows Media Player. Be careful not to violate copyright laws when you're copying music.

Record an Audio Clip

1. Start Windows Movie Maker from the Accessories submenu of the Start menu. If necessary, start a new project and create a new collection to hold your audio clips.
2. Click Record.

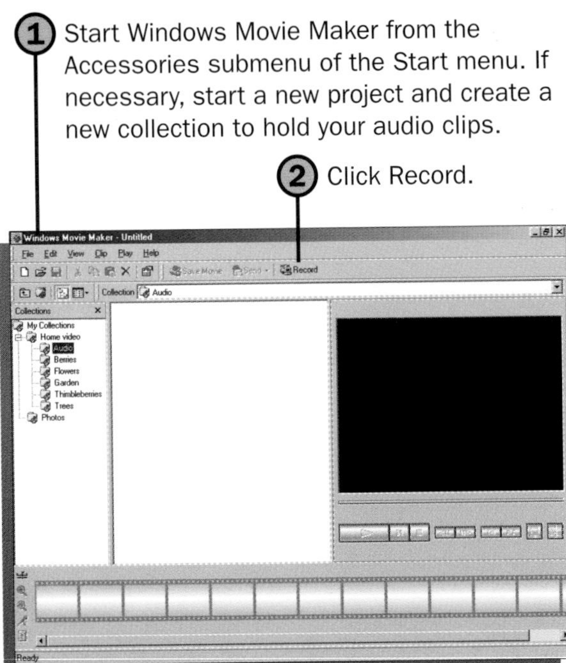

3. Select Audio Only.

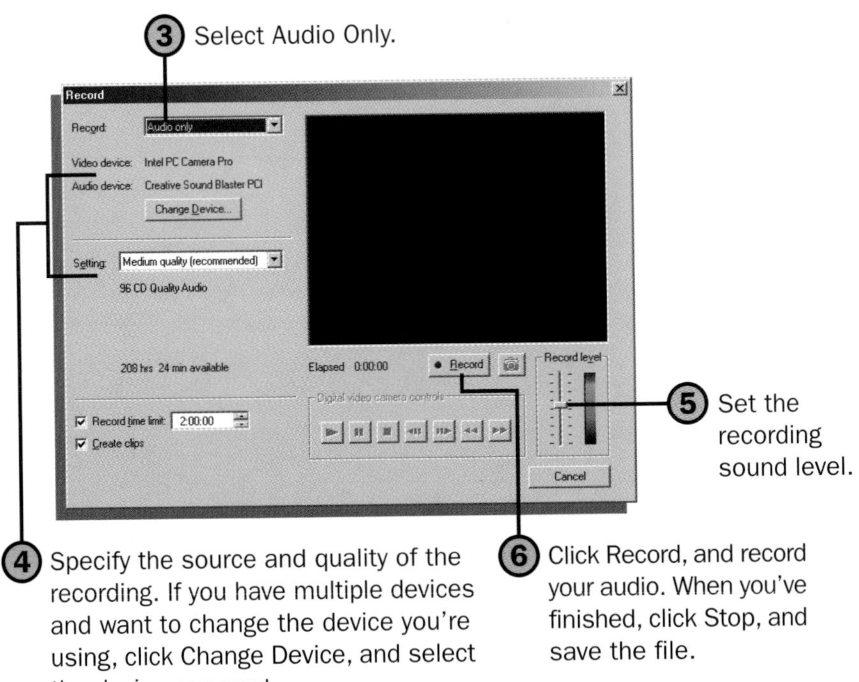

4. Specify the source and quality of the recording. If you have multiple devices and want to change the device you're using, click Change Device, and select the device you want.
5. Set the recording sound level.
6. Click Record, and record your audio. When you've finished, click Stop, and save the file.

Combine Clips

2 Choose Timeline from the View menu if the timeline isn't already displayed.

1 Record or import a series of audio clips and files. (Imported files can be in any format supported by Windows Movie Maker.)

4 Click Save Movie, and save the combined sound clip.

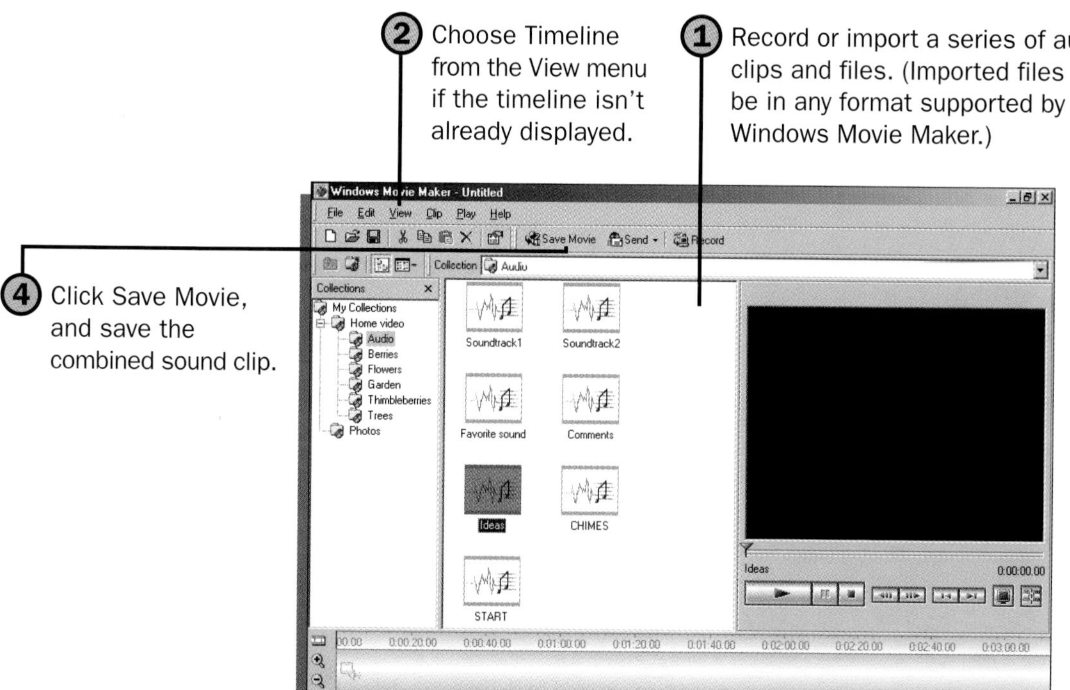

3 Drag the audio clips onto the timeline one at a time and in the order you want them to be played.

SEE ALSO: For information about cropping clips and using transitions between clips, see "Editing Your Movie" on page 98.

TRY THIS: Create and insert several audio clips. Click a clip, and drag the Start Trim or End Trim indicator on the timeline to crop the clips. Drag the left border of the clip onto the clip at the left to create a transition. Click the beginning of the timeline, and click the Play button to preview the audio track.

TIP: You can crop audio clips and insert transitions between clips exactly as you do with video clips.

TIP: Click the Set Audio Levels button at the left of the timeline to set the audio level for the whole audio track. (You can't adjust the level for individual clips.)

Controlling the Volume

If the sound your computer emits to signal an event—the logon or logoff sound, for example—is an ear-splitting assault, relief in the form of adjusting the volume is just a click away. You can also use the Volume Control to keep your music and other sounds muted so that you don't disturb other people, or, when you're the only person around, you can crank up the sound level and blast away! Although many programs have individual controls, you can use the volume control to set all your sound levels.

Set the Master Volume Level

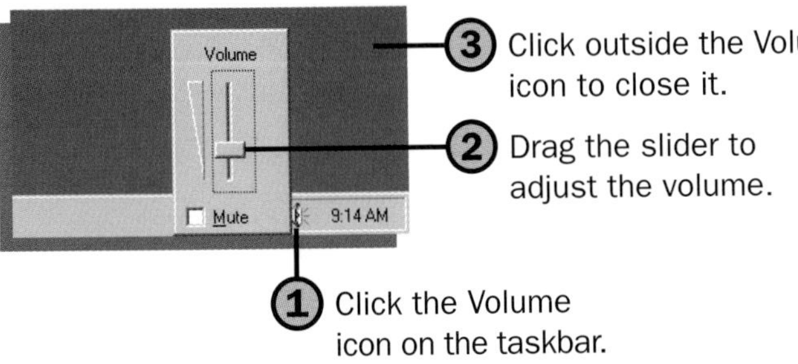

3. Click outside the Volume icon to close it.
2. Drag the slider to adjust the volume.
1. Click the Volume icon on the taskbar.

TIP: If the Volume icon doesn't appear on the taskbar, open the Control Panel from the Settings submenu of the Start menu, double-click the Sounds And Multimedia icon, and, on the Sounds tab, turn on the Show Volume Control On The Taskbar check box.

TIP: If you're using a device that isn't listed in the Volume Control, choose Properties from the Options menu, and turn on the check box for the device.

SEE ALSO: For information about changing or removing the sounds Windows Me uses to signal an event, see "Associating a Sound with an Event" on the facing page.

Set the Volume for Individual Devices

1. Double-click the Volume icon on the taskbar.

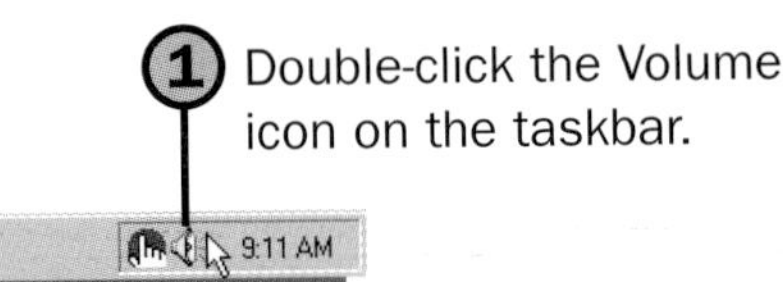

2. Adjust the settings for the device or devices whose volume you want to adjust, and then use the device or devices to check the sound level.

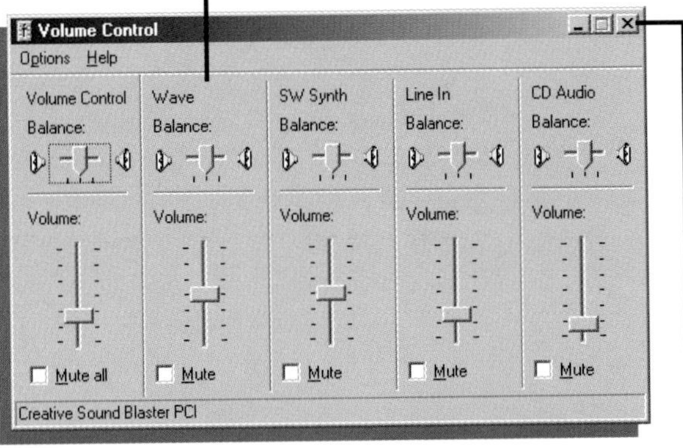

3. When the adjustments are correct, close the Volume Control.

Associating a Sound with an Event

If you want audio cues for events in Windows Me—the closing of a program or the arrival of new mail, for example—you can assign wave (WAV) sounds to these events.

TIP: Put any WAV audio files that you want to use for events into the Media subfolder of the Windows folder, and the files will appear in the Name list.

TIP: To remove a sound from an event, choose None from the Name list.

Assign a Sound to an Event

1. Open the Control Panel from the Settings submenu of the Start menu, and double-click the Sounds And Multimedia icon. If the item isn't displayed, click View All Control Panel Options in the Control Panel window.

The icon indicates that a sound has been assigned to the event.

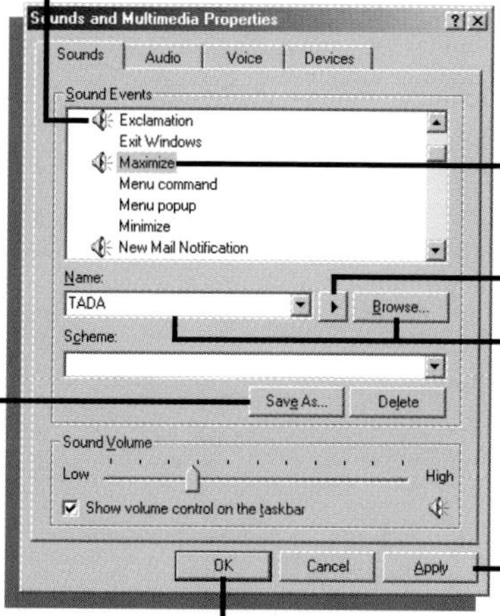

2. On the Sounds tab, select an event from the Sound Events list.

Click to hear the selected sound.

3. Select a sound from the Name list, or use the Browse button to find a sound in another folder. Continue selecting events and sounds until you've completed your sound scheme.

4. Click the Apply button.

5. Click Save As, enter a name for the sound scheme you've created, and click OK.

6. Click OK.

TIP: If you've created multiple sound schemes, or if you want to switch back to the default Windows Me sound scheme, select the appropriate scheme from the Scheme list, and click OK. If you want to remove all sound events, select No Sounds from the Scheme list.

SEE ALSO: For information about using a sound scheme that corresponds to an overall change in the appearance of Windows Me, see "Changing the Overall Look" on page 150.

Connecting

In this section

The ability to communicate electronically is one of a computer's most used and most valued features. In this section, we'll discuss the tools that Microsoft Windows Millennium Edition provides to enable you to reach out and connect with people.

Microsoft Outlook Express helps you organize and customize your e-mail and does double duty as a news reader. It can complete an address from your Contacts list when you type only the first couple of letters of your contact's name, and it can automatically add a signature to your messages. You can enclose files, or *attachments,* with your e-mail, and you can format messages with fonts and colors. You can even choose or create your own e-mail stationery. If several people use your computer, each individual can have his or her own mail and news accounts, folders, and Contacts list. And you can use the MSN Messenger Service to exchange instant messages with as many as five of your contacts whenever they're on line.

You can use Microsoft NetMeeting to conduct meetings or online working sessions over the Internet or your network. Meeting participants can confer using text "chats" or voice conversations, view video presentations, and share other material using NetMeeting's Whiteboard. And Phone Dialer is a handy tool that places phone calls for you, keeps a log of the calls you've made, and lets you automate your calls with the Speed Dial buttons.

Setting Up Your Connections

You can set up Outlook Express with one or more e-mail accounts and one or more news servers. When you set up a service such as Hotmail, the account will probably be added automatically to Outlook Express. You can, however, add more accounts yourself.

TIP: Some mail services, including AOL (America Online), cc:Mail, CompuServe, Microsoft Exchange Server (prior to version 5), and MS Mail, don't work with Outlook Express. Check the mail service's documentation to see which mail clients you can use.

TIP: Gather up the information you need from your Internet Service Provider (ISP) before you add a new service.

Specify Your Services

1. Start Outlook Express by double-clicking its icon on the Desktop or clicking its button on the Quick Launch toolbar.
2. Choose Accounts from the Tools menu to display the Internet Accounts dialog box.
3. On the Mail tab, check to see whether the account you want has already been set up.
4. If the account you want isn't listed, click the Add button, and choose Mail from the menu that appears.
5. Complete the steps of the Internet Connection Wizard to specify your mail account. If you don't have an existing account, select the option to sign up for a Hotmail account.
6. Click the News tab, click the Add button, choose News, and complete the wizard to set up any news accounts you want.
7. Click Close.

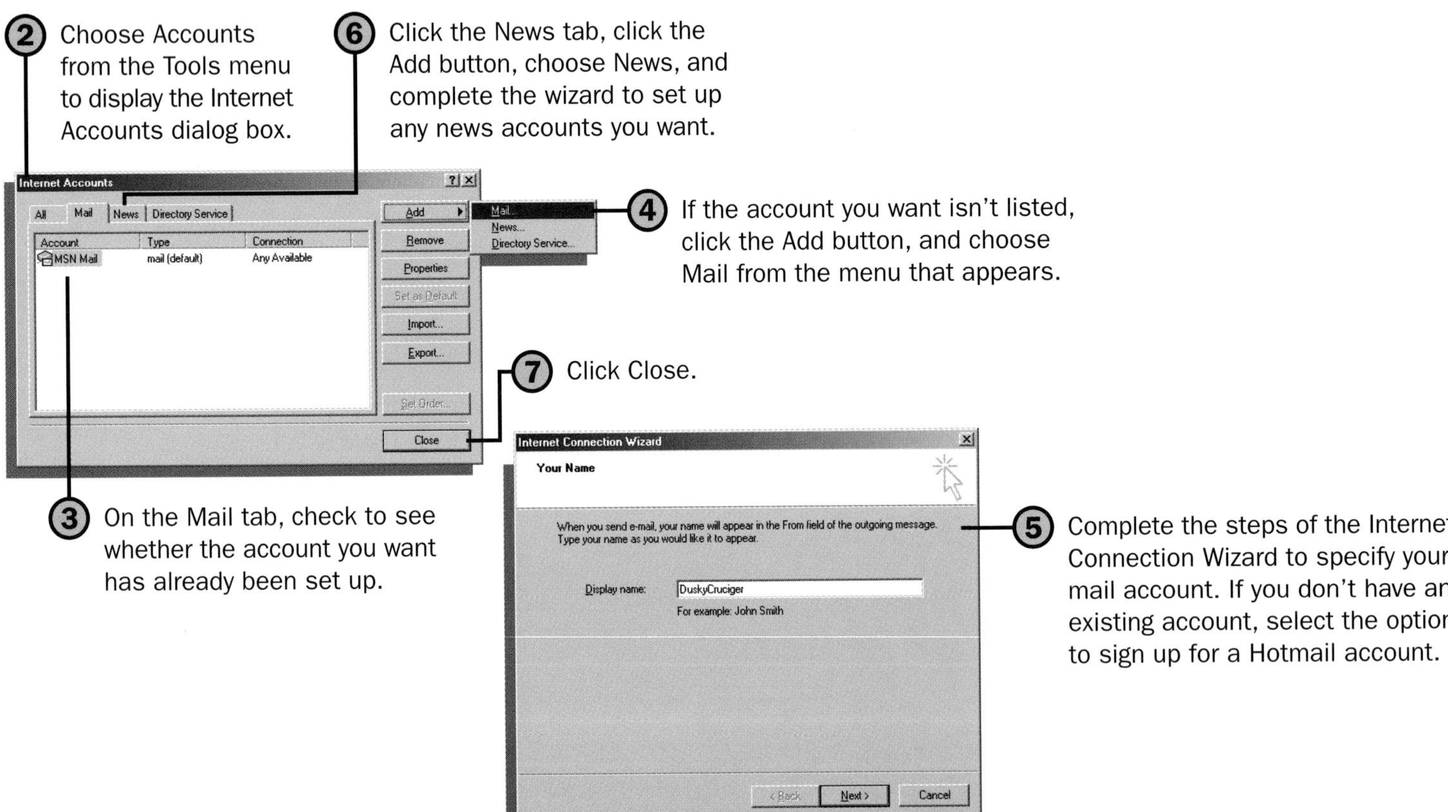

Sending E-Mail

You don't have to address an envelope or trek to the mailbox on a cold, rainy day. All you do is select a name, create a message, and click a Send button. Outlook Express and your mail server do the rest. What a great idea!

TIP: A From field is displayed if you have more than one e-mail account. If you want to send a blind copy but the BCC field isn't displayed, choose All Headers from the View menu.

Create a Message

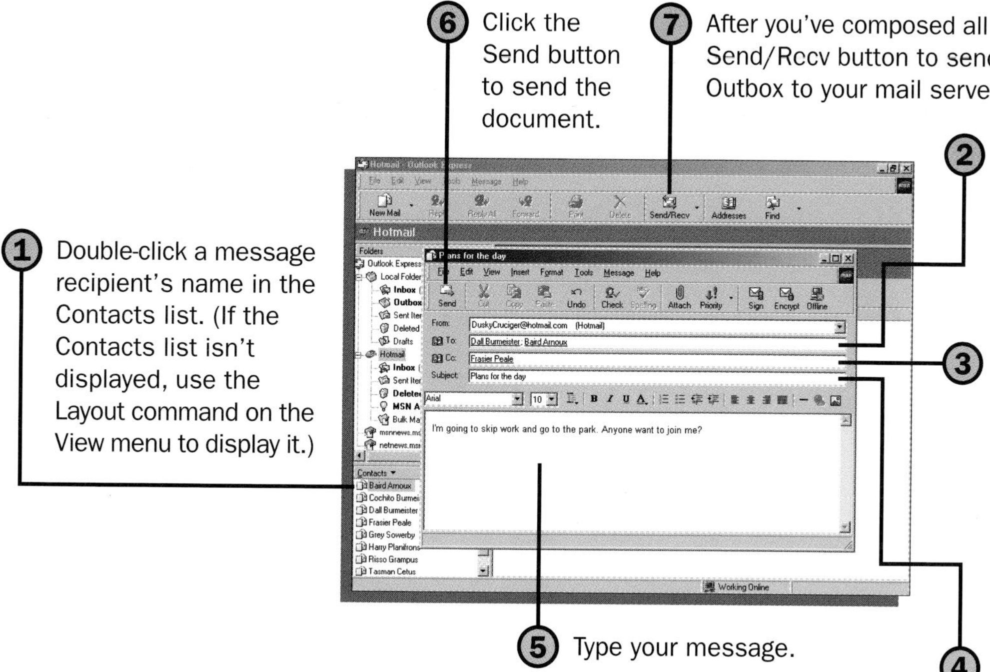

1. Double-click a message recipient's name in the Contacts list. (If the Contacts list isn't displayed, use the Layout command on the View menu to display it.)
2. To add more names, type a semicolon (;), and then start typing another recipient's name. Press Enter when Outlook Express completes the name based on the names in the Contacts list, or continue typing if the proposed name is incorrect.
3. Press the Tab key to move to the CC field, and type the names of the people who are to receive a copy of the message. Press the Tab key again to move the BCC field, if it's displayed. (The names in the CC field are included in all copies of the message; the names in the BCC—blind copy—field are not included in the messages sent to the people listed in the To and CC fields.)
4. Press the Tab key to move to the Subject line, type a subject, and press Tab again to move into the message area.
5. Type your message.
6. Click the Send button to send the document.
7. After you've composed all your messages, use the Send/Rccv button to send any messages in the Outbox to your mail server.

SEE ALSO: For information about adding formatting, pictures, or your signature, or to use a predefined format, see "Formatting a Message" on page 113 and "Designing Your Default Message" on page 114.

For information about adding names and e-mail addresses to your Contacts list, see "Managing Your Contacts" on page 122.

TIP: To find and add a name and address once you've started addressing your message, click the To, CC, or BCC button at the left of the address field.

Reading E-Mail

Outlook Express makes it simple to review your messages—you can see at a glance which messages have and haven't been read, or you can set the view to list unread messages only. When you select a message, the message header appears in the preview section of Outlook Express. If you want to read the entire message in a larger format, you can open it in its own window.

TIP: When you start Outlook Express, it checks for your mail, and it checks periodically thereafter while it's running. To receive mail immediately when you don't want to wait for the system to check your mailbox for you, click the Send/Recv button. To change the frequency with which Outlook Express checks for mail, choose Options from the Tools menu, and change the settings on the General tab.

Read Your Messages

1. Switch to the Inbox for the mail service you want to view if it's not the currently active folder.
2. On the View menu, specify how you want to view your messages:
   - Point to Current View, and choose the type of messages you want displayed.
   - Point to Sort By, and choose the way you want the messages to be ordered.
   - Choose Layout, specify whether and, if so, where you want the preview pane displayed, and click OK.

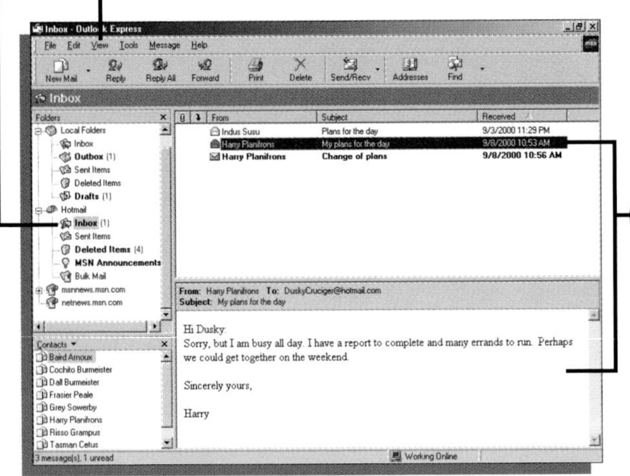

3. Click a message header, and read the message in the preview pane.
4. Double-click a message header to view the message in a separate window.

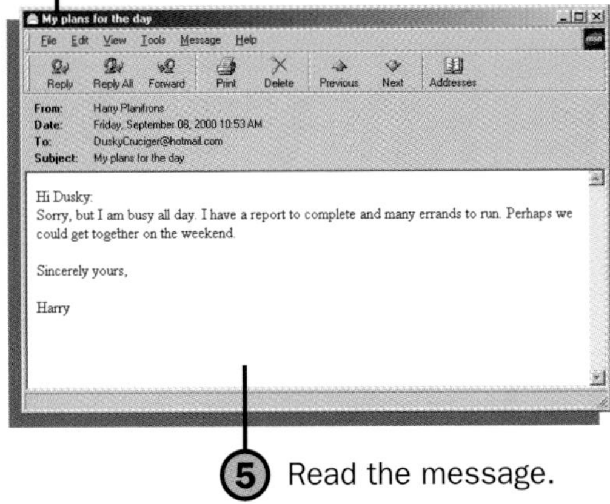

5. Read the message.

TRY THIS: On the Read tab of the Options dialog box, click the Fonts button. Select a new font in the Proportional Font list and a new font size in the Font Size list, and click OK. Close the Options dialog box, and look at the messages in the preview pane.

Formatting a Message

Although a plain text mail message is often all that's needed, you might want to enhance the appearance of your message with special text formatting, or by including a background color or picture.

TIP: Use Plain Text formatting if you're not sure whether the recipient has a mail reader that supports HTML formatting. Messages using Plain Text formatting are smaller and will download faster over a slow Internet connection than messages using Rich Text formatting, especially those that contain pictures.

Format a Message

1. Start a new message in Outlook Express, and complete the address and subject lines.
2. From the Format menu, choose Rich Text (HTML) if the command doesn't have a bullet next to it.
3. On the Format menu, do either of the following:
   - Point to Background, and choose a picture or a color for the background, or a sound that will be played when the message is opened.
   - Point to Apply Stationery, and choose a predefined layout, including background picture and font settings.
4. Use the items on the Formatting Bar to format the text and layout as you create the message.
5. Complete and send the message.

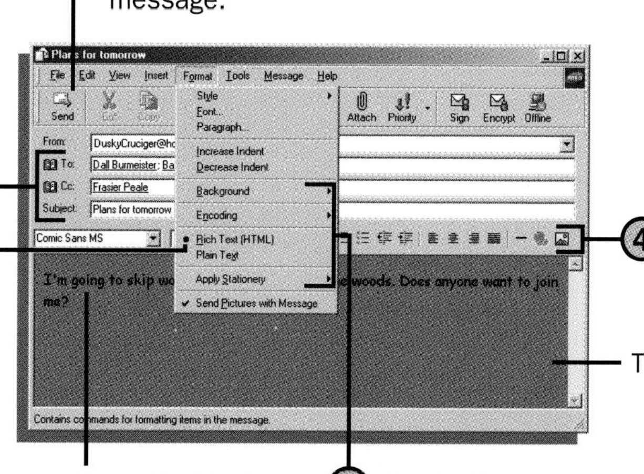

Formatted text

The background color

TIP: When you're composing a long message, it's a good idea to frequently choose Save from the File menu to save a copy of the message in the Drafts folder.

Designing Your Default Message

Why not let your computer do some of the work for you? When you design a default mail message, every new message that you start will look exactly the way you want, with all the elements in place—a specific background picture, perhaps; your signature automatically inserted at the end of the message; and a font that makes the message a little more "you."

TIP: If your message is in the HTML format, your signature file can be an HTML document too. If you enjoy experimenting with HTML, you can create anything from an attractive or ornate signature to a humorous or truly obnoxious one. The signature file, however, can't be any larger than 4 KB.

Add a Signature

1. In Outlook Express, choose Options from the Tools menu, and click the Signatures tab.

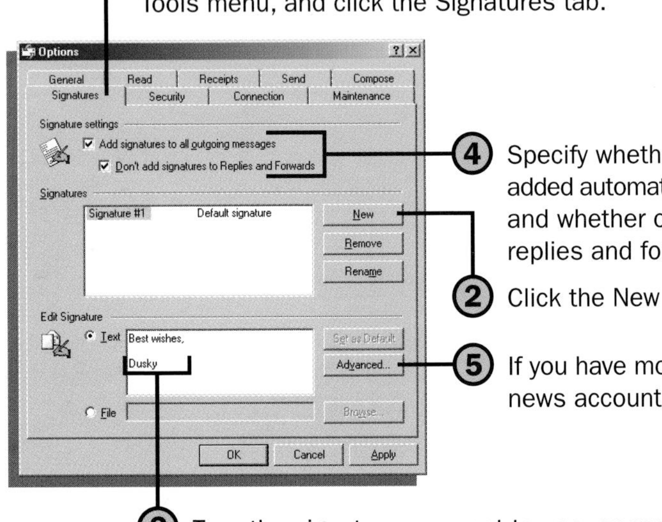

2. Click the New button.
3. Type the signature you want to use, or specify the text or HTML document that contains the signature.
4. Specify whether you want the signature added automatically to all outgoing messages and whether or not you want it included in replies and forwarded messages.
5. If you have more than one mail or news account, click Advanced.

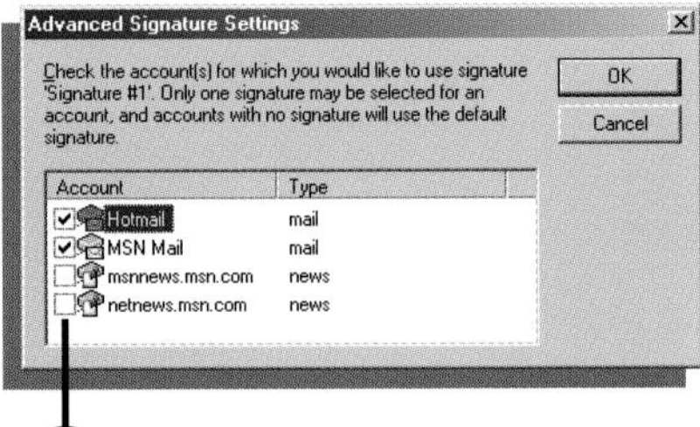

6. Specify which accounts will use this signature, and then click OK.

TIP: If you know that a certain contact can receive only text formatted messages, right-click his or her name in your Contacts list, choose Properties from the shortcut menu, and, on the Name tab, turn on the check box to send mail in plain text, and click OK. To send a message in plain text only once, choose Plain Text from the Format menu when you compose the message.

Select Your Stationery

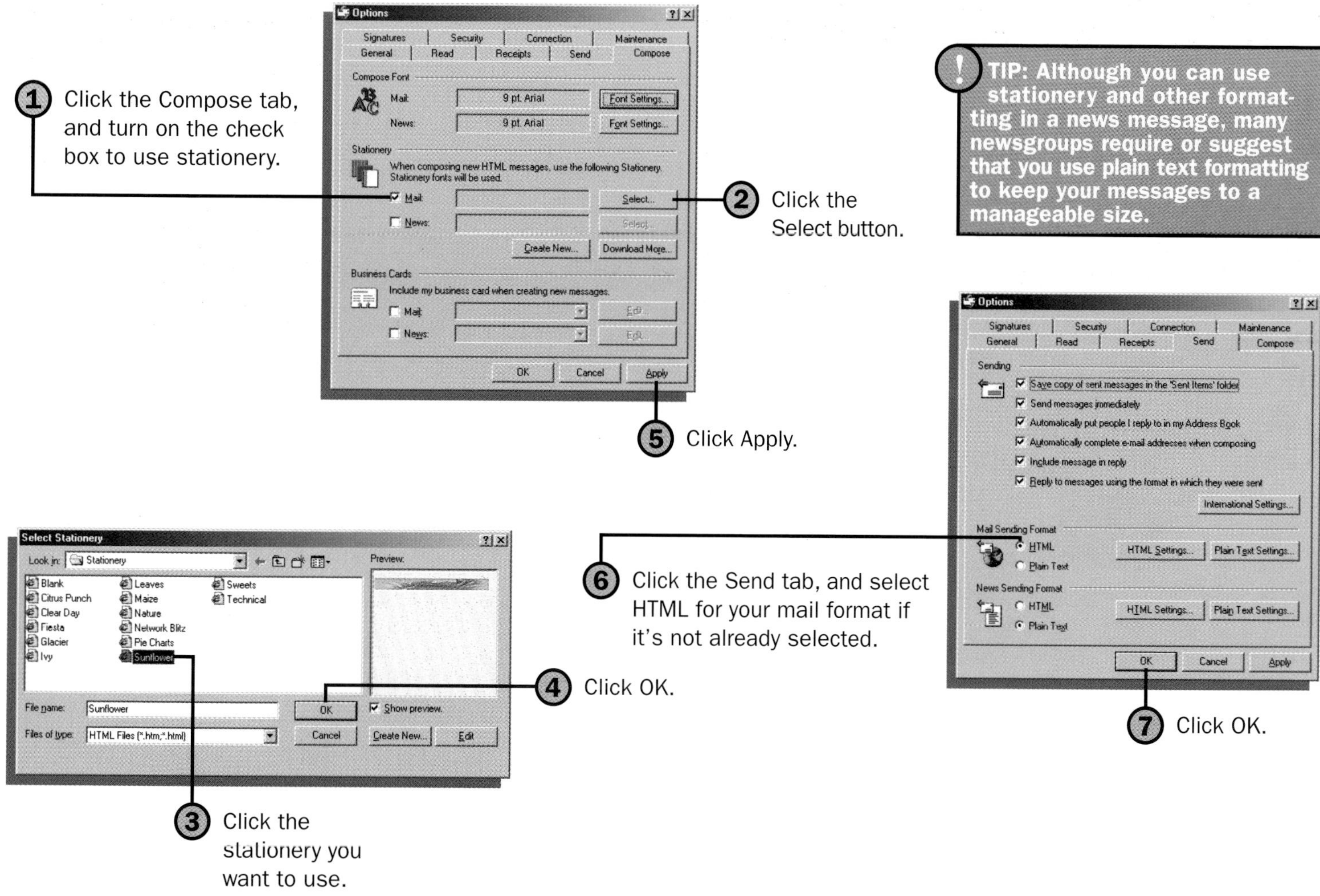

1. Click the Compose tab, and turn on the check box to use stationery.
2. Click the Select button.
3. Click the stationery you want to use.
4. Click OK.
5. Click Apply.
6. Click the Send tab, and select HTML for your mail format if it's not already selected.
7. Click OK.

TIP: Although you can use stationery and other formatting in a news message, many newsgroups require or suggest that you use plain text formatting to keep your messages to a manageable size.

TIP: To create your own e-mail stationery, click the Create New button on the Compose tab of the Options dialog box, and complete the Stationery Setup Wizard.

SEE ALSO: For information about using different formatting for each message, see "Formatting a Message" on page 113.

Sending or Receiving a File

A great way to share a file—a Word document, a picture, or even an entire program, for example—is to include it as part of an e-mail message. The file is kept as a separate part of the message—an *attachment*—that the recipient can save and open at any time.

SEE ALSO: For information about different methods of transferring files, see "Transferring Files" on page 118.

Include an Attachment

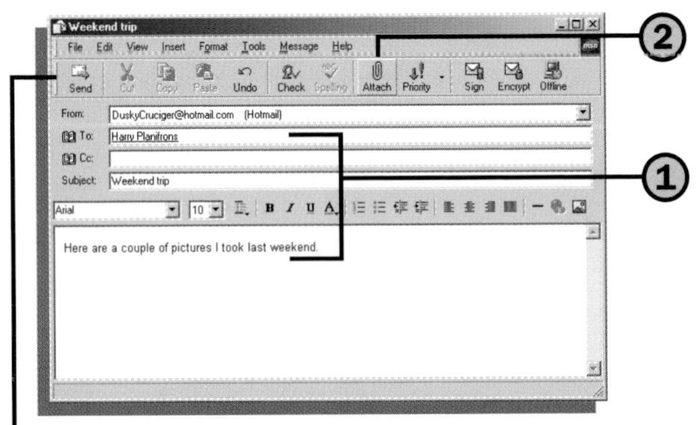

② Click the Attach button.

① Create and address a message, and type the message text.

③ In the Insert Attachment dialog box, select the file or files to be included.

④ Click Attach.

⑤ Send the message just as you'd send any other message.

TIP: Some mail systems can't accommodate attachments larger than about 1 MB, and some types of files can be corrupted when sent as attachments. In those cases, use other file-transfer methods, such as those available through NetMeeting or FTP services.

Open and Save an Attachment

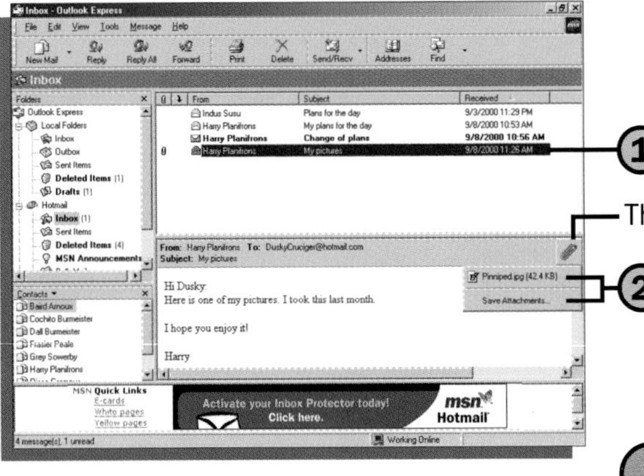

① Select a message you've received that contains an attachment.

The Attachment icon

② Click the Attachment icon, and, on the menu that appears, click

- The name of the file to open the file.
- Save Attachments to save the file to disk without opening it.

TIP: Viruses are often distributed in attached files. Never open an attachment you're not expecting without first saving the attachment to disk and using a virus-scanning program to inspect the file.

Replying to or Forwarding a Message

When you receive an e-mail message that needs a reply or that you want to forward to someone else, all it takes is a click of a button to create a new message. But be careful when you use the Reply All button—your message could be received by people for whom it wasn't intended!

TIP: When you reply to a message that has an attached file, the attachment isn't included with your reply. When you forward a message, though, the attachment is included.

Reply to or Forward a Message

1. Select the message.
2. Click the appropriate button:
   - Reply to send your reply to the writer of the message only
   - Reply All to send your reply to the writer of the message and to everyone listed in the original message's To and CC lines
   - Forward to send a copy of the message to another recipient
3. Add names to or delete names from the To and CC lines.
4. Type your reply message or any note associated with the forwarded message.
5. Click the Send button.

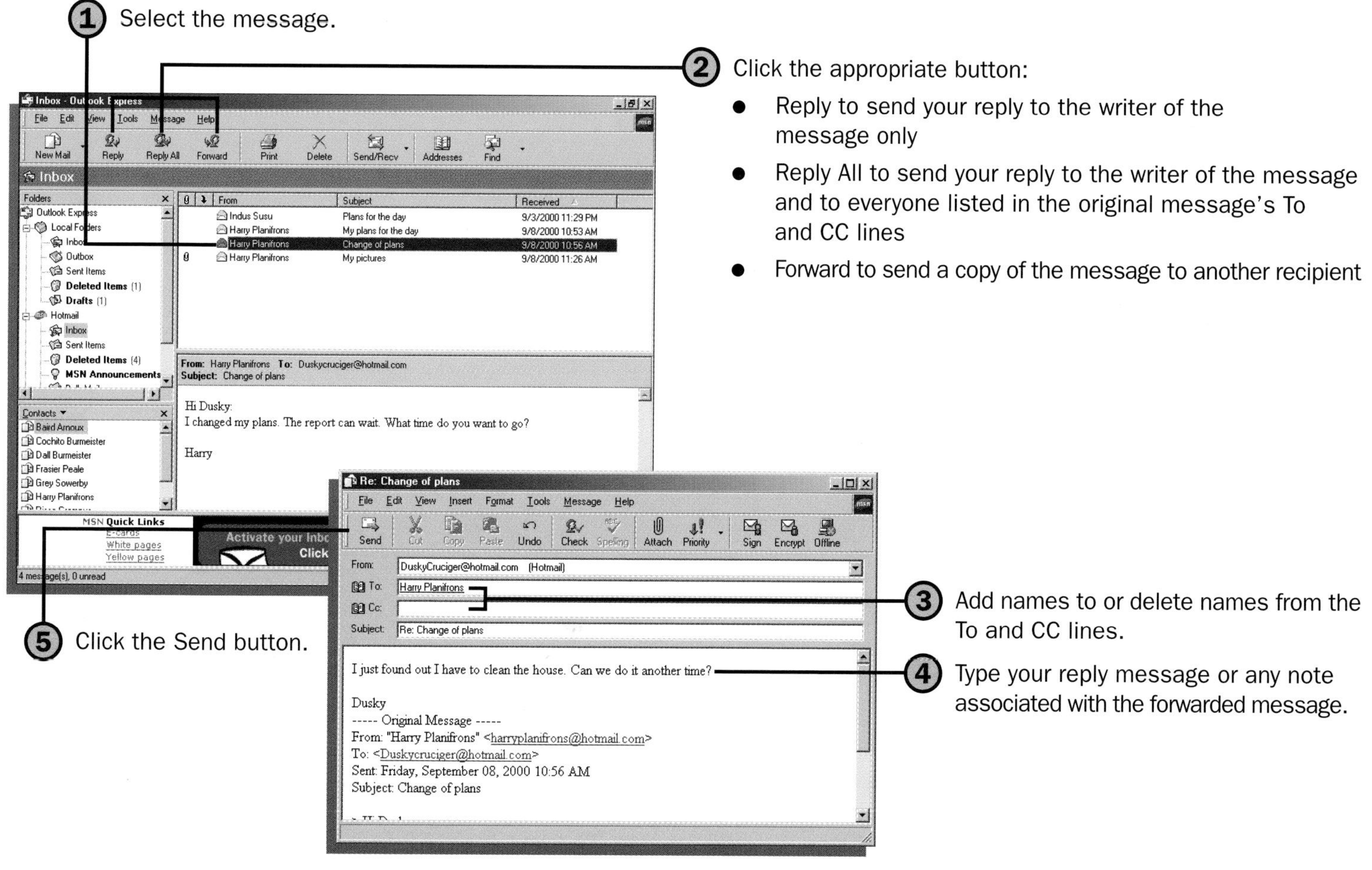

Transferring Files

In most cases, transferring files is a simple task: if you want to transfer a few small files, you can easily send them by e-mail or copy them to a floppy disk. On a network, you can simply move the files to a shared folder. If you're not connected to a business network, you can connect using a dial-up server or a VPN connection over the Internet. However, if you need to transfer a number of large files but don't have access to a network, there are several possible solutions. Listed below are additional methods for directly transferring files; you should find at least one among them that's appropriate for your situation. To find more information about any of these methods, look in the index of this book and/or search the Windows Me Help And Support Center.

Direct Cable Connection: A direct cable connection connects two computers with a special cable, using either the serial or parallel port on each computer. Once connected, you've established a network connection through which you have access to shared folders and files. However, this method works only with Windows-based computers.

Terminal: Terminal is a communications program that enables you to call and connect to another computer over a telephone line. The other computer must have a communications package (either Terminal or a compatible program). You can select from a list of different standard transfer protocols. You can use Terminal to connect to different types of computers and operating systems.

NetMeeting: You can connect over the Internet to another computer running NetMeeting, and you can transfer files while conducting a meeting. This is a simple procedure once NetMeeting is set up and running on both computers.

Dial-Up Server: You can set up your own computer as a dial-up server so that other computers can call in to connect and establish a network link through which files can be transferred to and from the server.

FTP Transfer: You can use FTP (File Transfer Protocol) to transfer files to an FTP server over the Internet. Use the FTP command in an MS-DOS window to start the FTP session, and make sure you have written directions from the site administrator detailing the commands to use to transfer the files. Some web sites automate FTP transfer; others allow you to navigate through the FTP site and transfer files as though the FTP location were just another hard drive.

Windows Me also provides two invaluable tools to assist you in transferring files: the Compressed Folders feature and the Windows Briefcase.

Compressed Folders: The Compressed Folders feature reduces the size of the files it contains and keeps all the compressed files in one location. When you transfer a compressed folder, the receiving computer sees either a compressed folder (if the Compressed Folders feature is installed) or a ZIP-type file that can be opened using one of several third-party programs.

Windows Briefcase: The Windows Briefcase is a file-management tool. It helps you keep track of different versions of a file when the file is edited on different computers. You copy files from your computer to the Briefcase and transfer the entire Briefcase to another computer, where the files can be edited and saved back into the Briefcase. When you return the Briefcase to your computer, the original files on your computer can be updated automatically.

Subscribing to Newsgroups

With so many newsgroups available, you'll probably want to be selective about the ones you review. You can do so in Outlook Express by *subscribing* to the newsgroups you like. Subscribed newsgroups appear in the message pane when you select the news server and on the Folder Bar, if it's displayed, when you expand the listing for a news server.

SEE ALSO: For information about setting up your connections to news servers in Outlook Express, see "Setting Up Your Connections" on page 110.

Select Your Newsgroups

1. With Outlook Express connected on line, select the news server you want to access.

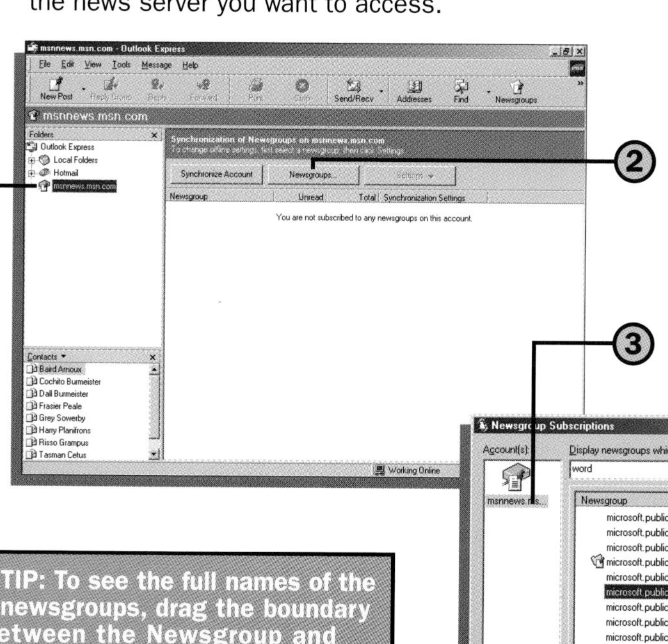

2. If Outlook Express doesn't automatically take you to the Newsgroup Subscriptions dialog box, click Newsgroups.
3. If you have more than one news server, select the one you want to use.
4. Search for the newsgroups you want to access.
5. Double-click a newsgroup to subscribe to it. Repeat to subscribe to all the newsgroups you want to access.
6. Click OK.

TIP: To see the full names of the newsgroups, drag the boundary between the Newsgroup and Description labels to widen the Newsgroup area.

Reading the News

Reading the news—or the gossip, tirades, and misinformation that often pass for news in Internet newsgroups—is as simple as reading your e-mail. All you do is select a newsgroup, select a message, and read it. When you select a newsgroup, the message headers are downloaded. When you select a message header, that message is downloaded and the other messages remain on the news server.

Select a Message

TIP: A "thread" is a series of messages in which one person posts a message and other readers reply to the message and/or to the replies to the original message.

1. In the Folders list, expand the list under the news server if necessary, and click the newsgroup.
2. On the View menu, point to Current View, and choose the view you want:
   - Show All Messages to see everything
   - Hide Read Messages to display only the messages you haven't read
   - Show Downloaded Messages to see the messages you've downloaded
   - Hide Read Or Ignored Messages to display only the messages you haven't read or that haven't been marked to be ignored
   - Show Replies To My Messages to see responses to your messages

The "torn page" icon shows that only the message header has been downloaded.

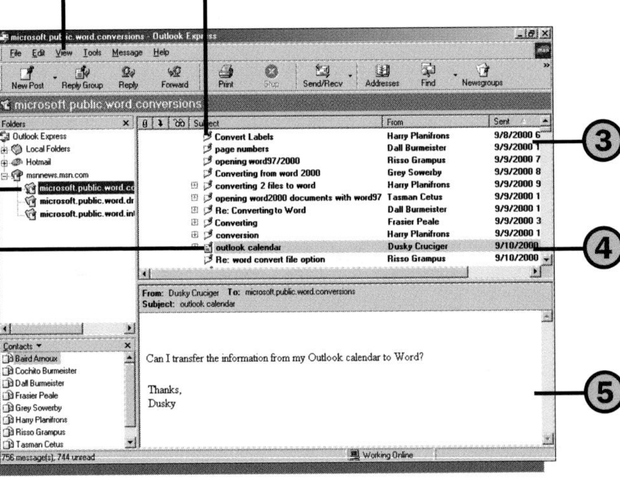

The "full page" icon shows that the message has been downloaded.

3. Read the message headers. A plus sign means there are additional messages in the thread under the message.
4. Click to display a message.
5. Read the message. Double-click the message header if you want to read the message in a separate window.

TIP: To download all the messages from the newsgroups that you've subscribed to so that you can read the messages while you're off line, select the news server and click Synchronize Account. Click the Settings button if you want to modify the type of messages to be downloaded.

Adding to the News

Most newsgroups are *interactive*—that is, you can post your own messages and you can reply to other people's messages. You can compose your messages on line or off line. If you compose a message when you're off line, the message is saved and will be posted to the newsgroup the next time you connect to the Internet.

Create a Message

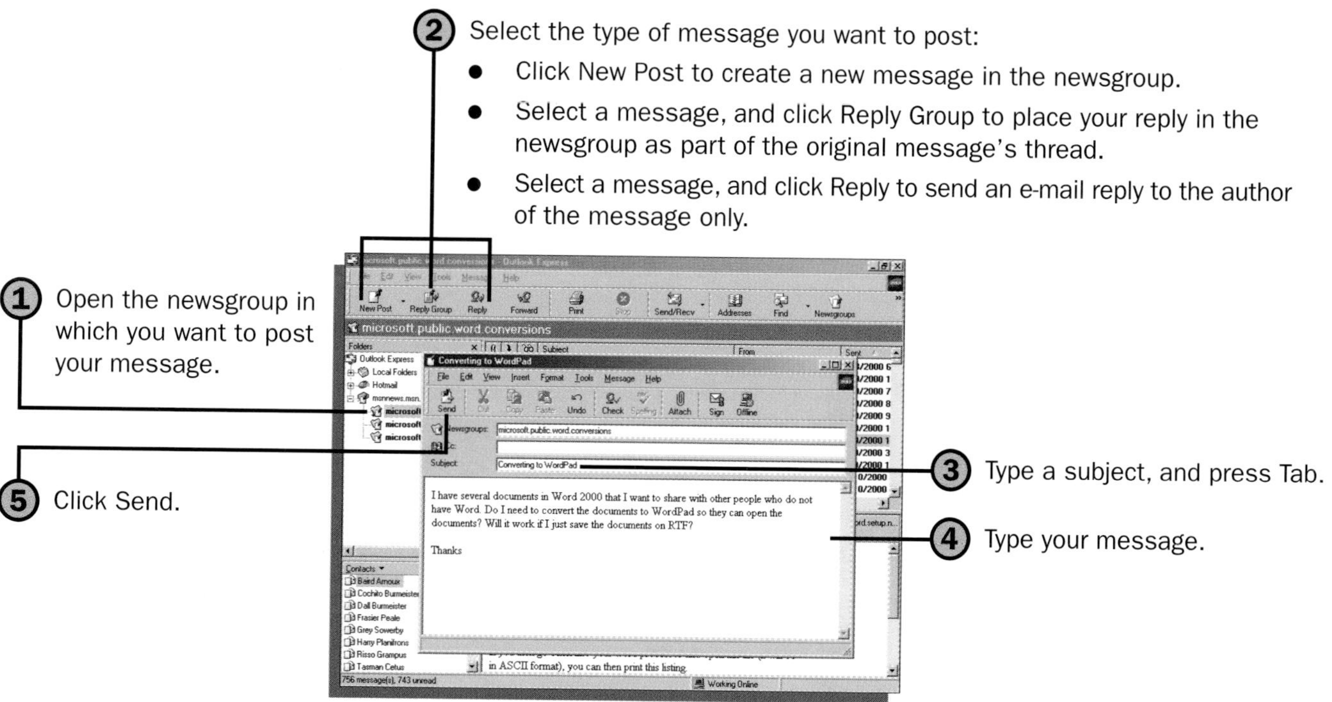

1. Open the newsgroup in which you want to post your message.
2. Select the type of message you want to post:
   - Click New Post to create a new message in the newsgroup.
   - Select a message, and click Reply Group to place your reply in the newsgroup as part of the original message's thread.
   - Select a message, and click Reply to send an e-mail reply to the author of the message only.
3. Type a subject, and press Tab.
4. Type your message.
5. Click Send.

TIP: Although you can create and send formatted messages, most newsgroups prefer messages to be in plain text to keep download time to a minimum.

TIP: To find the replies to your messages, point to Current View on the View menu, and choose Show Replies To My Messages.

Managing Your Contacts

When you're using e-mail, you don't need to type an address every time you send a message; you can retrieve addresses from the Contacts list. All the names shown in the Contacts list are actually stored in your Address Book, a separate program that works with Outlook Express and other programs. If you frequently send one message to the same group of people, you can gather all their addresses into a *group,* and then all you need to find is that one address item. How convenient!

Create a New Address

1. In Outlook Express, click Contacts at the top of the Contacts pane, and click New Contact on the menu that appears.
2. On the various tabs of the Properties dialog box, enter the information you want to record.
3. Click OK.

Add an Address from a Message

1. In the Inbox, right-click the message.

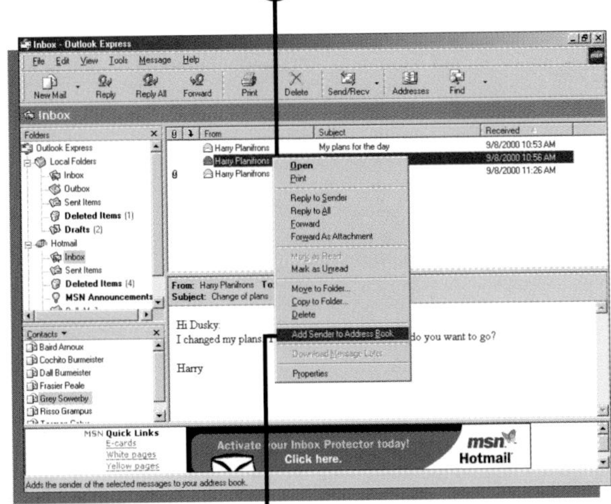

2. Choose Add Sender To Address Book from the shortcut menu. If the command is grayed (unavailable), click the message to download it, and then right-click it and choose the command again.

TIP: To add to your Address Book someone whose name is listed in the CC line of a message, double-click the message to open it in a separate window, and then right-click the name you want to add.

Create a Group

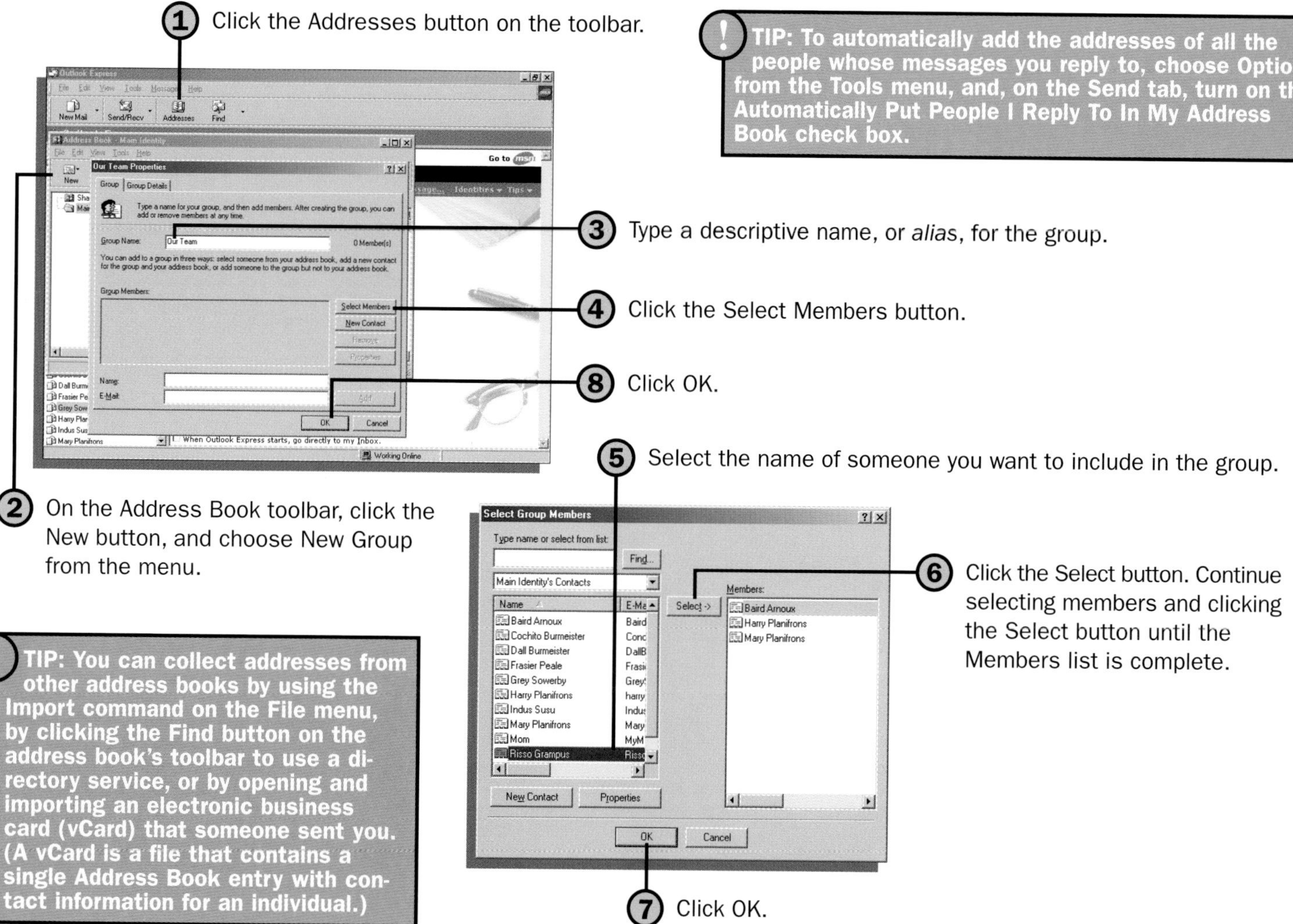

1. Click the Addresses button on the toolbar.
2. On the Address Book toolbar, click the New button, and choose New Group from the menu.
3. Type a descriptive name, or *alias*, for the group.
4. Click the Select Members button.
5. Select the name of someone you want to include in the group.
6. Click the Select button. Continue selecting members and clicking the Select button until the Members list is complete.
7. Click OK.
8. Click OK.

TIP: To automatically add the addresses of all the people whose messages you reply to, choose Options from the Tools menu, and, on the Send tab, turn on the Automatically Put People I Reply To In My Address Book check box.

TIP: You can collect addresses from other address books by using the Import command on the File menu, by clicking the Find button on the address book's toolbar to use a directory service, or by opening and importing an electronic business card (vCard) that someone sent you. (A vCard is a file that contains a single Address Book entry with contact information for an individual.)

Sending and Receiving Instant Messages

Using the MSN (Microsoft Network) Messenger Service, you can exchange instant messages with your designated contacts whenever they're on line. Your contacts must have the MSN Messenger Service installed and must have their own Microsoft Passports. You can have as many as 75 different contacts and can include up to five people in a conversation. Each message can be as long as 400 characters.

Set Up Your Account

TIP: To quickly log on to the MSN Messenger Service, double-click its icon on the taskbar.

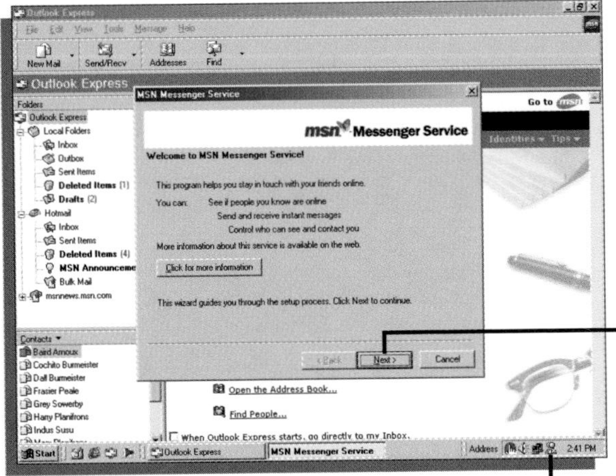

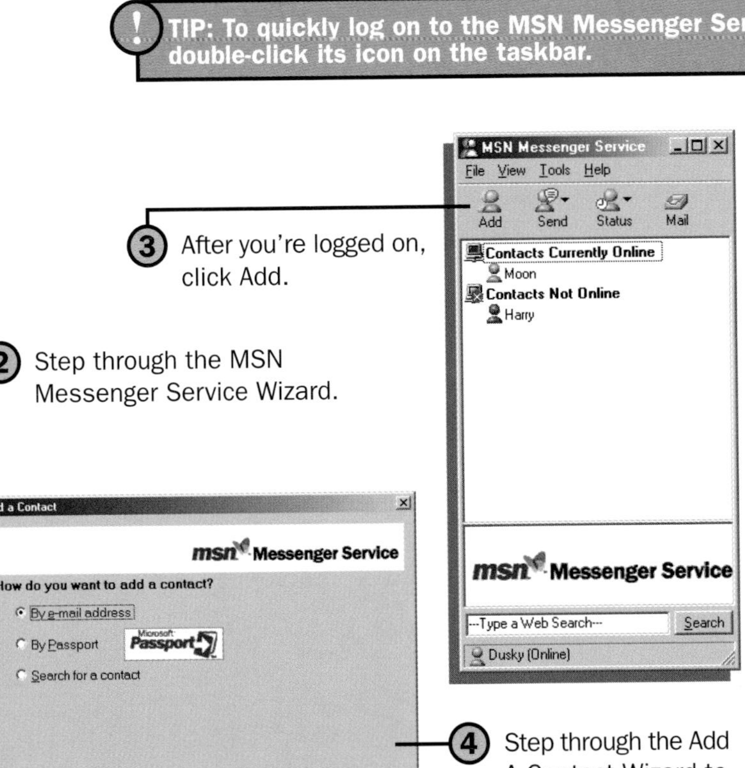

1. If the MSN Messenger Service isn't already running or displayed, start it by clicking the icon on the taskbar or, if the icon isn't displayed, choosing it from the Communications submenu of the Start menu. Connect to the Internet if you're not already connected.
2. Step through the MSN Messenger Service Wizard.
3. After you're logged on, click Add.
4. Step through the Add A Contact Wizard to add your contacts.

TIP: You don't have to be an MSN member to use the MSN Messenger Service, but you do need to have a Microsoft Passport. If you're not an MSN member, the easiest way to obtain a Passport is to sign up for a Hotmail e-mail account.

Send a Message

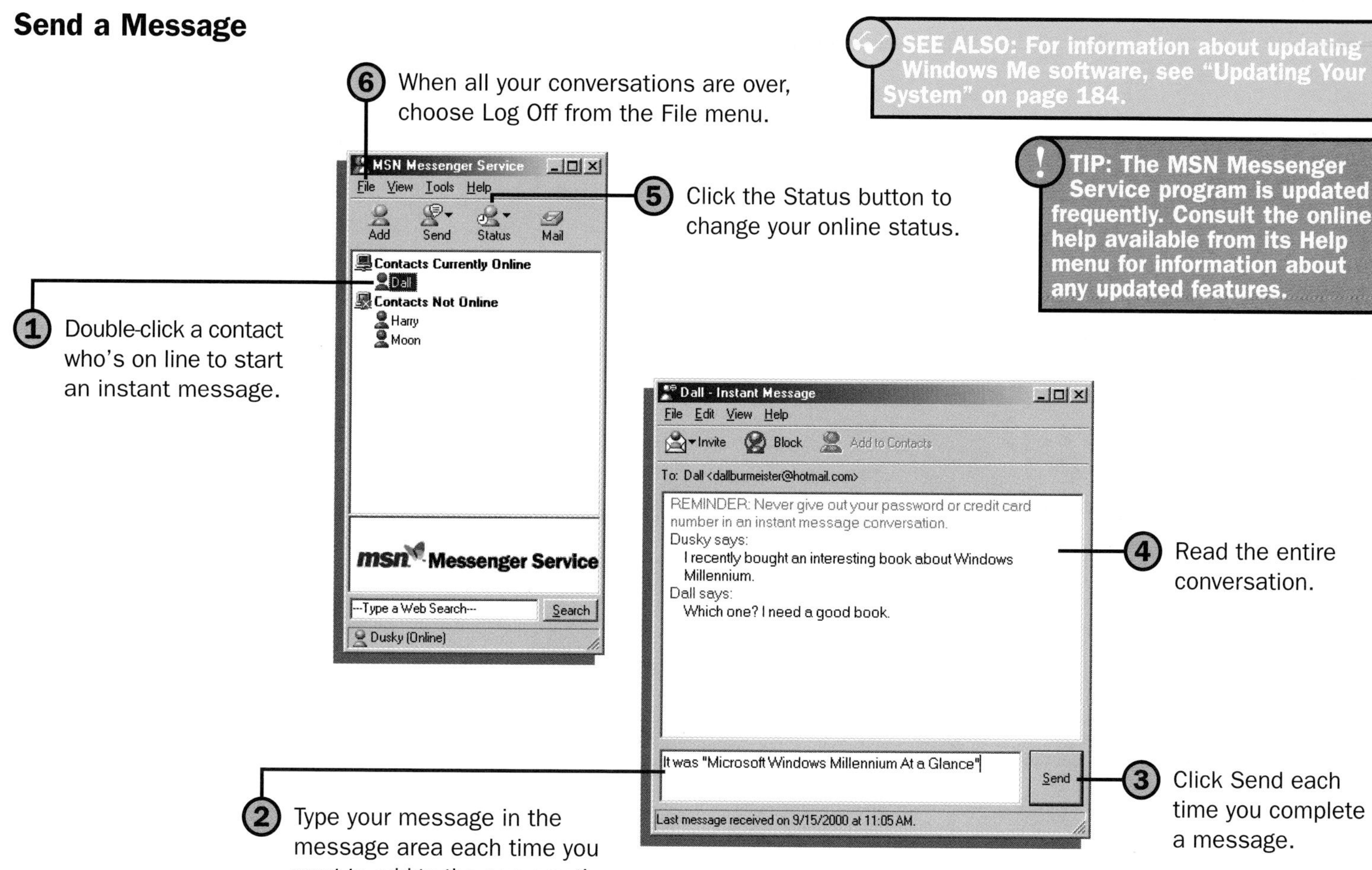

SEE ALSO: For information about updating Windows Me software, see "Updating Your System" on page 184.

TIP: The MSN Messenger Service program is updated frequently. Consult the online help available from its Help menu for information about any updated features.

TIP: When you're logged on to the MSN Messenger Service, your online contacts appear in your Contacts list. To send a message, right-click the contact's name, and choose Send An Instant Message.

TIP: The MSN Messenger Service is designed to work with Outlook Express and your Contacts list. To add someone from your Contacts list in Outlook Express to the MSN Messenger Service, right-click his or her name, and choose Set As Online Contact.

Customizing Outlook Express for Different Users

If more than one person uses Outlook Express on your computer, you can create individual identities so that each person has his or her own mail and news accounts, folders, and Contacts list.

Define an Identity

1. In Outlook Express, point to Identities on the File menu, and choose Add New Identity from the submenu to display the New Identity dialog box.

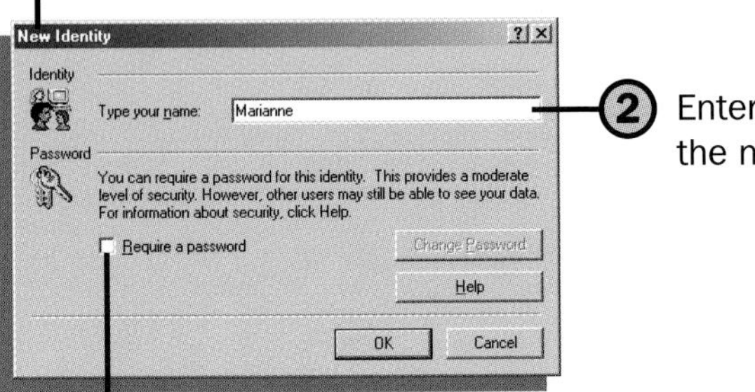

2. Enter a name for the new identity.
3. Specify whether you want to require a password to switch to this identity, and click OK.

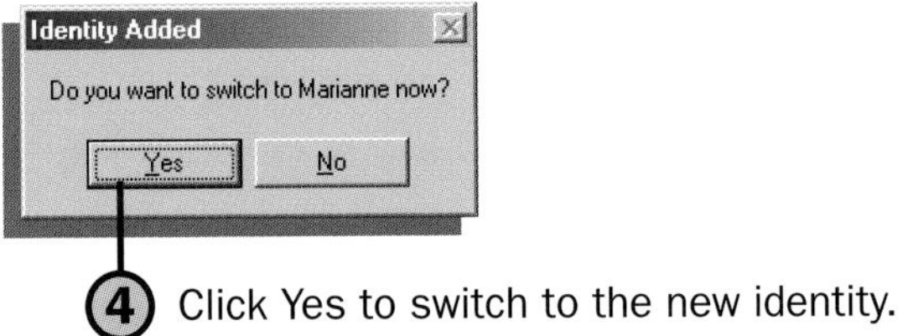

4. Click Yes to switch to the new identity.

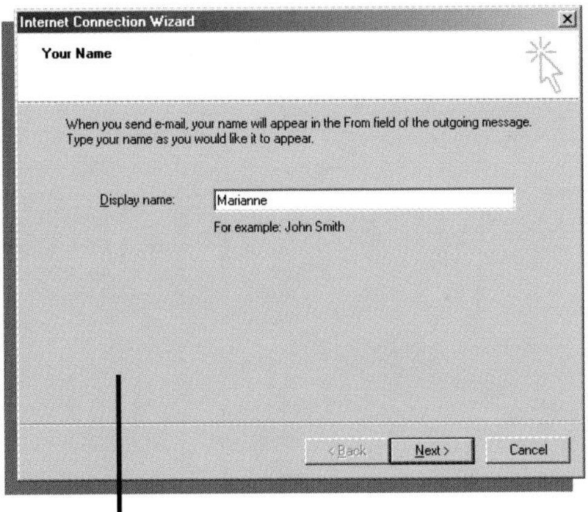

5. Complete the Internet Connection Wizard to specify or set up an Internet e-mail account for the new identity.

TIP: If Outlook Express is set up to use different identities, the names in the Contacts list are the names listed in the Address Book for the current identity plus any names in the Shared Contacts folder of the Address Book.

TIP: The Address Book stores information for individual identities in separate folders. To share addresses, open the Address Book, choose Folders And Groups from the View menu, and copy addresses into the Shared Contacts folder.

Switch Identities

1. In Outlook Express, choose Switch Identities from the File menu to display the Switch Identities dialog box.

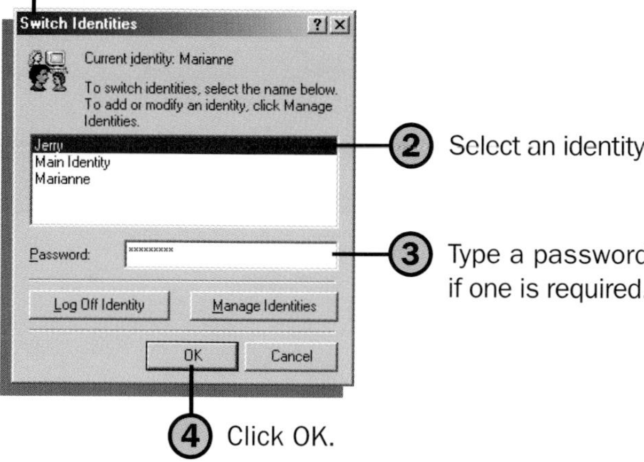

2. Select an identity.
3. Type a password if one is required.
4. Click OK.

TIP: The Main Identity contains all the connections, settings, and addresses that you specified before you established the first new Identity. To make all these contacts available to all the identities while you're logged on to the Main Identity in the Address Book, move all the contacts into the Shared Contacts folder.

TIP: Click the Manage Identities button in the Switch Identities dialog box to add or delete an identity or to specify which identity is to be used when Outlook Express is started.

Share Your Contacts

1. Click the Addresses button on the Outlook Express toolbar to display the Address Book for the current identity.

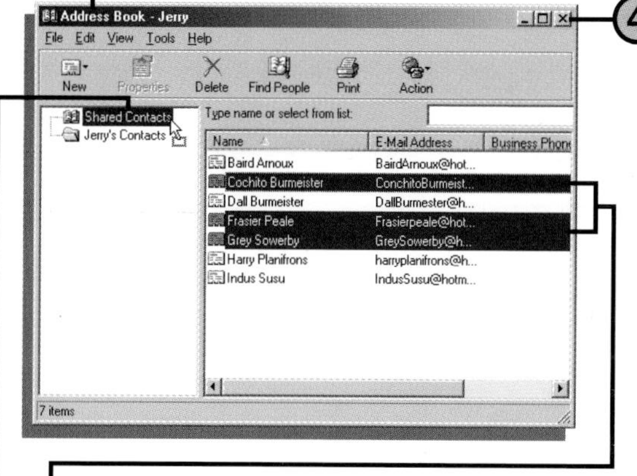

2. Hold down the Ctrl key and click the addresses you want to share with others.
3. Drag the selected addresses into the Shared Contacts folder.
4. Close the Address Book when you've finished.

TIP: If the folder containing your contacts and shared contacts isn't displayed, choose Folders And Groups from the View menu.

Conferring on the Net

Microsoft NetMeeting provides services that let you hold a private meeting over the Internet or your network. The easiest way to connect over the Internet is to connect to the online contacts you established for the MSN Messenger Service. Once you're connected, you can use the connection like a telephone for voice conversations or as a conferencing tool for a video presentation. You can also share programs, exchange notes using a text "chat," or view illustrations and other material using the Whiteboard. The first time you run NetMeeting, a wizard walks you through the setup and asks you to provide the necessary information.

Call a Contact

1. Start NetMeeting from the Communications submenu of the Start menu. If you haven't completed the NetMeeting Wizard, do so now.

SEE ALSO: For information about setting up your online contacts, see "Sending and Receiving Instant Messages" on page 124.

2. Log on to the MSN Messenger Service and establish contact with the person you want to meet with.

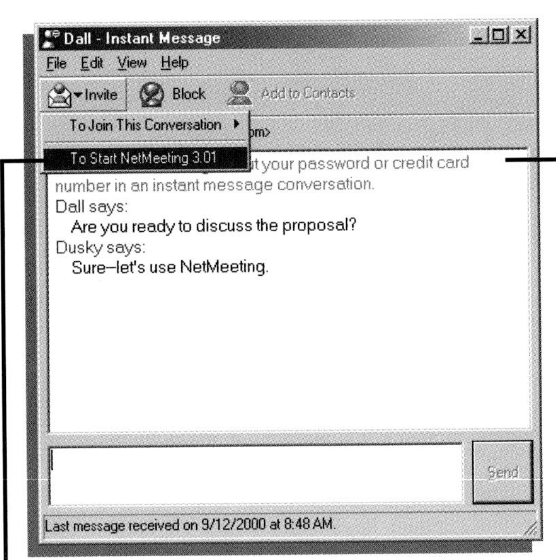

3. Click Invite, and choose To Start NetMeeting.

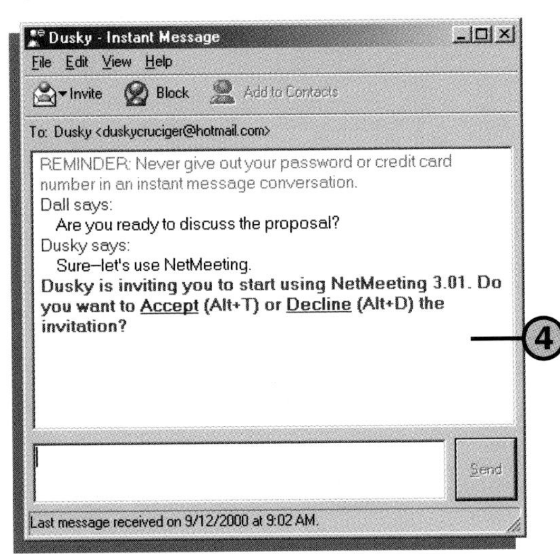

4. Wait for your contact to click Accept in his or her instant message. If NetMeeting isn't already running on your contact's computer, it will start automatically.

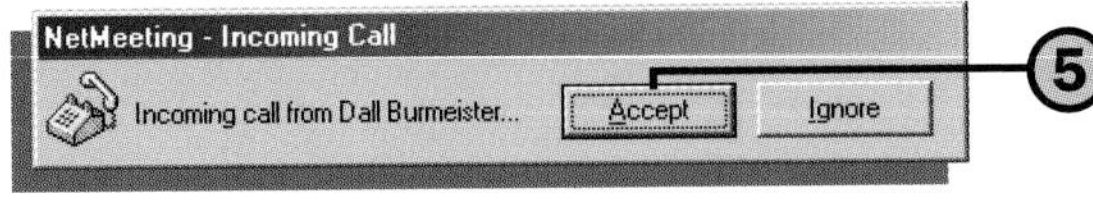

5. Accept the call from your contact to start the NetMeeting session.

TIP: To connect to an individual who isn't one of your online contacts but who is using a conferencing server, add him or her to your Contacts list, and, on the NetMeeting tab of the Properties dialog box, enter the name of the conferencing server and the individual's e-mail address (or a specific conferencing address), and then click Call Now to connect.

Connect over a Network

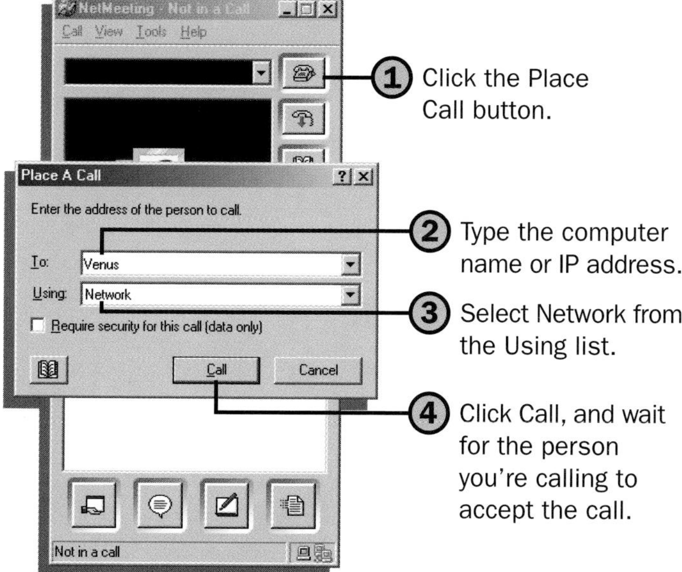

TIP: NetMeeting provides advanced videoconferencing features that are available if your computer is equipped with a video modem or if you can connect to a videoconferencing server. See NetMeeting Help and your hardware documentation for details.

Hold a Meeting

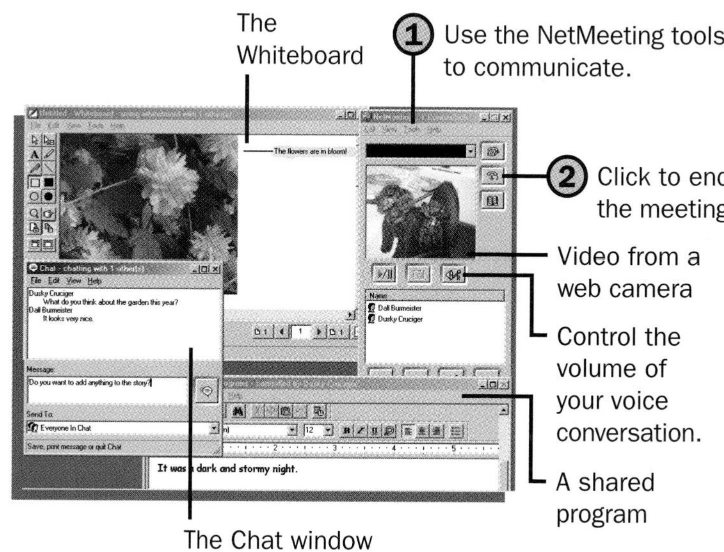

TIP: For simultaneous voice communications, your computer needs a full-duplex modem. If you're using a half-duplex modem, you must wait for the other person to finish speaking before you can respond. See your modem documentation to identify the type of modem you have.

SEE ALSO: For information about using NetMeeting to control another computer remotely, see "Controlling Your Computer Remotely" on page 46.

For information about connecting using the MSN Messenger Service, see "Sending and Receiving Instant Messages" on page 124.

Making a Phone Call

If you have a headset or a telephone connected to your modem, you can use a Windows Me accessory program called Phone Dialer to place the call for you and to keep a log of all your calls. You can automate the process even further by using the Speed Dial buttons.

SEE ALSO: For information about installing Phone Dialer if it doesn't appear on the Start menu, see "Adding or Removing Windows Me Components" on page 170.

Dial a Number

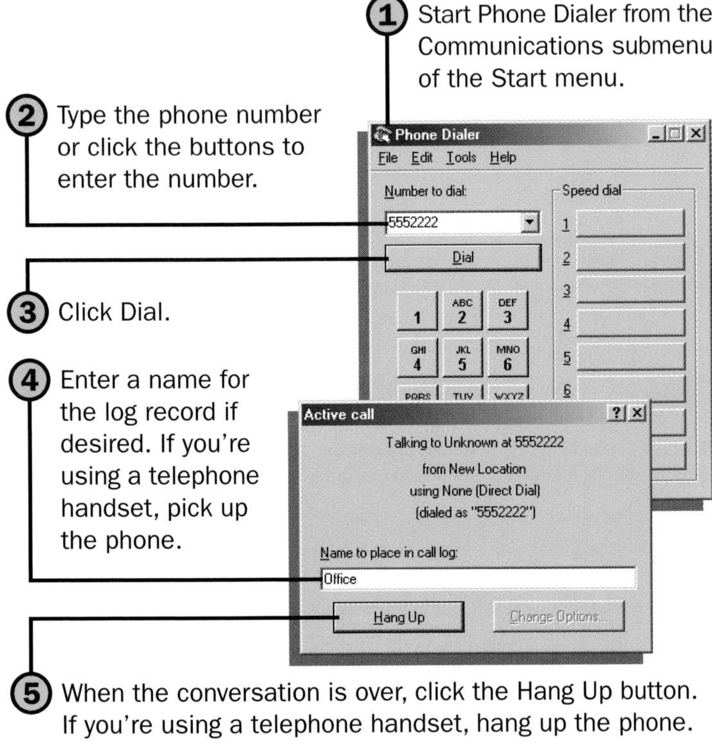

1. Start Phone Dialer from the Communications submenu of the Start menu.
2. Type the phone number or click the buttons to enter the number.
3. Click Dial.
4. Enter a name for the log record if desired. If you're using a telephone handset, pick up the phone.
5. When the conversation is over, click the Hang Up button. If you're using a telephone handset, hang up the phone.

Speed It Up

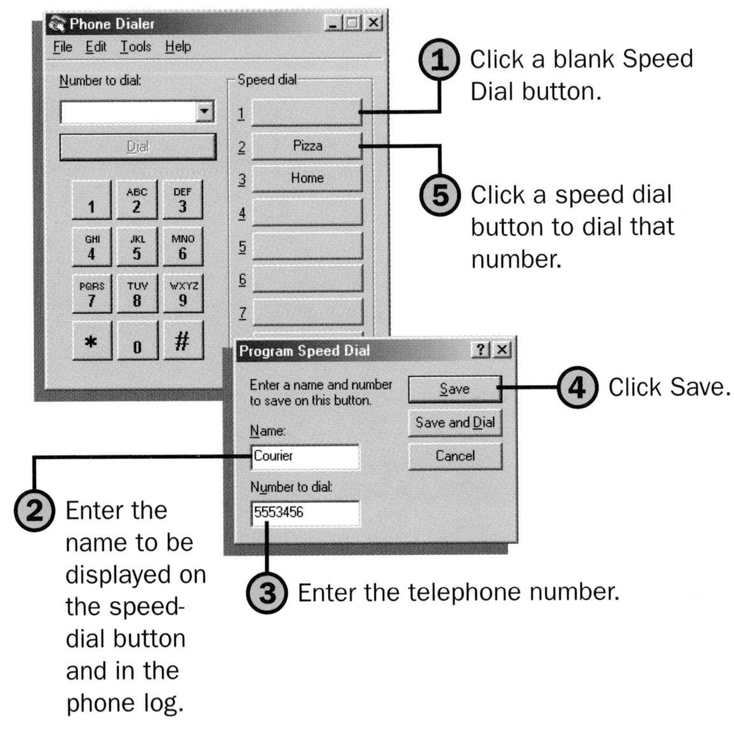

1. Click a blank Speed Dial button.
2. Enter the name to be displayed on the speed-dial button and in the phone log.
3. Enter the telephone number.
4. Click Save.
5. Click a speed dial button to dial that number.

TIP: To modify an existing speed-dial name or number, choose Speed Dial from the Edit menu.

TIP: To see a list of the calls you've made, choose Show Log from the Tools menu.

10 Customizing

In this section

You can customize your computer so that it looks and works exactly the way you want it to. With Microsoft Windows Millennium Edition installed on your computer, you can keep the classic Windows look, change the look to that of a web page, or design your own look with elements from both styles. You can change the size and color of almost everything; set items to open with one click instead of two; rearrange or hide the taskbar, toolbars, Start menu, and Desktop items; create your own toolbars; and customize your Active Desktop with pictures, animated items, and links.

You can use a single window in which to open all your folders, or use a separate window for each folder; and you can customize folder windows with colors, pictures, and comments. You can choose a screen saver, use the Magnifier to enlarge anything on your screen, try different mouse pointers, and change your mouse's behavior.

If you have any problems with your vision, hearing, or manual dexterity—or if you simply want to try different ways of working—you can use some innovative tools: press key combinations one key at a time instead of simultaneously, use high-contrast color schemes for better visibility, control mouse movements with the numeric keypad, specify visual cues to replace the computer's beeps, or use the On-Screen Keyboard.

Reorganizing the Start Menu

The Windows Me Start menu is a wonderful resource for organizing and starting your programs and associated documents. You can organize the Start menu by adding and deleting programs, and by moving programs around to create an arrangement that's logical and convenient for the way you work.

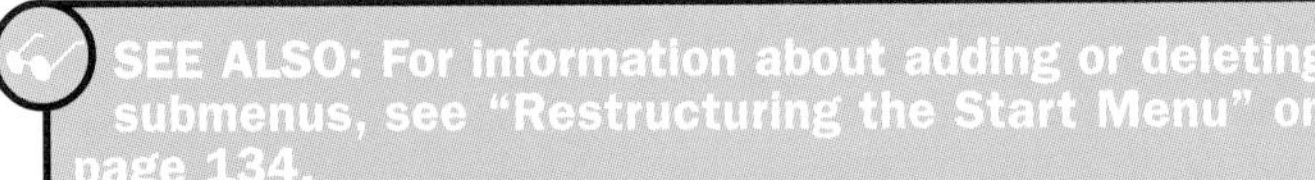

SEE ALSO: For information about adding or deleting submenus, see "Restructuring the Start Menu" on page 134.

Add an Item

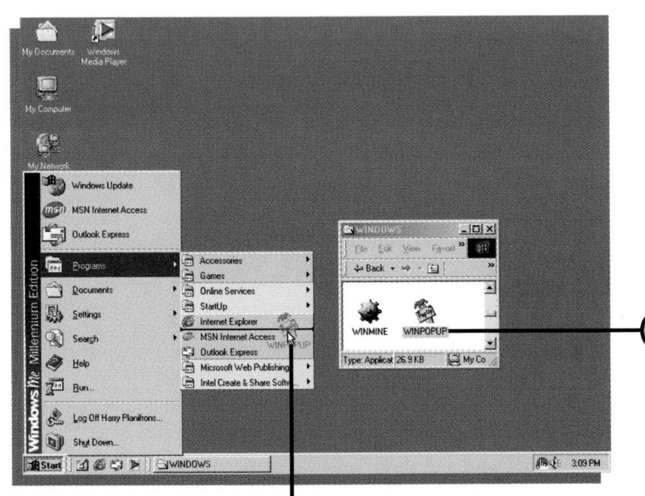

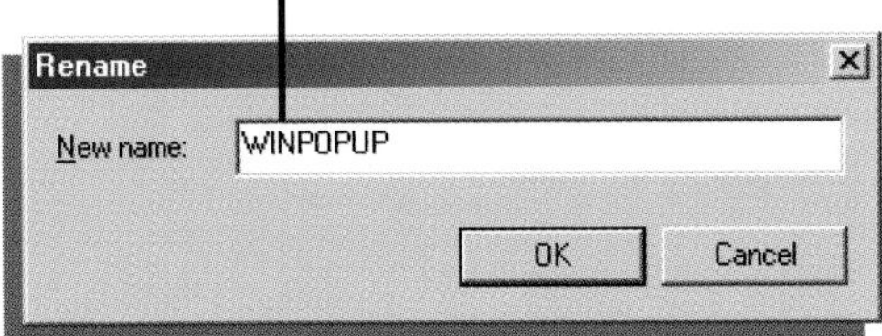

1. Use My Computer to locate the item you want to add.
2. Drag the item onto the Start button and hold it there until the Start menu opens. Then drag the item onto the Programs menu item, and either drag the item onto the Programs submenu, or continue dragging and pointing to submenus until you reach the desired location, and then place the item.
3. If you want to rename the item, right-click it, choose Rename from the shortcut menu, type a new name, and click OK.

TIP: When you move an item onto the Start button, the item will appear at the top of the Start menu.

TIP: The programs listed on the Start menu are not the programs themselves but shortcuts to the programs. When you add, move, or delete an item whose name appears on the Start menu, you're affecting only the shortcut to the program, not the program itself.

Move an Item

1. Open the Start menu, and the submenus if necessary, until you locate the item you want to move.

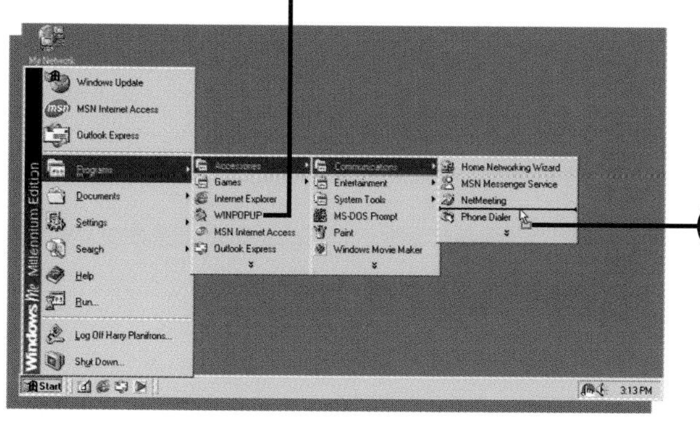

2. Drag the item into a new location.

TIP: If you've been adding, deleting, or moving items and the menu has become a bit disorganized, right-click any item on the menu, and choose Sort By Name from the shortcut menu to list the items alphabetically.

TIP: Any items that you add to the StartUp folder (on the Programs submenu of the Start menu) will start when Windows Me starts.

Delete an Item

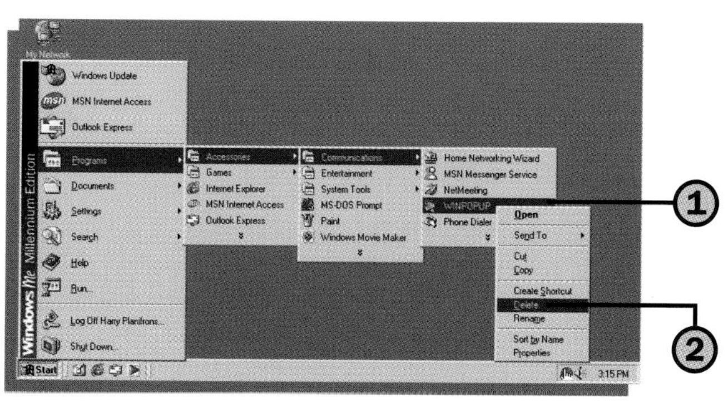

1. Open the Start menu, and the submenus if necessary, until you locate the item you want to delete.
2. Right-click the item, and choose Delete from the shortcut menu.

Confirm File Delete

Are you sure you want to send 'WINPOPUP' to the Recycle Bin?

Yes No

3. When prompted, confirm that you want to delete the item.

Restructuring the Start Menu

The beauty of Windows Me is the flexibility it gives you to change things around. For example, if you'd like to restructure the Start menu so that it works more logically for you, you can do so by creating or deleting submenus. Windows Me uses folders to organize the Start menu, so you have to create a subfolder to create a submenu. You can also specify which items are displayed and how they appear.

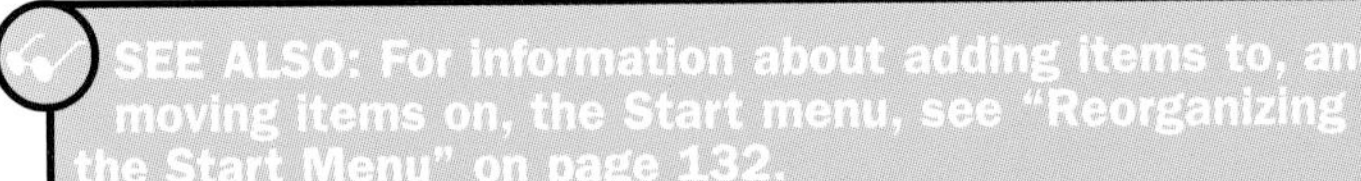

SEE ALSO: For information about adding items to, and moving items on, the Start menu, see "Reorganizing the Start Menu" on page 132.

For information about hiding or displaying the taskbar, see "Hiding the Taskbar" on page 143.

Add a Submenu

1. Right-click the Start button, and choose Explore from the shortcut menu.
2. In the window that appears, select the folder (and thereby the Start-menu submenu) in which you want to create a submenu.
3. Open the File menu, point to New, and choose Folder from the shortcut menu.
4. Name the folder, using the name you want to appear on the submenu.
5. Close the window.
6. Open the Start menu, and drag your program or document into the new submenu.

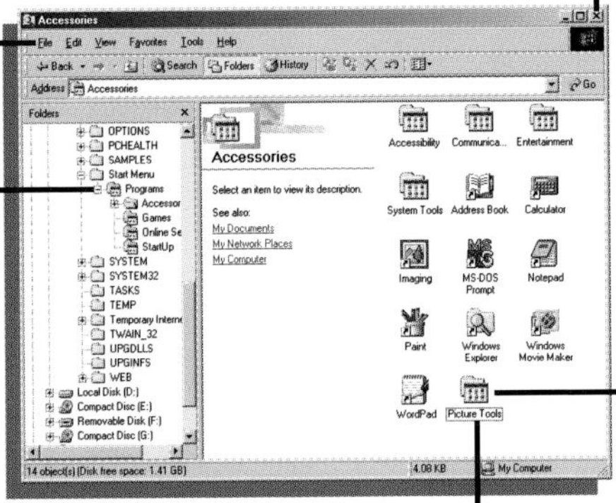

By creating this new folder...

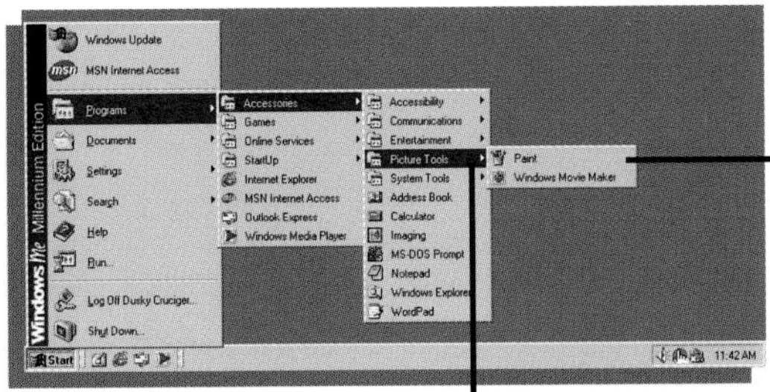

...you create this new submenu.

TIP: You delete a subfolder the same way you delete any Start-menu item—right-click it, and choose Delete from the shortcut menu.

Change What's Displayed

1. Right-click a blank spot on the taskbar, and choose Properties from the shortcut menu to display the Taskbar And Start Menu Properties dialog box.

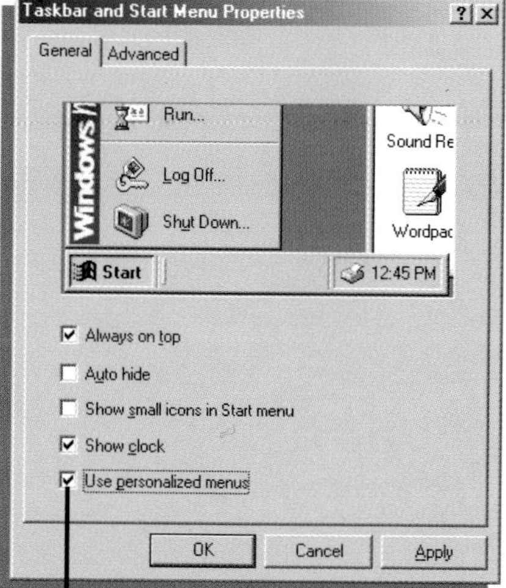

2. On the General tab, turn on the Use Personalized Menus check box to initially display only the menu items you use, or turn off the check box to always display all the menu items.

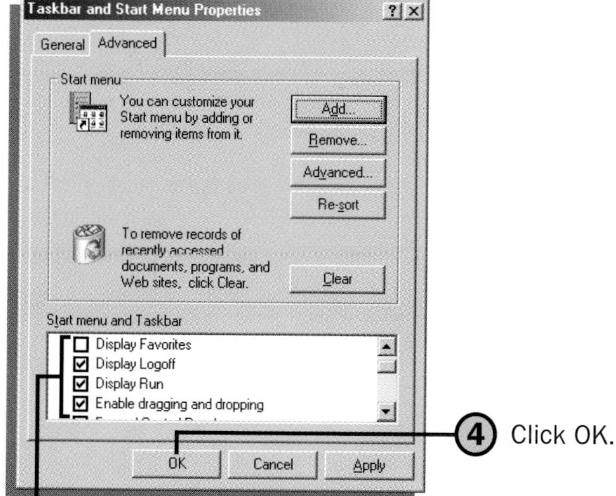

3. On the Advanced tab, turn on the check boxes for the features you want, and turn off the check boxes for the features you don't want:
   - Display... to display the specified item on the Start menu or taskbar
   - Expand... to display a submenu for the item, showing its contents
   - Scroll Programs to add scroll bars to the Programs listing if you have too many programs to fit on the screen in a single column
   - Enable Moving And Resizing to permit changes to the location or size of the taskbar
4. Click OK.

TIP: After you've added items to a submenu, right-click it, and choose Sort By Name to arrange the items in alphabetical order.

TRY THIS: Press Ctrl+Esc to open the Start menu, press S, and then press T to display the Taskbar And Start Menu Properties dialog box using the keyboard.

Customizing the Desktop

Just as your physical desktop might be constructed from solid oak, printed plastic, or glass, your Windows Me Desktop can have a patterned surface. You can add a picture for more interest, and you can have it occupy the entire Desktop surface or only part of it. You can even combine a picture with a patterned background. Keep experimenting until you find the look you like.

TIP: To create your own Desktop pattern, select a pattern you'd like to modify, and click Edit Pattern. In the Pattern Editor dialog box, click in the pattern to add or remove parts of it. Click Change to save the changes, and click Done to close the dialog box.

Add a Pattern

1. Right-click a blank spot on the Desktop, and choose Properties from the shortcut menu to display the Display Properties dialog box.
2. Click the Background tab if it's not already selected.
3. Click the Pattern button.
4. Select the pattern you want to use.
5. Click OK.
6. Click Apply to see the pattern on your Desktop.

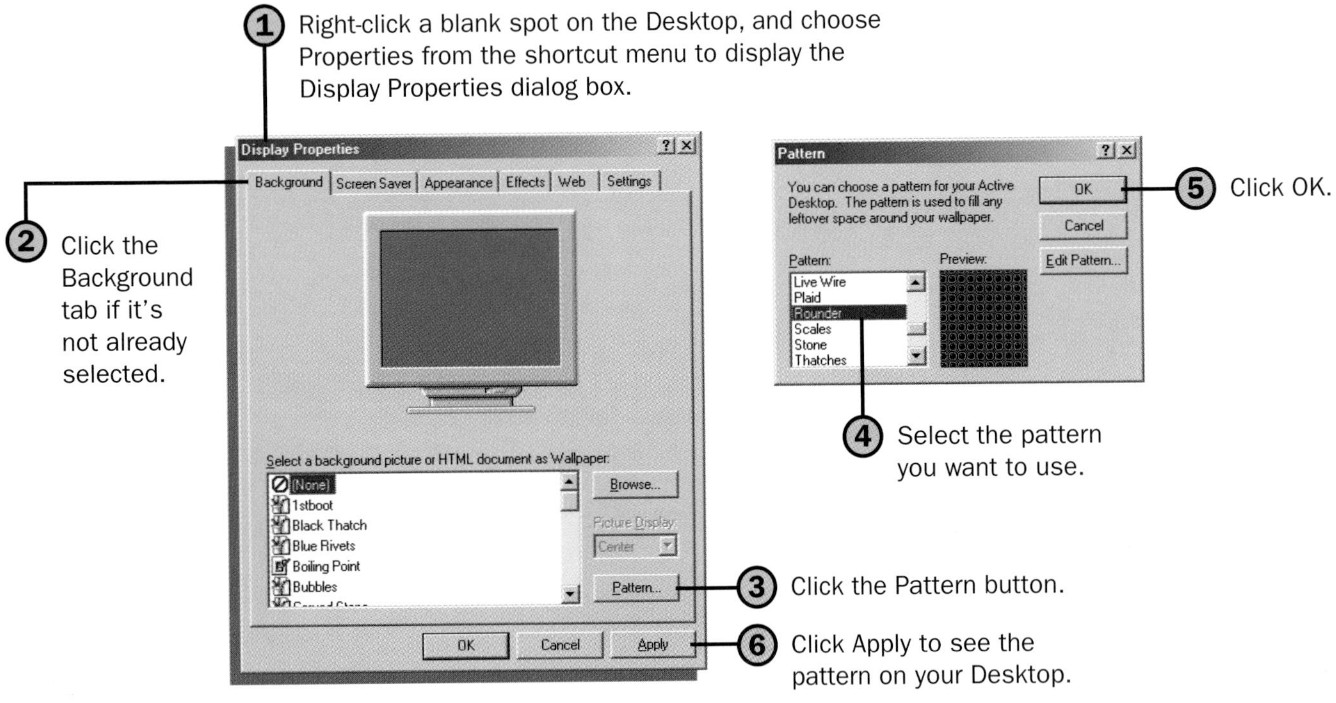

TIP: The background for the pattern and for the Desktop-icon text is set to the Desktop color that was specified on the Appearance tab.

Add a Picture

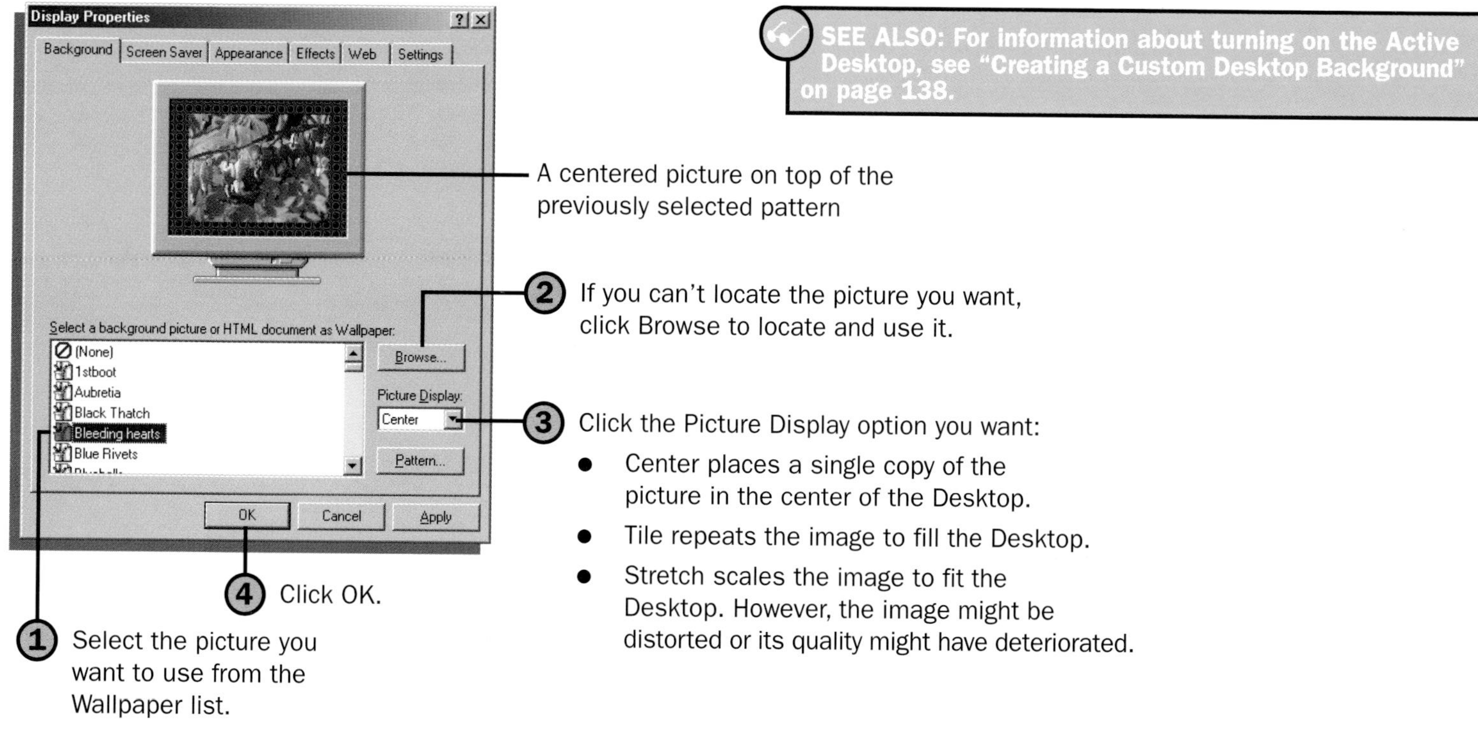

A centered picture on top of the previously selected pattern

1. Select the picture you want to use from the Wallpaper list.
2. If you can't locate the picture you want, click Browse to locate and use it.
3. Click the Picture Display option you want:
   - Center places a single copy of the picture in the center of the Desktop.
   - Tile repeats the image to fill the Desktop.
   - Stretch scales the image to fit the Desktop. However, the image might be distorted or its quality might have deteriorated.
4. Click OK.

SEE ALSO: For information about turning on the Active Desktop, see "Creating a Custom Desktop Background" on page 138.

TIP: When you use a Wallpaper picture, it's always placed on top of any pattern you select. You'll see the pattern only when the Wallpaper picture is centered rather than tiled or stretched and when the picture is smaller than the whole screen. When you have the wallpaper and the pattern both set to None and the Active Desktop has been deactivated, the Desktop will be the solid color that was specified on the Appearance tab.

TIP: You can use only Paint-type bitmap pictures for Desktop patterns and pictures unless you turn on the Active Desktop. With the Active Desktop, you can use JPEG and GIF graphics formats that are designed for HTML documents.

Creating a Custom Desktop Background

With the Active Desktop enabled—that is, when the Desktop is set to show web content—you can place pictures, web pages, and other components as part of the background for your Desktop. Although the items are in the background, they're still active, so you can have some web pages that are automatically updated while you're connected to the Internet and others that are updated only at your command.

Choose an Active Desktop Item

TIP: To hide the background, right-click a blank spot on the Desktop, point to Active Desktop on the shortcut menu, and choose Show Web Content. Choose Show Web Content again to redisplay your custom Desktop.

1. Right-click a blank spot on the Desktop, point to Active Desktop on the shortcut menu, and choose New Desktop Item to display the New Active Desktop Item dialog box.

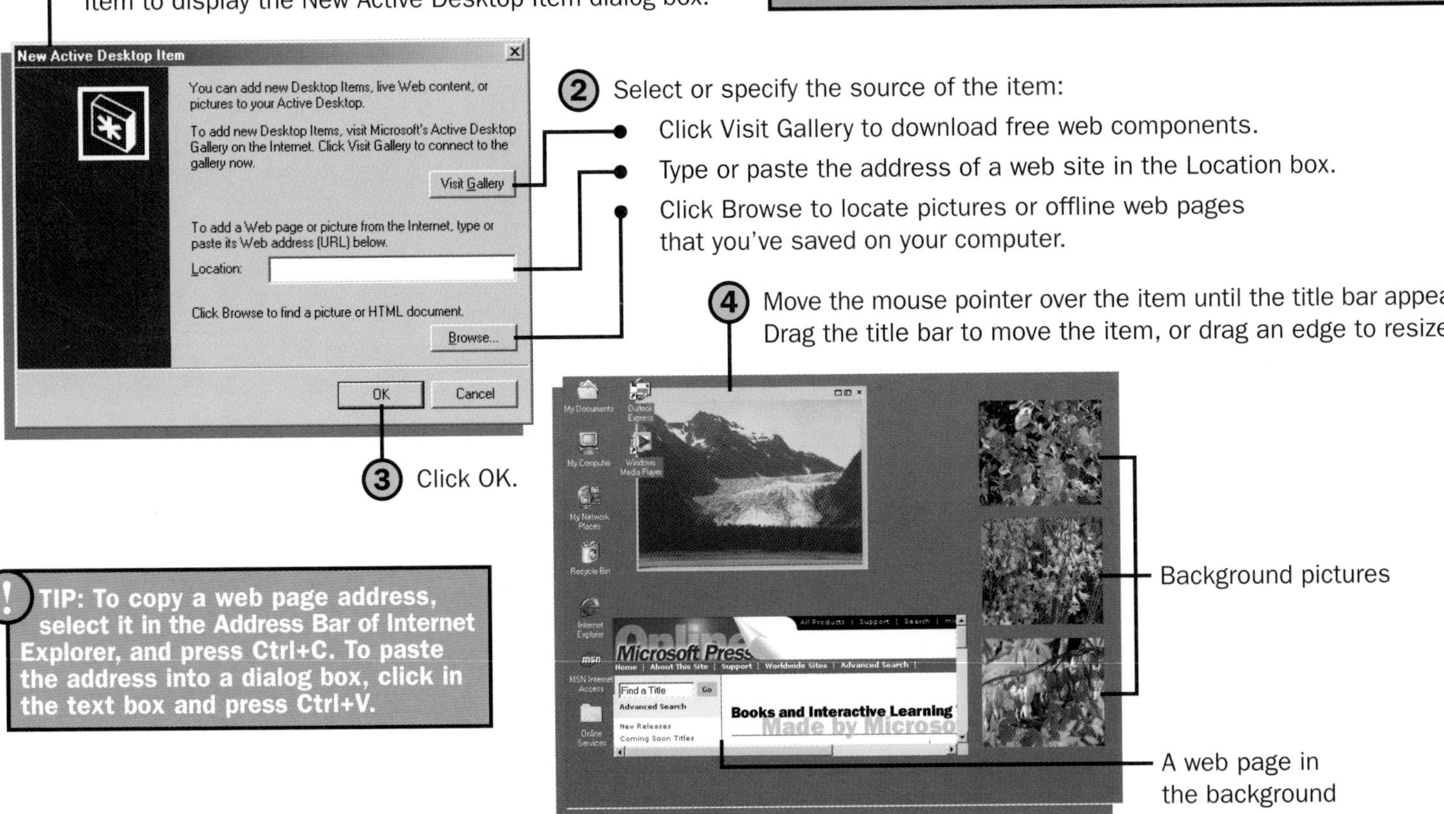

2. Select or specify the source of the item:
   - Click Visit Gallery to download free web components.
   - Type or paste the address of a web site in the Location box.
   - Click Browse to locate pictures or offline web pages that you've saved on your computer.
3. Click OK.
4. Move the mouse pointer over the item until the title bar appears. Drag the title bar to move the item, or drag an edge to resize it.

TIP: To copy a web page address, select it in the Address Bar of Internet Explorer, and press Ctrl+C. To paste the address into a dialog box, click in the text box and press Ctrl+V.

Hide the Desktop Icons

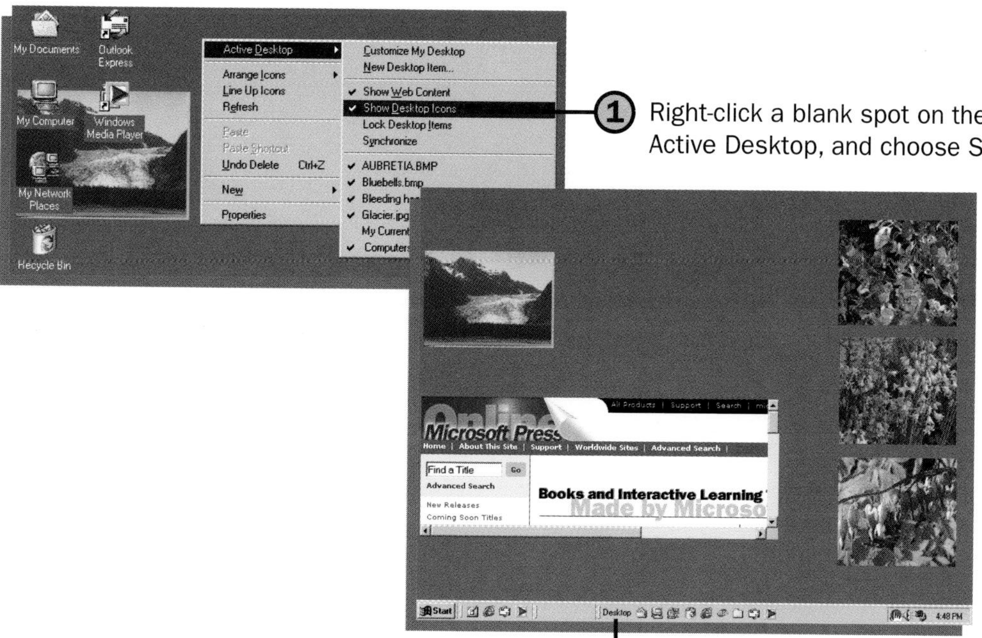

1. Right-click a blank spot on the Desktop, point to Active Desktop, and choose Show Desktop Icons.
2. Right-click a blank spot on the taskbar, point to Toolbars, and, if it isn't already checked, choose Desktop to display the Desktop toolbar. Use the Desktop toolbar to access items that would normally be displayed as icons on the Desktop.

TIP: When you add a new Desktop item, the Desktop automatically switches to show web content if it isn't already set to do so.

SEE ALSO: For more information about working with toolbars, see "Displaying and Arranging Toolbars" on page 141.

TIP: To display the compact form of the Desktop toolbar, as shown on this page, right-click a blank spot on the toolbar, and choose Show Text from the shortcut menu.

Creating a Shortcut to a File or Folder

If you use a particular file or folder frequently, you can access it quickly by placing a shortcut to it on the Desktop, on the Start menu, or just about anywhere you want. A shortcut to a document opens the document in its default program; a shortcut to a program file starts the program; a shortcut to a folder opens the folder in a window.

TIP: You can also create shortcuts to network, intranet, and Internet locations.

Create a Shortcut to a File or Folder

1. Open the window containing the file or folder.

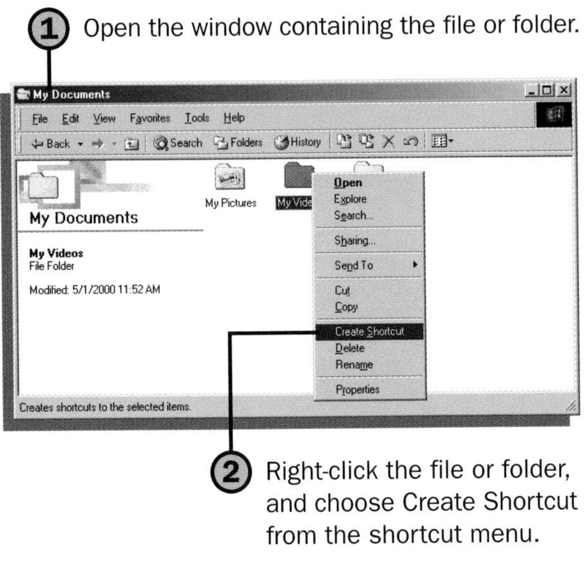

2. Right-click the file or folder, and choose Create Shortcut from the shortcut menu.

3. Right-click the shortcut, and choose Rename from the shortcut menu if you want to change the shortcut's name.

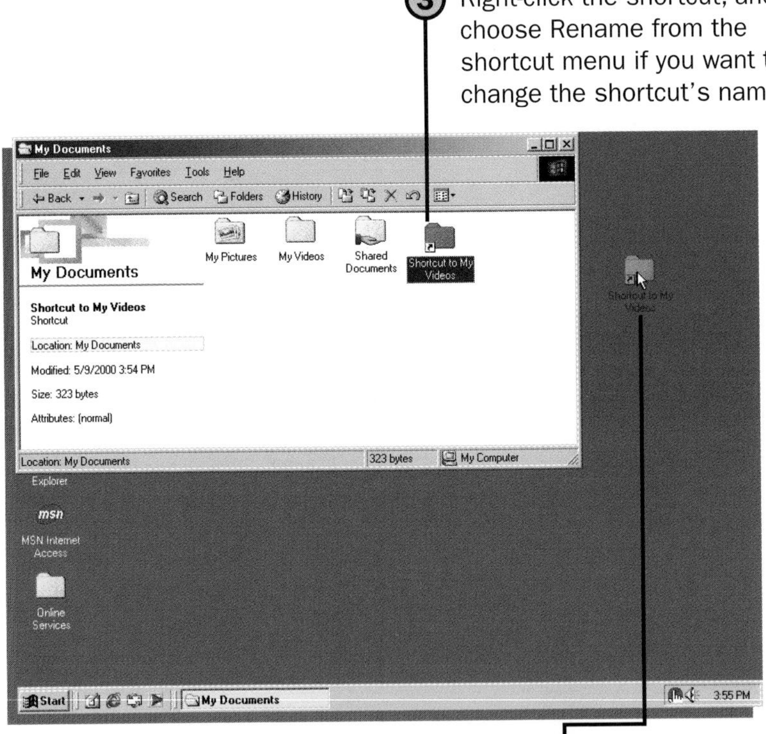

4. Drag the shortcut to the desired location.

SEE ALSO: For information about adding items to and arranging items on the Start menu, see "Reorganizing the Start Menu" on page 132.

For information about creating shortcuts that you can access from a toolbar, see "Creating Your Own Toolbars" on page 142.

Displaying and Arranging Toolbars

The taskbar and the toolbars are indispensable tools for working efficiently in Windows Me. If you want, you can rearrange them so that they're tailored even more closely to your working style. For example, you can change the size of a toolbar or the taskbar, and you can "dock" either at any of the four sides of your screen. You can also "float" the toolbars—but not the taskbar—anywhere on your Desktop.

Display a Toolbar

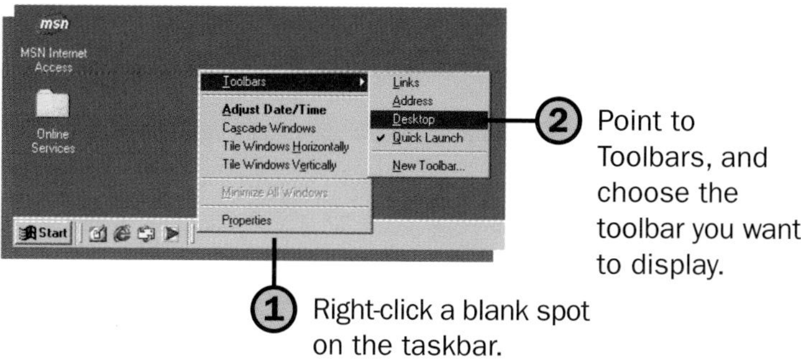

1. Right-click a blank spot on the taskbar.
2. Point to Toolbars, and choose the toolbar you want to display.

Move It

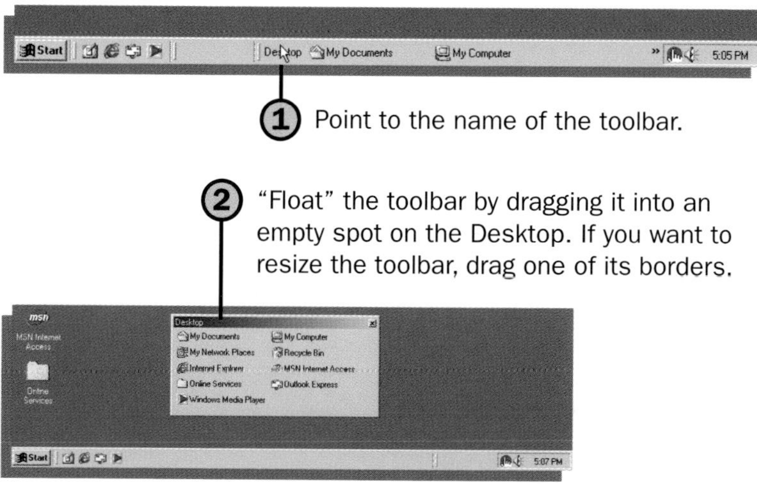

1. Point to the name of the toolbar.
2. "Float" the toolbar by dragging it into an empty spot on the Desktop. If you want to resize the toolbar, drag one of its borders.
3. Drag the floating toolbar by its title bar and "dock" it at the top, bottom, or either side of your screen.

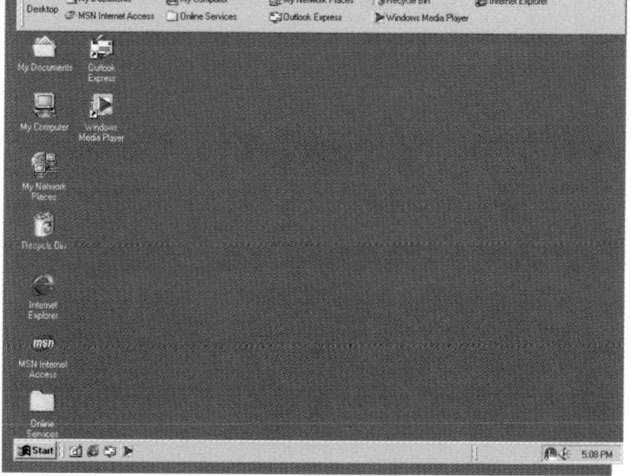

SEE ALSO: For information about creating a new toolbar, see "Creating Your Own Toolbars" on page 142.

For information about the Auto Hide option, see "Hiding the Taskbar" on page 143.

TIP: To change the size at which icons are displayed on a toolbar, right-click a blank spot on the toolbar, point to View on the shortcut menu, and choose Large or Small. To show or hide a text label to identify each icon, right-click the toolbar, and choose Show Text from the shortcut menu. To show or hide a text label to identify a docked toolbar, right-click the toolbar, and choose Show Title from the shortcut menu.

Creating Your Own Toolbars

The toolbars that come with Windows Me are invaluable, but if they don't precisely meet your needs you can easily create your own customized toolbars by connecting to a folder in which you've placed all the items you want to appear on your toolbar.

TIP: If you no longer need a custom toolbar and want to delete it permanently, right-click it, and choose Close from its shortcut menu. The toolbar will go away but the contents of the folder to which it was connected will be unchanged.

Create a Toolbar

1. Create a folder containing the documents, folders, and shortcuts that you want to appear on the toolbar.

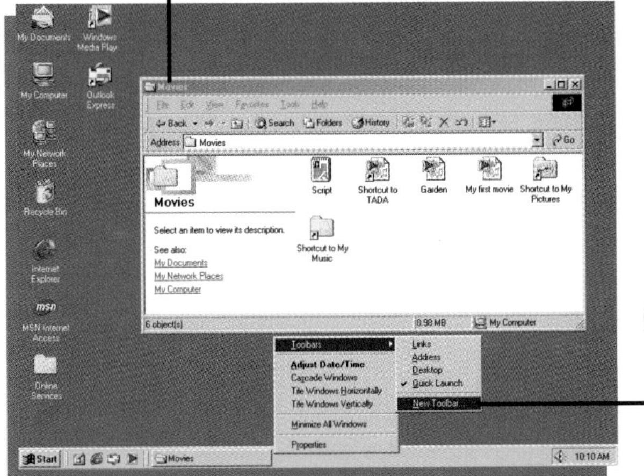

2. Right-click a blank spot on a toolbar or on the taskbar, point to Toolbars, and choose New Toolbar.
3. Navigate to the folder you created, and select it.

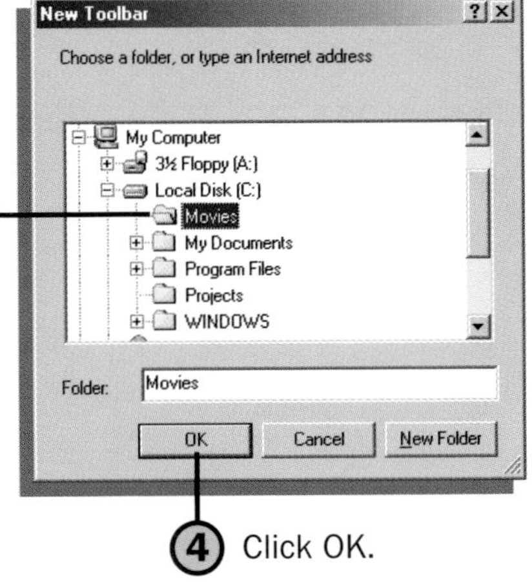

4. Click OK.

TRY THIS: Create a new toolbar. Drag any documents, folders, or programs from other windows onto the toolbar. Note that a shortcut to each item is added to the folder on which the toolbar is based.

5. Customize and use the toolbar just as you use any other toolbar.

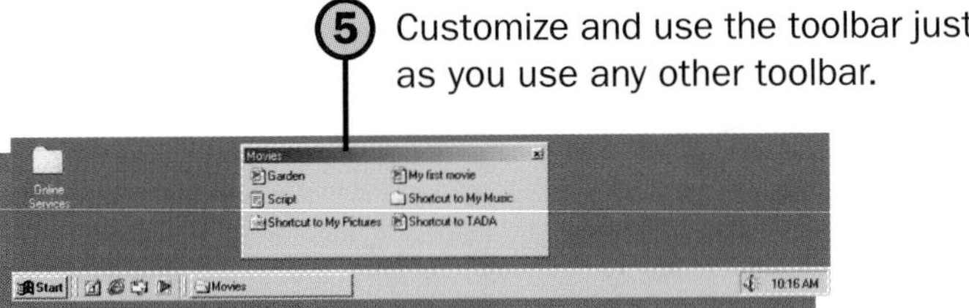

Hiding the Taskbar

The taskbar is a handy navigational device, but it can sometimes get in your way. If you want to, you can hide the taskbar and have it appear only when you need it.

TIP: If you can't find the taskbar because it's hidden or because something else is on top of it, press the Ctrl+Esc key combination. This will display the taskbar with the Start menu open.

Hide the Taskbar

1. Right-click a blank spot on the taskbar, and choose Properties from the shortcut menu to display the Taskbar And Start Menu Properties dialog box.
2. Turn on the Always On Top check box.
3. Turn on the Auto Hide check box.
4. Click OK.

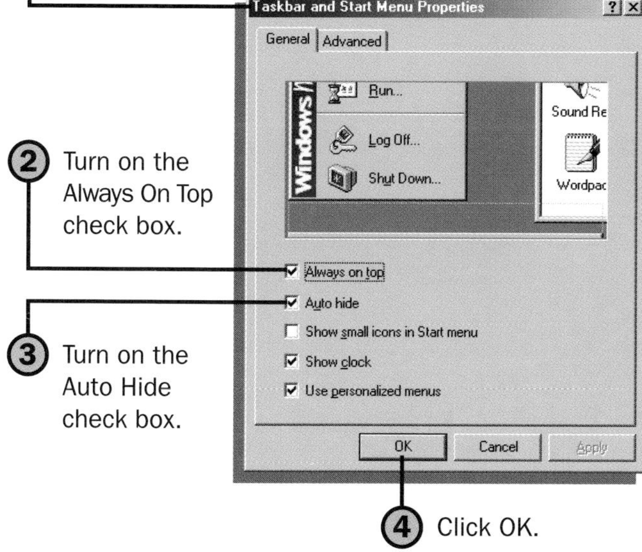

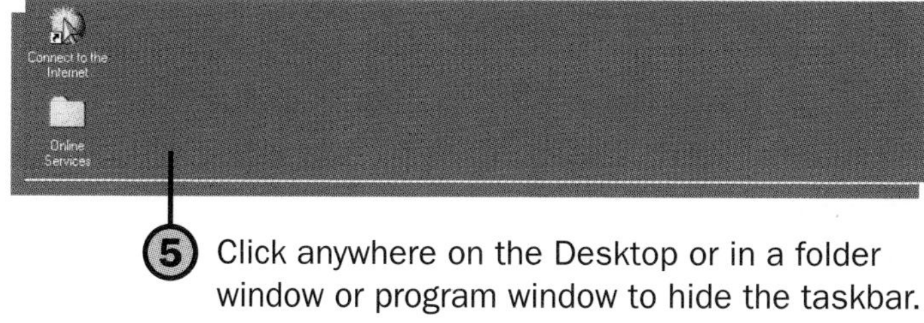

5. Click anywhere on the Desktop or in a folder window or program window to hide the taskbar.

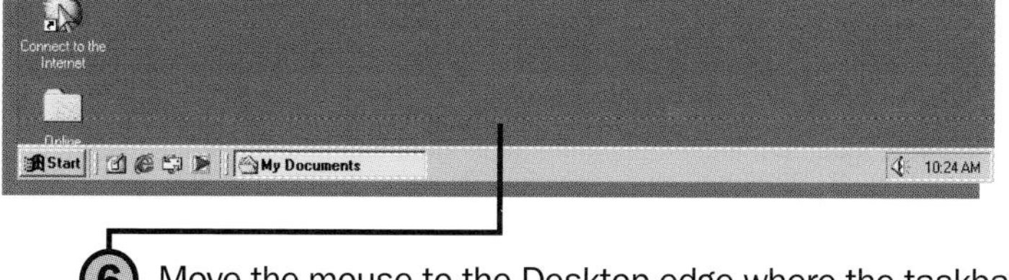

6. Move the mouse to the Desktop edge where the taskbar is hidden and wait until the taskbar reappears.

TIP: Any toolbar that's connected to the taskbar will be hidden when the taskbar is hidden and displayed when the taskbar is displayed.

TIP: To hide a toolbar that's docked but not connected to the taskbar, right click the toolbar, and choose Auto-Hide from the shortcut menu.

Customizing a Folder Window

You can customize your folder windows to display the type of information you want and the way you want to see it. For example, if you want the contents of several folders displayed at the same time, you can tell Windows Me to open a new window for each folder you open instead of replacing the contents of the current window with the newly opened folder. If you want to maximize the area for file listings, you can turn off the web content and see only the files and folders in that folder. You can also specify which items are displayed in a folder, add a personalized comment to a folder, or change its appearance by adding a background picture.

Set the Layout

1. In a folder window, choose Folder Options from the Tools menu to display the Folder Options dialog box.

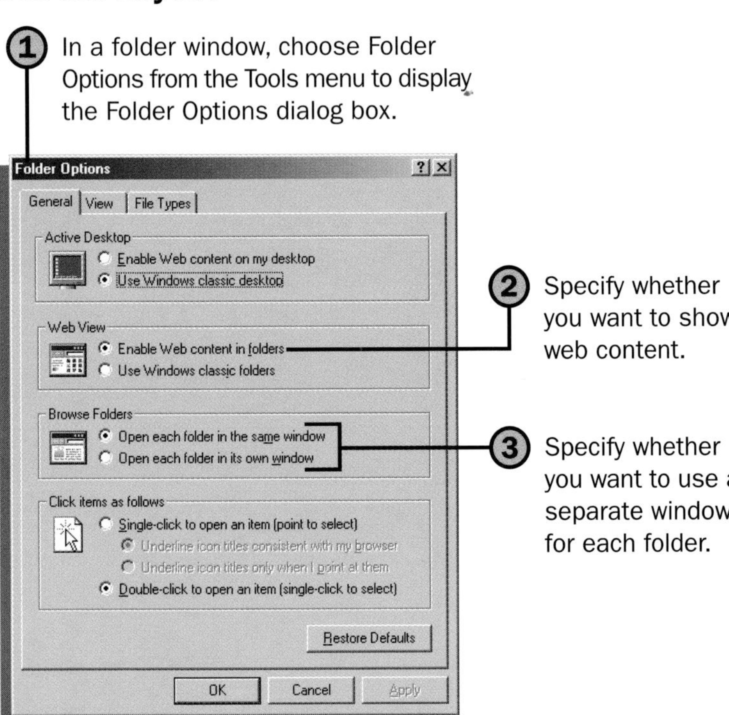

2. Specify whether you want to show web content.
3. Specify whether you want to use a separate window for each folder.

TIP: To learn more about the function of each option on the View tab, click the Help button at the top right of the dialog box, and then click the item.

TIP: To use the same view settings in all folders, click the Like Current Folder button before you click OK.

4. On the View tab, turn on the options you want and turn off the options you don't want.

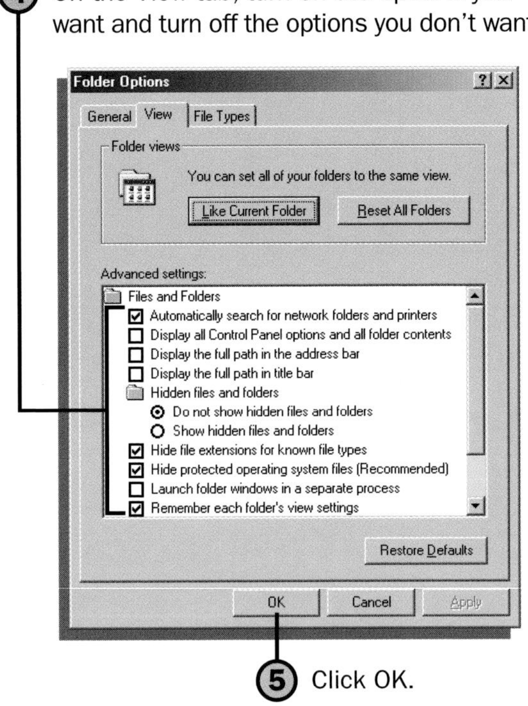

5. Click OK.

Change the Appearance

1 From the View menu of the folder window you want to modify, choose Customize This Folder to display the Customize This Folder Wizard.

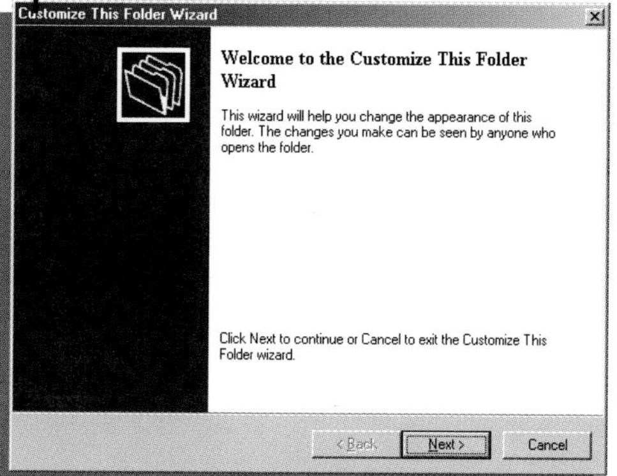

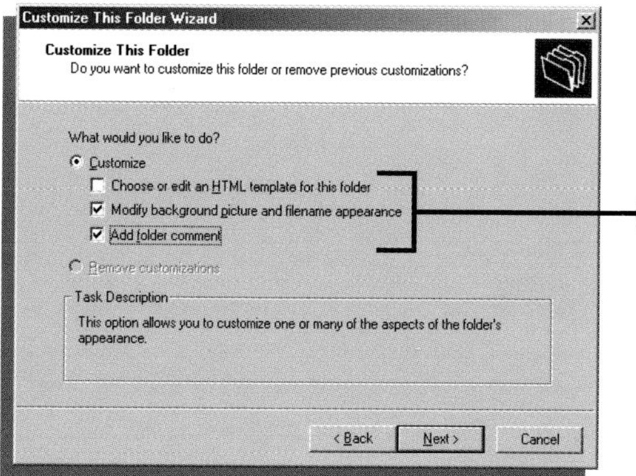

2 Step through the wizard, specifying whether you want to use a background picture and/or add a comment to the folder window. Complete the wizard, selecting the background picture and/or the comment you want included.

3 Inspect the folder window. If you're not satisfied with the changes, rerun the wizard, and use the Remove Customizations option to return the folder to its original state.

TIP: If the Customize This Folder command doesn't appear on the menu, you can't customize that folder.

SEE ALSO: For information about modifying the window's template, see "Customizing a Folder for Pictures" on page 84.

TIP: If you create a comment but don't see it immediately in the folder window, close the window and then reopen it. The comment should now be visible.

Customizing Your Mouse

Few things are more frustrating than an uncooperative mouse that doesn't do what you want it to do. A dirty—and thus unhappy—mouse is often the cause of many problems, but, if you've attended to your mouse's *toilette* and you're still having problems, you can make some simple adjustments for better mouse performance.

SEE ALSO: For information about specifying the way Windows Me responds to your mouse clicks, see "Setting Your Click" on page 148.

For information about using the keyboard to control mouse actions, see "Using Alternative Ways of Working" on page 151.

Change the Way Your Mouse Works

1. Open the Control Panel from the Settings submenu of the Start menu, and double-click the Mouse icon to open the Mouse Properties dialog box.

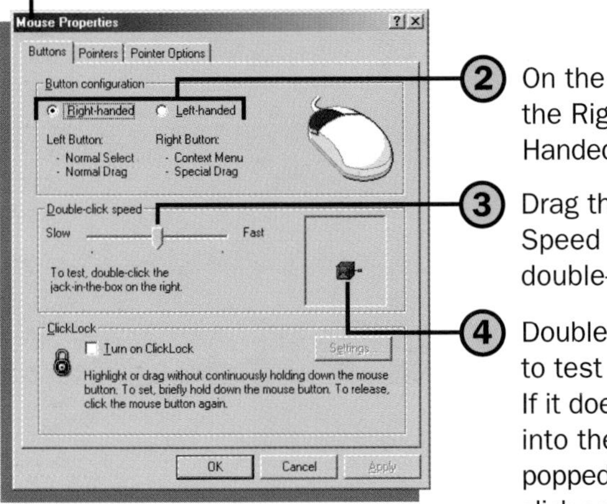

2. On the Buttons tab, select the Right-Handed or Left-Handed button configuration.
3. Drag the Double-Click Speed slider to set your double-click speed.
4. Double-click the jack-in-the-box to test the double-click speed. If it doesn't pop up (or go back into the box if it's already popped up), change the double-click speed and repeat the test.

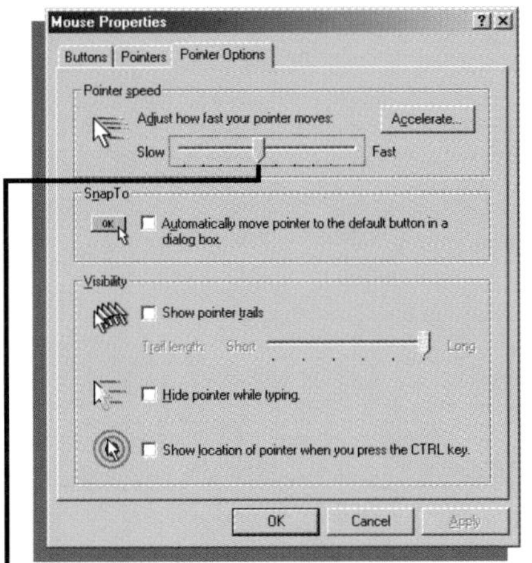

5. On the Pointer Options tab, drag the Pointer Speed slider to set the speed at which the pointer moves when you move the mouse. Use the Accelerate button to fine-tune the movement.

TIP: If the Mouse icon isn't displayed in the Control Panel, click the View All Control Panel Options item to display all the items that are available in the Control Panel.

Change the Pointers

1. On the Pointers tab, select the pointer scheme you want to use.

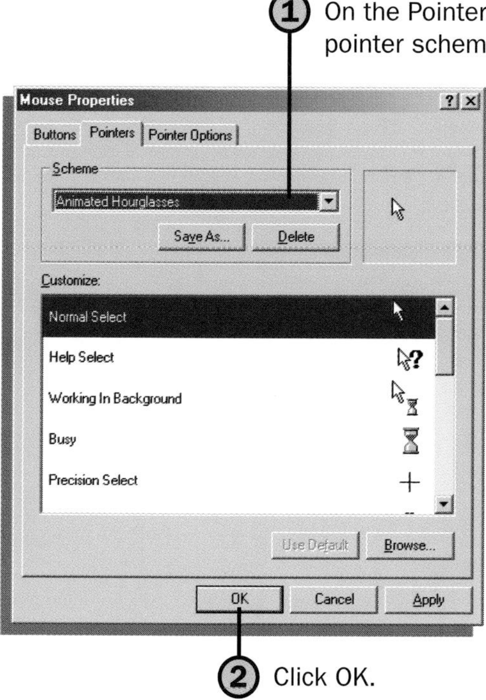

2. Click OK.

TIP: To enable the mouse pointer to snap to a button in a dialog box, one button must be defined as the default button. Because some programs don't always define a default button, you won't be able to use the SnapTo Default option in those programs.

More Mouse Options

Option	Function
ClickLock	Allows multiple selection or dragging without holding down the mouse button.
SnapTo	Moves the pointer to the default button of a dialog box when the dialog box is first opened.
Show Pointer Trails	Temporarily displays a series of pointers to show the movement of the mouse.
Hide Pointer While Typing	Removes the pointer from the screen when you type your text. The pointer reappears when you move the mouse.
Show Location Of Pointer When You Press The Ctrl Key	Displays concentric circles around the pointer when you press the Ctrl key; helps you locate the pointer on your screen.

TRY THIS: On the Pointers tab, click a pointer, and then click Browse. Select a different pointer, and click Open. Click Save As, and save your custom mouse-pointer scheme.

TIP: If you have Desktop Themes installed, you'll find many more pointers available in the Themes folder, which is located in the Plus! subfolder of the Program Files folder.

Setting Your Click

One of the big differences between exploring your computer with Windows Me and exploring the Internet with Internet Explorer is the way you use a single or double mouse-click. If you prefer to use the single-click style of the web browser, just let Windows Me know your preference.

Set the Style

1. In any folder window, choose Folder Options from the Tools menu to open the Folder Options dialog box.

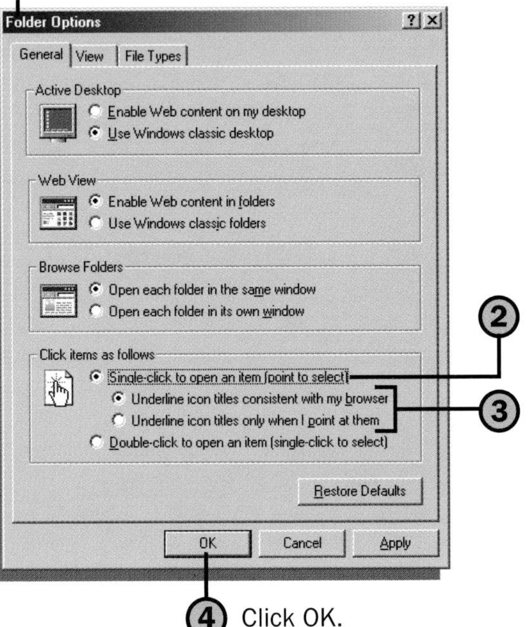

2. On the General tab, select the Single-Click To Open An Item (Point To Select) option.
3. Select an option to determine when icon text is underlined:
   - Underline Icon Titles Consistent With My Browser to use the same settings as those used by Internet Explorer or other browsers for underlining links
   - Underline Icon Titles Only When I Point At Them to have the icon text underlined only when the mouse pointer is pointing to the icon
4. Click OK.

TIP: To specify the way Internet Explorer underlines links, choose Internet Options from the Tools menu of Internet Explorer, and change the setting on the Advanced tab. The table below describes the way Internet Explorer's settings for underlining links affect the way icons are underlined.

Internet Explorer's Icon-Underlining Options

Use browser settings when browser is set to	For this icon underlining
Always	All the icons are underlined.
Hover	Only the icon you point to is underlined.
Never	No icons are ever underlined.

Displaying a Screen Saver

When you work at a computer, it's good for your eyes—and for your mental health—to take a break and look at something different once in a while. If you work with other people, you might not want them to be able to read your screen—albeit unintentionally—any time your computer is unattended. A screen saver can provide a nice little respite from your work as well as some privacy. To prevent anyone from using your computer—but still allowing network access to it—when you're away from your desk, you can use the password option. You'll need to enter the password to end the screen saver when you're ready to get back to work.

Choose a Screen Saver

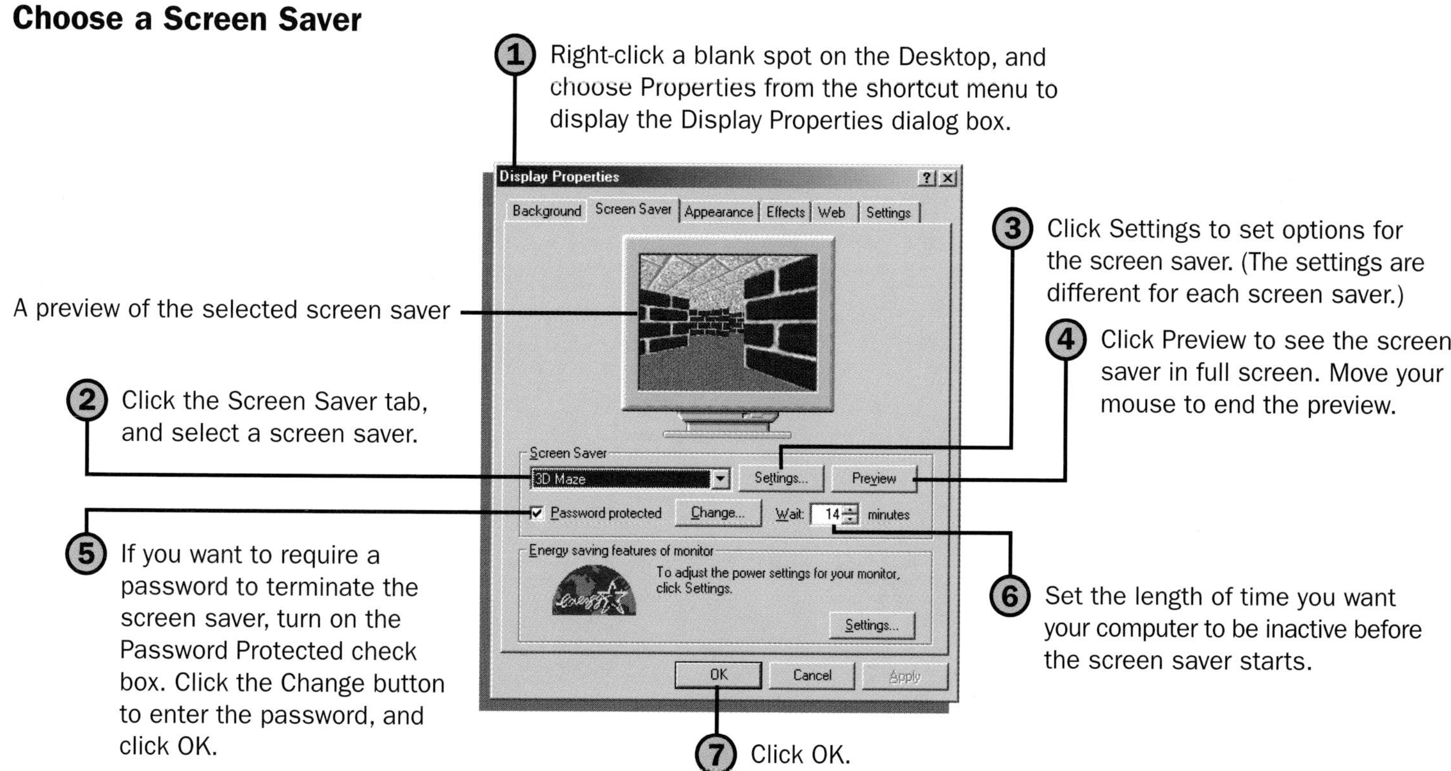

TRY THIS: Create a folder and put some pictures in it that you'd like to display as a screen saver. Select the My Pictures screen saver in the Display Properties dialog box, and click the Settings button. Set the timing and specify the size of the pictures, and then use the Browse button to locate and specify the folder of pictures that you just set up. Finish setting your screen saver.

Changing the Overall Look

You can change the entire appearance of your computer with Desktop Themes. Using one of the themes, you can change not only the background picture and your screen saver, but the mouse pointers, sounds, icons, colors, and fonts—all at the same time.

SEE ALSO: For information about installing Desktop Themes if you don't see the Desktop Themes icon in the Control Panel, see "Adding or Removing Windows Me Components" on page 170.

Switch Themes

1. Open the Control Panel from the Settings submenu of the Start menu, and double-click the Desktop Themes icon. (If only a few items are displayed, click View All Control Panel Options at the left of the window.)
2. Select a theme from the drop-down list.
3. Turn on the check boxes for the items to which you want to apply the changes.
4. Click to preview the screen saver.
5. Click to preview the mouse pointers, sounds, and visual-elements schemes.
6. Make sure you like the way the changes look before you put them into effect.
7. Click OK.

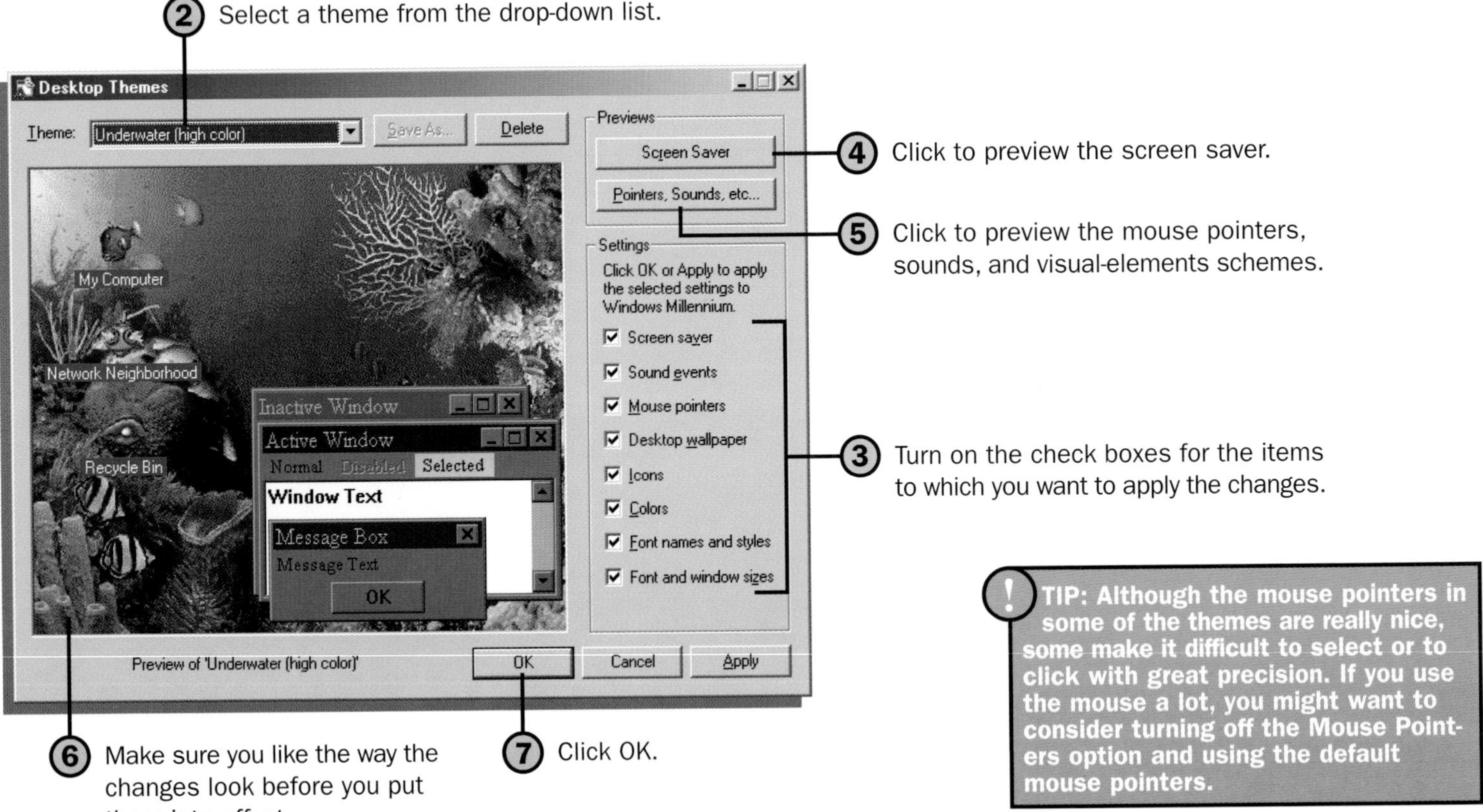

TIP: Although the mouse pointers in some of the themes are really nice, some make it difficult to select or to click with great precision. If you use the mouse a lot, you might want to consider turning off the Mouse Pointers option and using the default mouse pointers.

Using Alternative Ways of Working

Windows Me provides several tools that let you change the way you enter information into, or receive information from, the computer. These tools—although designed primarily for those who experience difficulty when typing, using the mouse, seeing details on the screen, or hearing sounds—can be used by anyone who wants to try some alternative ways to work on the computer. For example, the keyboard can be used to execute mouse actions, or the mouse or another pointing device can be used for keyboard input. Some other tools that can help you customize keyboard input are described in the table.

Set the Options

1. Open the Control Panel from the Settings submenu of the Start menu, and double-click the Accessibility Options icon to display the Accessibility Properties dialog box.
2. On the various tabs of the dialog box, turn on the options you want to use, as described in the table. Click the Settings button for each option you select, and specify how you want the option to function. Click OK.
3. On the General tab, specify whether you want the features you selected to be turned off after the computer has been idle for a specified period of time.
4. Click OK to close the dialog box.

TIP: You can use the Accessibility Wizard on the Accessibility submenu of the Start menu to provide a quick way to set up several tools at one time and to help you identify which tools you might want to use.

Tools for Alternative Ways of Working

Feature	What it does
StickyKeys	Sets key combinations with the Alt, Ctrl, and Shift keys to be pressable one key at a time.
FilterKeys	Ignores repeated characters or too-rapid key presses.
ToggleKeys	Makes different sounds when you turn the Caps Lock, Num Lock, or Scroll Lock key on or off.
MouseKeys	Sets the numeric keypad to control mouse movements.
SerialKey devices	Provides support for alternative input devices.
SoundSentry	Flashes a specified screen component when the system beeps.
ShowSounds	Displays text instead of sounds for programs that support this feature.
High Contrast	Sets the color scheme for Windows Me to High Contrast to improve the visibility of components.
Cursor Blink Rate	Sets the speed at which the cursor (the insertion point in WordPad, for example) blinks.
Cursor Width	Sets the width of the cursor in programs.

SEE ALSO: For information about increasing the visibility of items on the screen, see "Enlarging the View" on page 152.

Enlarging the View

If you have difficulty seeing the items on your screen, you can use Microsoft Magnifier to enlarge, or magnify, all the elements on the screen, whether they're Windows Me components or items from other programs you've installed. Because of the increase in size, you can enlarge only portions of the window at one time.

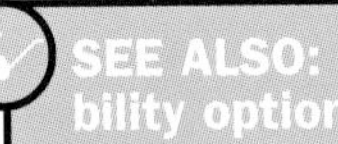

SEE ALSO: For information about setting other accessibility options, see "Using Alternative Ways of Working" on page 151 and "Typing with the Mouse" on page 154.

Set Up the Magnifier

1. If you didn't start the Magnifier from the Accessibility Wizard, choose Magnifier from the Accessibility submenu of the Start menu to display the Magnifier Settings dialog box.
2. Set a magnification level.
3. Turn on check boxes to specify how you want the Magnifier to follow your actions and whether you want high-visibility colors.
4. Click the Minimize button to remove the dialog box from view.

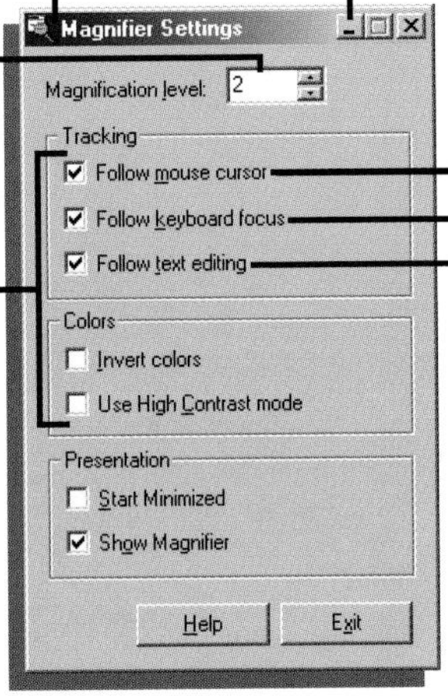

The Magnifier follows the movements of the mouse.

Shows the element that has focus—that is, the selected item.

Centers on the insertion point when you're editing text.

TIP: To temporarily hide the Magnifier, turn off the Show Magnifier check box.

TIP: To increase the size of only some Windows Me components, run the Accessibility Wizard from the Accessibility submenu of the Start menu. Many programs, including Microsoft Office programs, have zoom controls that let you increase the size of text as it's being viewed on the screen. Many programs also have options that let you display large icons.

TIP: The Invert Colors option affects only the Magnifier. The Use High Contrast Mode option changes the color scheme for all Windows Me elements.

Use the Magnifier

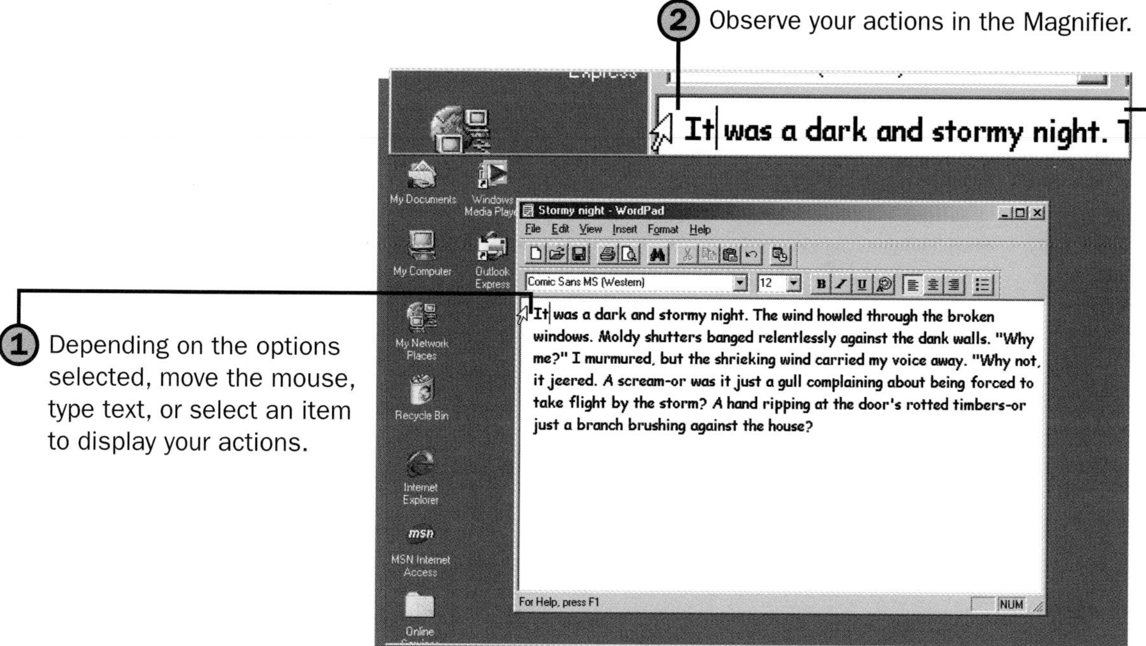

1. Depending on the options selected, move the mouse, type text, or select an item to display your actions.
2. Observe your actions in the Magnifier.
3. When you've finished, right-click in the Magnifier, and choose Exit.

TIP: When you're sure that your settings are correct, turn on the Start Minimized check box. When the Magnifier starts, the Magnifier Settings dialog box won't be displayed. You can, however, click Magnifier Settings on the taskbar to display the dialog box at any time.

TIP: To start the Magnifier whenever Windows Me starts, move the Magnifier item from the Accessibility submenu of the Start menu to the StartUp submenu of the Start menu.

TRY THIS: Right-click in the Magnifier window, and choose Hide from the shortcut menu. Use Windows Me without the Magnifier. If you've minimized the Magnifier Settings dialog box, click it on the taskbar to display it. Turn on the Show Magnifier check box, and use the Magnifier again.

Typing with the Mouse

If you have difficulty using a keyboard, or simply prefer not to, the On-Screen Keyboard lets you use your mouse or other pointing device to enter text and choose commands just like a traditional keyboard.

TIP: The keyboard layout reflects the regional settings. If you change your regional settings, the keyboard characters will change accordingly. Use the Regional Settings item in the Control Panel to change the locale for which your computer is set.

Use the On-Screen Keyboard

1. Choose On-Screen Keyboard from the Accessibility submenu of the Start menu to display the On-Screen Keyboard.

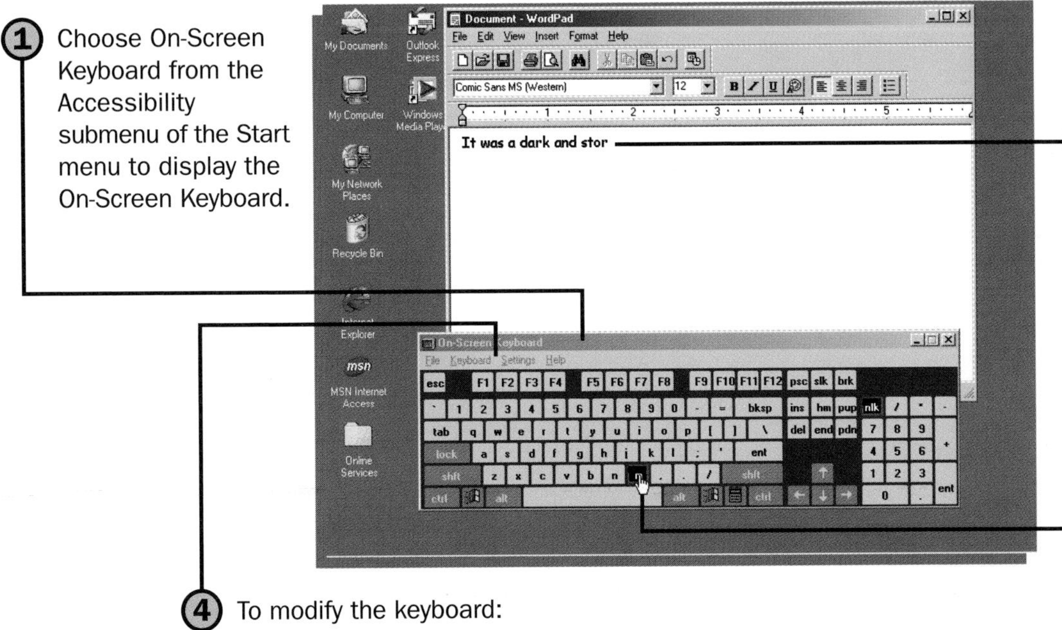

2. Click in a program window or dialog box where you want to enter some text. Use the tools in that program to format your text—to set the font and point size, for example.

3. Click a character to have it appear in the program window. Continue clicking characters to enter your text.

4. To modify the keyboard:
   - Use the Keyboard menu to choose a keyboard type and layout style, and the number of keys to be displayed.
   - Use the Settings menu to change the font in which the characters on the keyboard will be displayed, and to specify the typing mode (that is, whether characters will be selected by clicking them, hovering the pointer over them, pressing a keyboard key, or using a device such as a joystick).

11 Improving Security

In this section

In days of old, only the administrators of large corporate networks needed to worry about computer security. These days, however, what with the proliferation of computer viruses, constant connections to the Internet, home networks, and sophisticated hacking techniques used by an ever-growing cadre of snoops and pranksters, everyone has to be vigilant.

In this section you'll find valuable information about the various ways you can protect your files, your privacy on the Internet, and so on. For example, you can protect your e-mail messages from prying eyes on the Internet by *encrypting* your messages so that only people with the correct *digital ID* can read them. You can secure your sensitive files by disabling the computer's setting for sharing files. If you do share your files over a network, you can protect them with passwords so that only the people who have the passwords can access the files.

When you visit an Internet site that requests personal information, you can restrict the amount of information you provide by creating a special profile for that purpose. And you can also prevent "cookies," those little files that can be used by web sites to keep track of your visits and preferences and that are sometimes misused to compile too much personal information about you. If several people use your computer, you can use Content Advisor—a feature in Microsoft Internet Explorer—to restrict access to Internet sites that contain material you find inappropriate. You can specify the acceptable level of material that can be accessed or you can set up a password to allow access to restricted sites. And to maintain your overall security, you need an effective password, and you should make a point of changing it occasionally.

Securing Your E-Mail Messages

The Internet can be a dangerous place for e-mail. If you're worried about your e-mail being modified en route or being sent by an impostor, you can use a digital ID to digitally sign your e-mail, and you can use other people's digital IDs to authenticate their identity.

Set Up Your Security

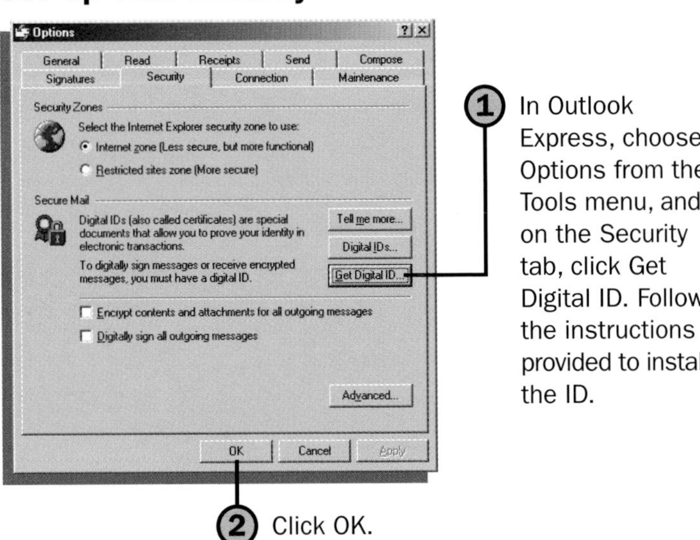

1. In Outlook Express, choose Options from the Tools menu, and, on the Security tab, click Get Digital ID. Follow the instructions provided to install the ID.
2. Click OK.

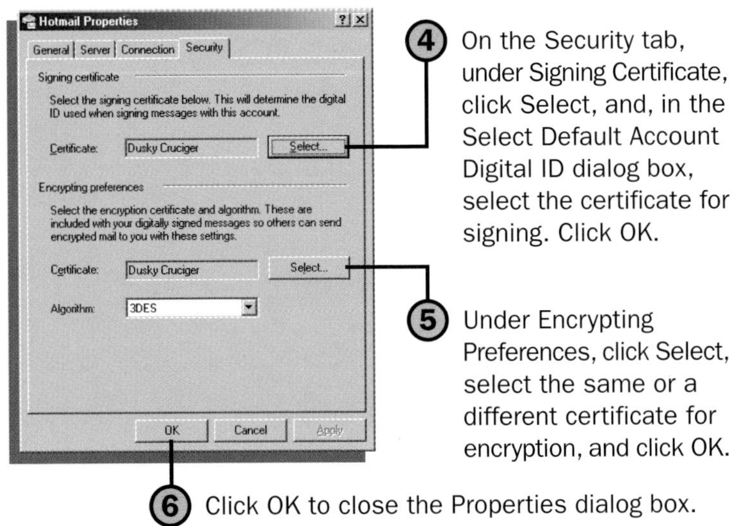

4. On the Security tab, under Signing Certificate, click Select, and, in the Select Default Account Digital ID dialog box, select the certificate for signing. Click OK.
5. Under Encrypting Preferences, click Select, select the same or a different certificate for encryption, and click OK.
6. Click OK to close the Properties dialog box.

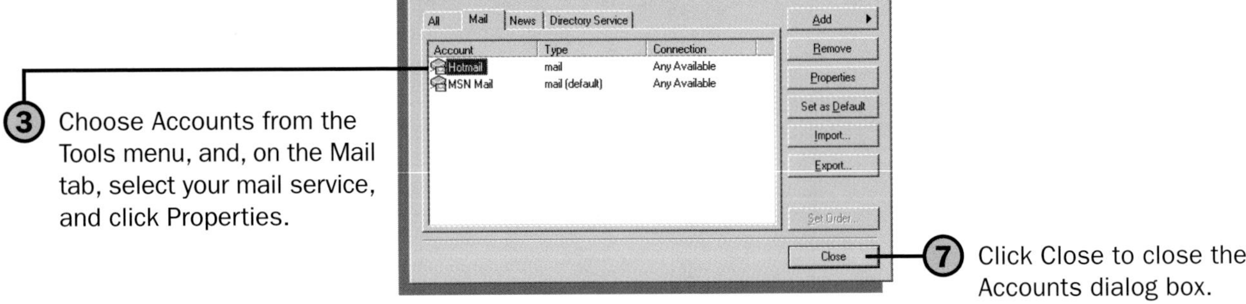

3. Choose Accounts from the Tools menu, and, on the Mail tab, select your mail service, and click Properties.
7. Click Close to close the Accounts dialog box.

Exchange Digital IDs

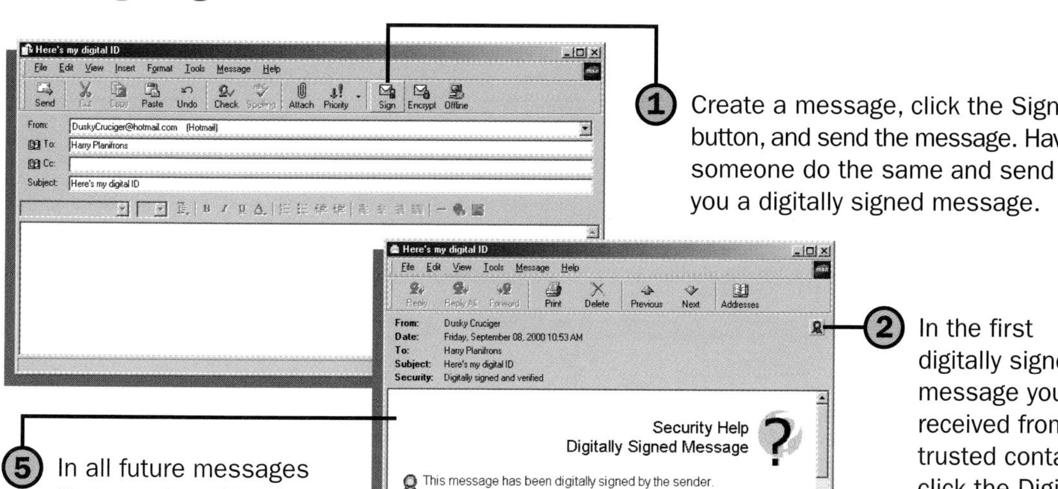

1. Create a message, click the Sign button, and send the message. Have someone do the same and send you a digitally signed message.

2. In the first digitally signed message you've received from a trusted contact, click the Digital Signature button.

3. On the Security tab, click View Certificates.

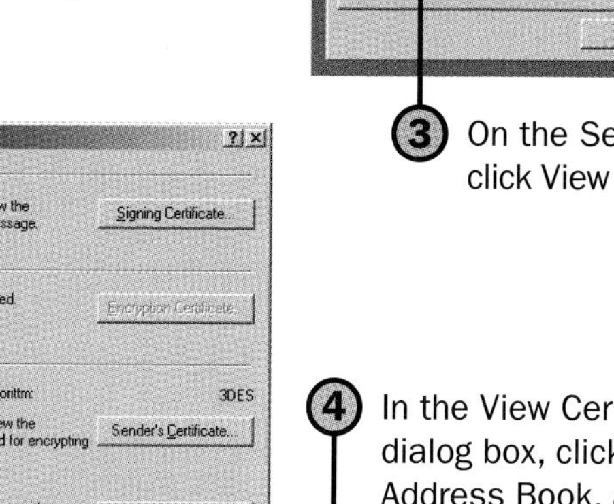

4. In the View Certificates dialog box, click Add To Address Book, and click OK. Click OK again to close the message's Properties dialog box.

5. In all future messages that are signed by the contact, use the security information to verify that the message is from a valid source and hasn't been tampered with.

TIP: You can also exchange digital IDs using electronic business cards (vCards) or an e-mail locator service.

SEE ALSO: For information about sending encrypted messages to protect the contents from unauthorized viewing, see "Sending an Encrypted E-Mail Message" on page 158.

Sending an Encrypted E-Mail Message

When you send sensitive information over the Internet in an e-mail message, you can *encrypt* the message so that no one but the recipient can read it. You do so by using the recipient's digital ID to encrypt the message. When the encrypted message is received, the private section of the recipient's digital ID automatically unscrambles the message.

Send an Encrypted Message

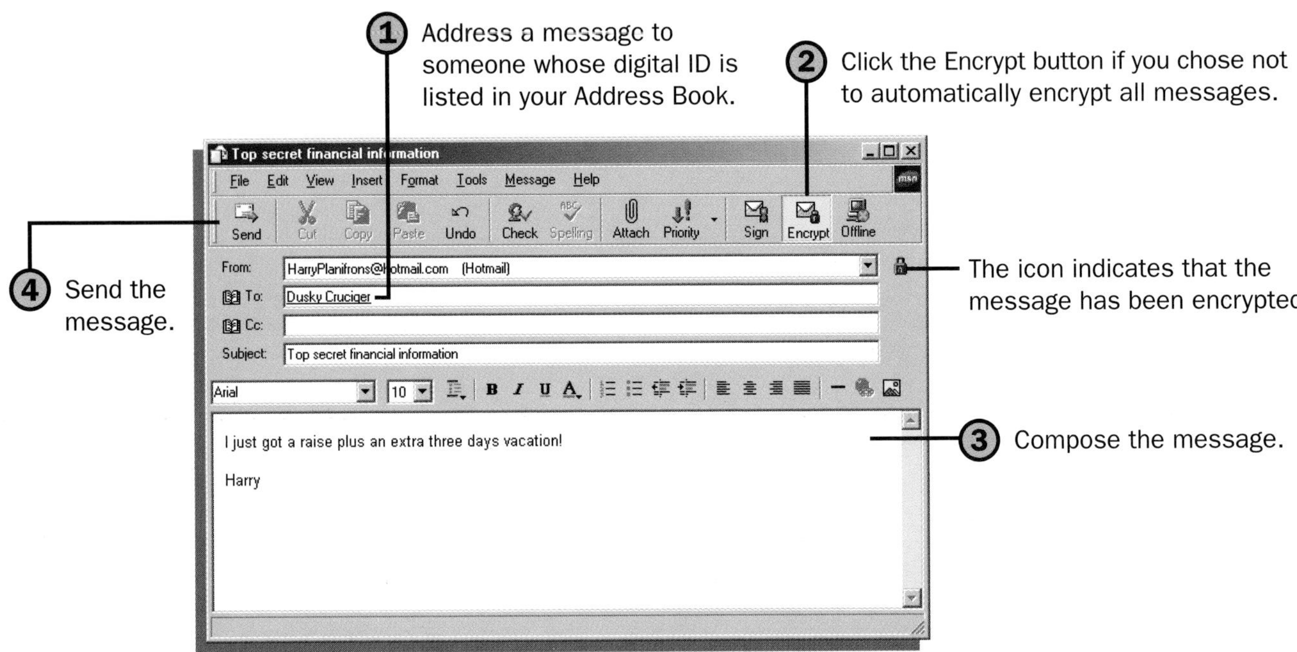

TIP: The digital ID you send out is your "public key." A private key is stored in your computer and is used along with the public key to decrypt messages. The private key exists only on your computer, so you can read encrypted messages only on that computer.

SEE ALSO: For information about obtaining and exchanging digital IDs, see "Securing Your E-Mail Messages" on page 156.

TRY THIS: Click the down arrow next to the Find button on the Outlook Express toolbar, and select People. Select a directory service, type the e-mail address of the person to whom you want to send an encrypted message, and click Find Now. Select the person in the list, and click Add To Address Book. You should now have the public key to that person's digital ID.

The Need for Security

To protect your personal information and sensitive files, you'll need to do a little extra work, but if it prevents someone from hacking into your computer or intercepting your messages, you'll consider it time well spent.

Viruses. Computer viruses can be spread in e-mail attachments, in downloaded or transferred files, and in pirated software. Other than avoiding these sources, your best protection is to install good virus-protection software and to *use* it! Most of the companies that sell such software maintain web sites where you can keep your software up to date. When you receive an e-mail attachment or download a file, always save the file to your hard disk and then scan it with your virus-protection software before you open it. You should also scan all transferred files before you open them.

Passwords. Passwords to log on, to access folders, or to retrieve e-mail can provide good security only if your password is an effective one. Too many people use their name or a password as obvious as "password." A secure password should be at least eight characters long and, for added security, should contain one or more numerals. For passwords that are case-sensitive (such as Hotmail passwords), incorporate both uppercase and lowercase letters into the password. (Your Microsoft Windows Millennium Edition password isn't case-sensitive.)

Firewalls. Corporate networks use software programs to construct a "firewall" that prevents unauthorized access to the network via the Internet. If your computer is always connected to the Internet, it's vulnerable. Firewall programs are available either free or for purchase, although some are a bit challenging to set up on your computer. If you use Internet Connection Sharing to connect to the Internet through your network, all the computers on the network except the host computer—that is, the one that has the connection to the Internet—should be secure enough that they don't need a firewall.

Secure Internet connections. Material sent over the Internet can be intercepted unless you take special precautions. If you're sending sensitive information to a web site, first make sure the web site is legitimate and that it has a security policy in place. Then verify that it's providing you with a secure connection, as indicated by the "lock" icon on the status bar of Internet Explorer.

Encryption. It's an unhappy fact that your e-mail can be intercepted and read by others when you send it over the Internet. To keep a message with sensitive information secure, you can encrypt the message so that only the designated recipient can read it. Encryption is also a powerful tool to protect sensitive documents, whether they're on your computer or on that floppy disk you lost somewhere.

Direct access to your computer. Anyone who has physical access to your computer can gain access to almost anything on it—without discovering your password! Although you can prevent others from viewing what's currently on your screen—by requiring a password to deactivate a screen saver or to return from Standby or Hibernate mode, for example—someone who *really* wants to invade your privacy can simply turn off the computer and then turn it back on. Doing so circumvents the password and accesses your computer. To avoid such a situation, check your computer's documentation for information about requiring a password to start the computer. You can also encrypt files on your computer, use a program's security features (if available) to require a password, or buy and install a security program.

Security patches. Microsoft and other software manufacturers usually respond quickly to security problems in their programs by issuing software patches. These programs automatically modify and fix the existing program on your computer. If any security patches are issued for Windows Me, you can install them using the Automatic Updates tool. For updates to other programs, go to the software vendor's web site.

Securing Your Files

When you're directly connected to the Internet or to a network, there's a possibility that your computer could be accessed by some nasty person who might copy your data, destroy your files, or infect your computer with a virus. If you have a stand-alone computer, or if your computer is on a network but you don't want others on the network to have access to it, you can disable the computer's settings for sharing files.

TIP: If your computer is on a large network, check with the systems administrator before you disable sharing. Sharing is often required for administrative reasons.

Disable Sharing

1. Right-click My Network Places, and choose Properties from the shortcut menu to display the Network dialog box.

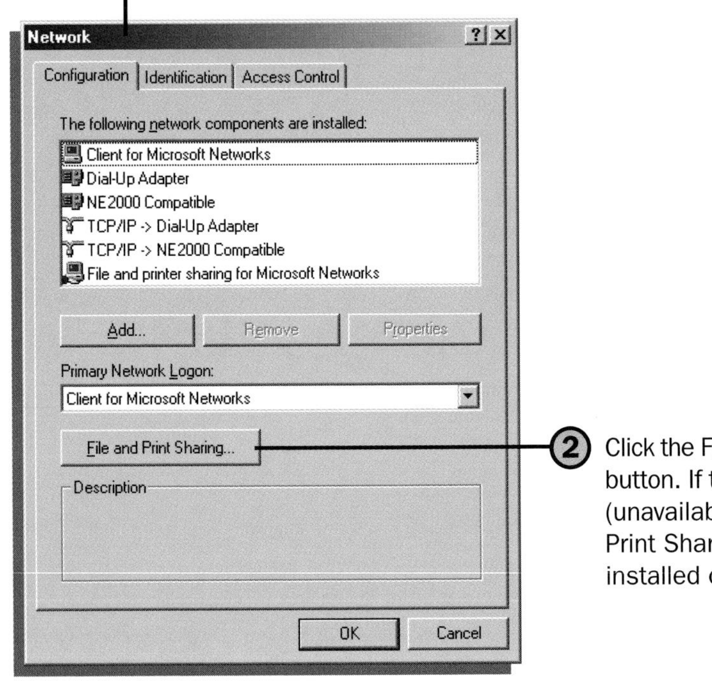

2. Click the File And Print Sharing button. If the button is grayed (unavailable), the File And Print Sharing feature isn't installed on your computer.

3. Turn off any boxes that are checked, and click OK.

File and Print Sharing

I want to be able to give others access to my files.

I want to be able to allow others to print to my printer(s).

OK Cancel

4. Click OK, and restart your computer when prompted.

SEE ALSO: For information about securing shared resources without disabling all sharing, see "Restricting Access to Files" on the facing page.

Restricting Access to Files

If you want to share files on a network, you can protect the files with passwords. With the Net Watcher utility program, you can see all the items that are shared and can quickly adjust the sharing status of each item.

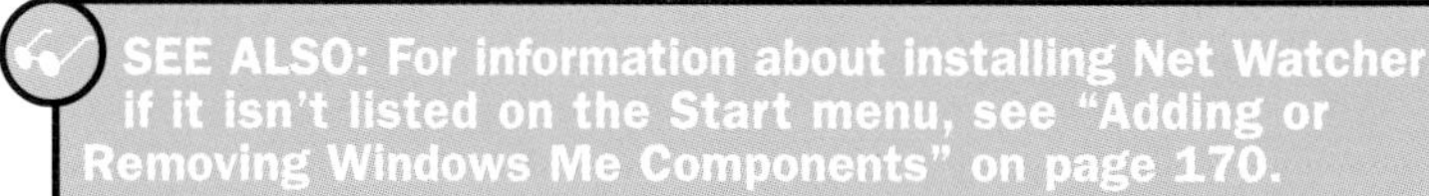
SEE ALSO: For information about installing Net Watcher if it isn't listed on the Start menu, see "Adding or Removing Windows Me Components" on page 170.

Find and Protect Shared Items

1. Start Net Watcher from the System Tools submenu of the Start menu.
2. Click the Show Shared Folders button.
3. Select a shared item, and press Alt+Enter.

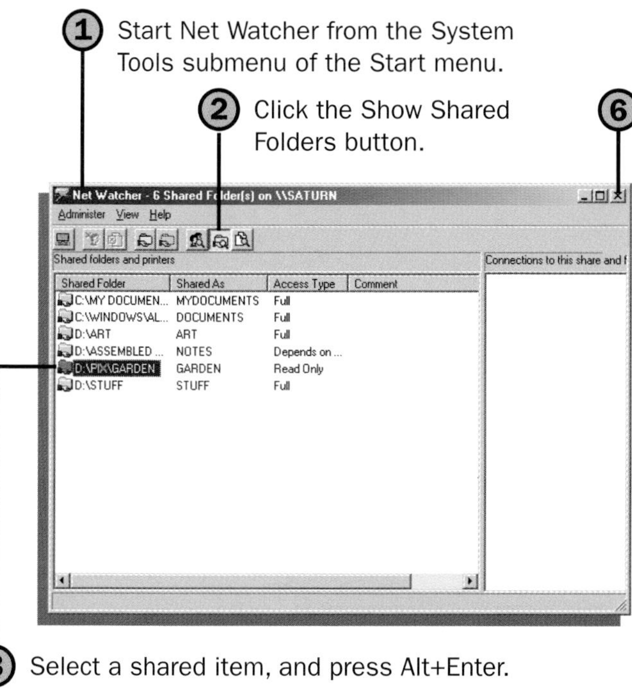

4. Do any of the following:
   - Disable sharing.
   - Change the access type.
   - Require a password.
5. Click OK.
6. When you've adjusted all the shared items, close Net Watcher.

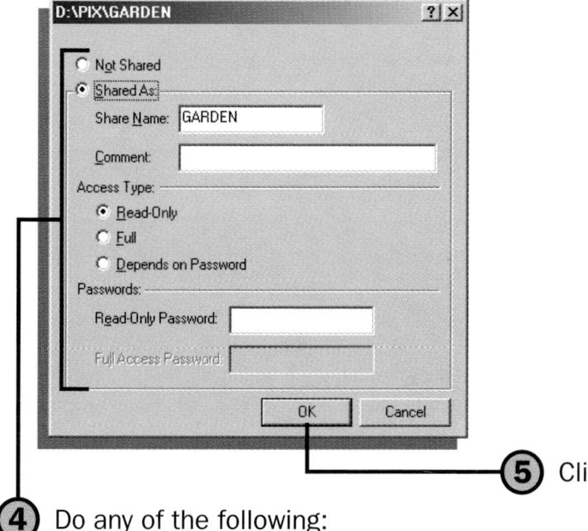

TIP: If you're sure you know which folders or drives are shared (and if there are only a few shared items), you can use My Computer to locate each shared item, right-click it, and choose Sharing to adjust its sharing properties.

Restricting Internet Access

The Internet provides access to many items, some of which might not be appropriate for everyone who uses the computer. To restrict access to certain types of sites—sexually explicit or violent material, for example—you can use Content Advisor.

Set the Restrictions

1. Right-click the Internet Explorer icon on the Desktop, choose Properties from the shortcut menu, and click the Content tab.

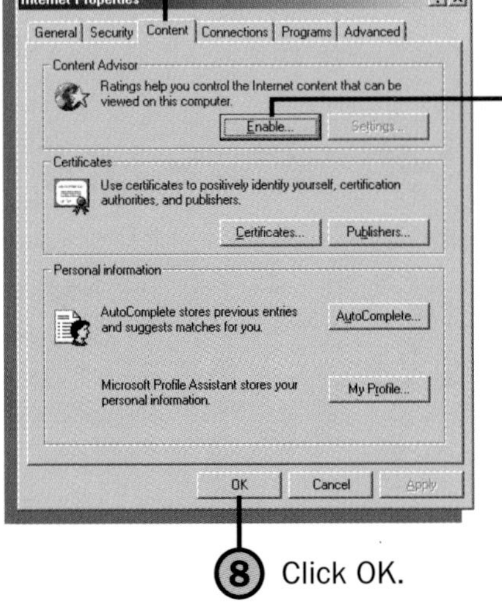

2. Click Enable.
3. Select a category.
4. Move the slider to adjust the acceptable level of the material that can be accessed. Repeat to set levels for the other categories.
5. On the General tab, specify whether unrated sites may be accessed and whether a password may be used to allow access to restricted sites.
6. Click Change Password, enter your password three times, and click OK.
7. Click OK.
8. Click OK.

TIP: You must use a password; otherwise, anyone can disable Content Advisor.

TIP: Content Advisor provides good protection, but a determined individual (or an unscrupulous and inventive web-page designer) can get around the restrictions. The best protection is supervision.

TIP: Use the Approved Sites tab to allow or deny access to a specific site regardless of the site's rating.

Preventing Cookies

"Cookies" are little files that are written by a web site and stored on your computer. These files remember your previous visits to the site, often recording a user name, preferences, or other information. Some sites, however, use these cookies to keep track of your web visits for advertising, demographic data, or other purposes. If you don't want such data stored, you can prevent cookies from being stored on your computer.

TIP: Some sites permit access only when you allow cookies. Other sites might not work properly when cookies are disabled.

TRY THIS: Make your security settings changes. Start Internet Explorer, and visit a few sites. If you have problems accessing some sites or if you find that you want to keep your custom settings, return to the Security Settings dialog box, and use the Reset Custom Settings section to restore your original settings.

Disable Cookies

1. Right-click the Internet Explorer icon on the Desktop, choose Properties from the shortcut menu, and click the Security tab.

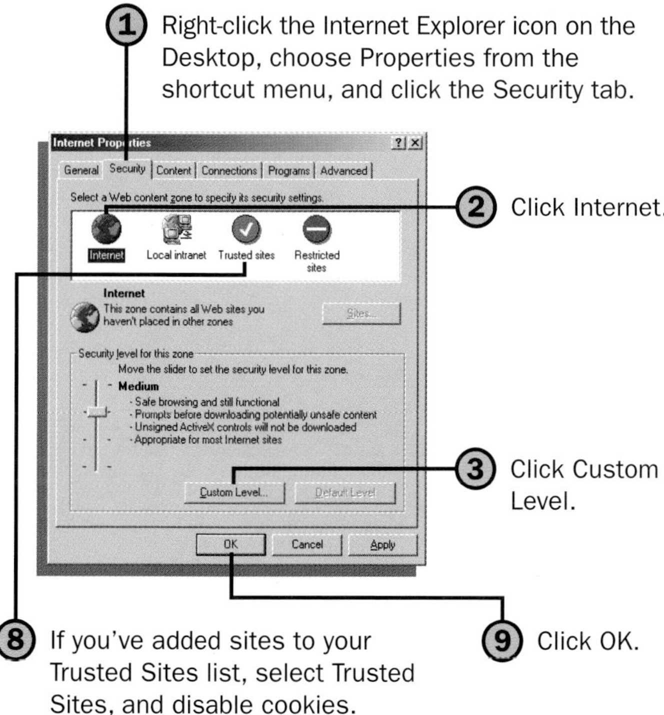

2. Click Internet.
3. Click Custom Level.
4. Select to disable cookies or to require a dialog box prompt to appear whenever a cookie is about to be stored.
5. Select to disable or to prompt for temporary cookies.
6. Make any other security settings you want, being careful not to disable features that protect your computer from viruses.
7. Click OK, and confirm that you want to make the security changes.
8. If you've added sites to your Trusted Sites list, select Trusted Sites, and disable cookies.
9. Click OK.

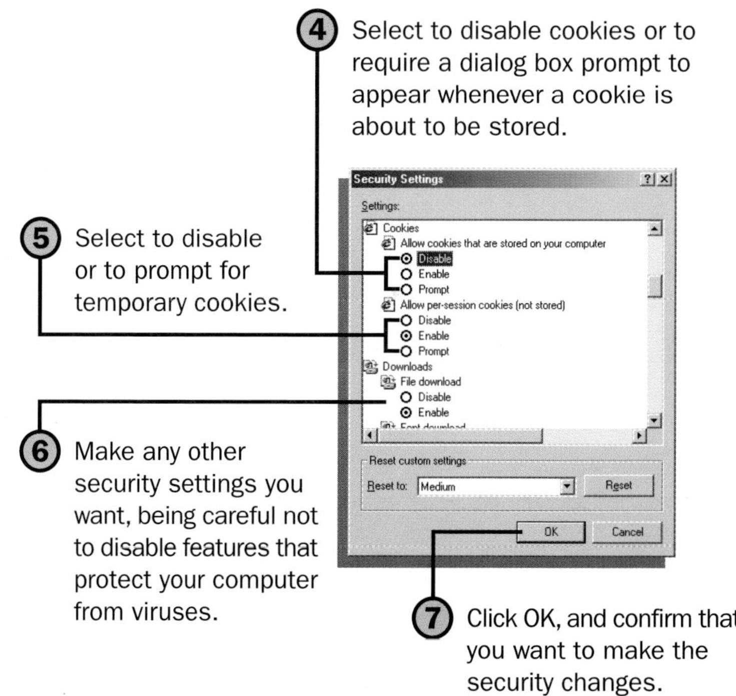

Protecting Your Personal Information

Some web sites request personal information such as your name and e-mail address. You can set up a profile to provide this information if you want, or you can edit your profile to limit or change the information you provide.

> TIP: You can edit your profile information directly in your Address Book or by clicking the My Profile button on the Content tab of the Internet Properties dialog box. To delete the profile, delete the information from your Address Book.

Set Your Profile

1. Right-click the Internet Explorer icon on the Desktop, choose Properties from the shortcut menu, and click the Content tab.

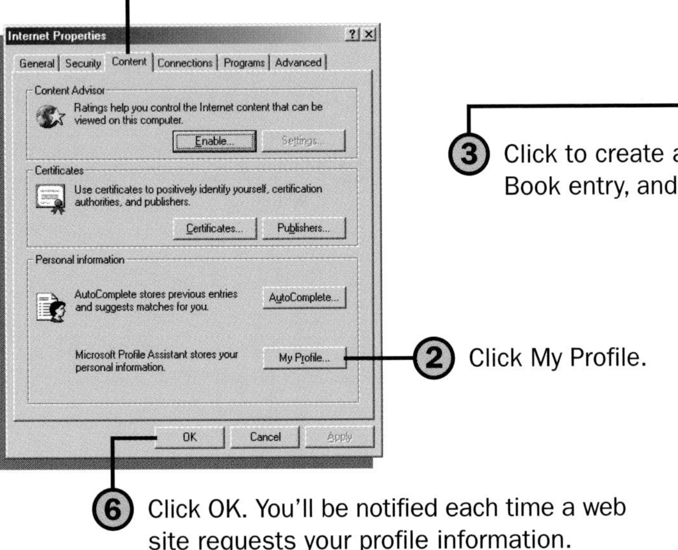

2. Click My Profile.
3. Click to create a new Address Book entry, and click OK.

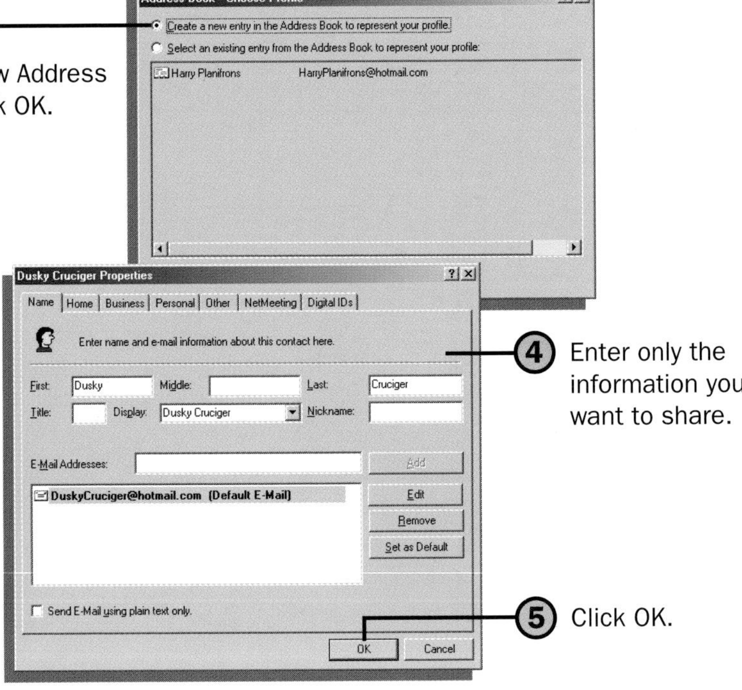

4. Enter only the information you want to share.
5. Click OK.
6. Click OK. You'll be notified each time a web site requests your profile information.

> TIP: You can create more than one profile for yourself in the Address Book, using one profile for web sites, and using another, more detailed one as an electronic business card (vCard) that you share with your e-mail contacts.

Changing Your Password

A secure password is one of the vital keys to maintaining security on your computer. Another is to change your password occasionally. Windows Me makes it easy to change your Windows password and, if your computer is connected to a network that requires a password, to change the network password as well.

> **TIP:** Some networks require you to use different tools for changing your network password. If you can't change your network password using these procedures, consult your network documentation.

Change Your Password

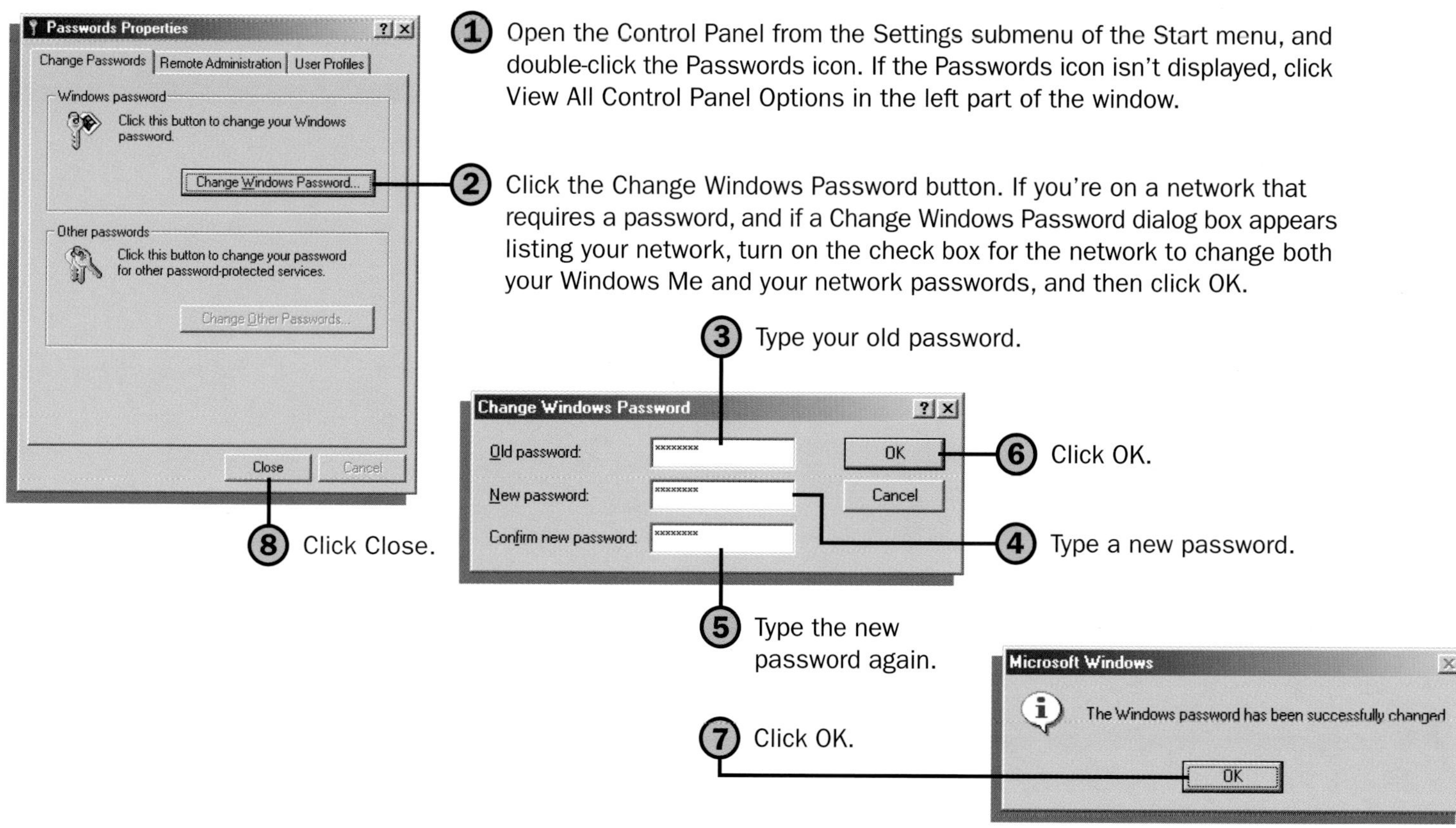

1. Open the Control Panel from the Settings submenu of the Start menu, and double-click the Passwords icon. If the Passwords icon isn't displayed, click View All Control Panel Options in the left part of the window.
2. Click the Change Windows Password button. If you're on a network that requires a password, and if a Change Windows Password dialog box appears listing your network, turn on the check box for the network to change both your Windows Me and your network passwords, and then click OK.
3. Type your old password.
4. Type a new password.
5. Type the new password again.
6. Click OK.
7. Click OK.
8. Click Close.

Protecting Your Files with a Password

If your files contain sensitive information and you want to make sure that others can't access it without a password, place the files in a compressed folder, create a password that will cause the files to become encrypted, and—whether the files are stored on your computer, in a shared folder on a network, or on that floppy disk you lost—the files will be protected from unauthorized viewing.

TIP: When you encrypt a file, the encryption is good for one time only. That is, if you use the password to open a file in an encrypted compressed folder, the contents of the compressed folder are no longer encrypted, even if you close the compressed folder. To maintain security, you must use the Encrypt command each time you've finished accessing the compressed folder.

Encrypt a Compressed Folder

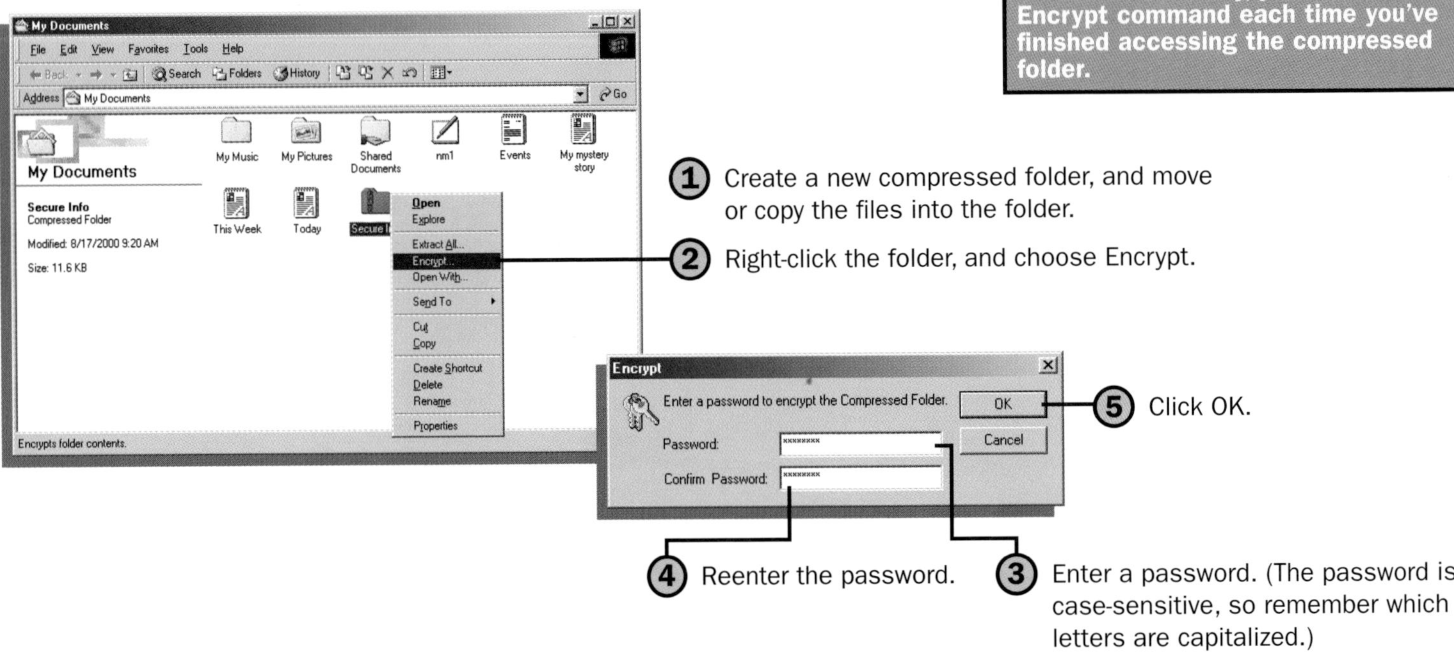

1. Create a new compressed folder, and move or copy the files into the folder.
2. Right-click the folder, and choose Encrypt.
3. Enter a password. (The password is case-sensitive, so remember which letters are capitalized.)
4. Reenter the password.
5. Click OK.

SEE ALSO: For information about working with compressed folders, see "Compressing Files" on page 27.

For information about encrypting e-mail messages, see "Sending an Encrypted E-Mail Message" on page 158.

Access a File

1. Open the compressed folder by double-clicking it.
2. Double-click the file.

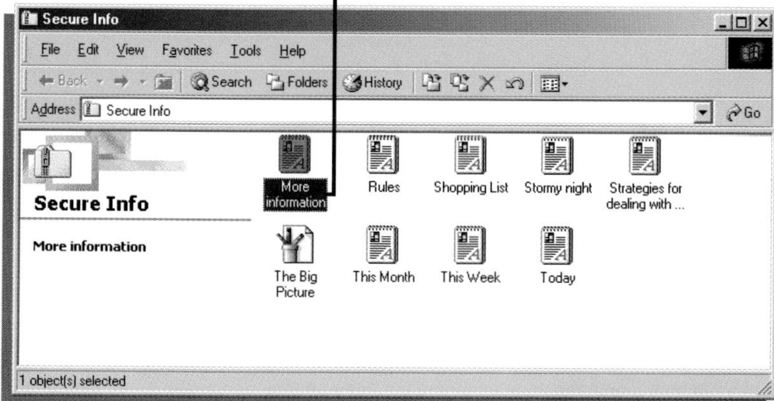

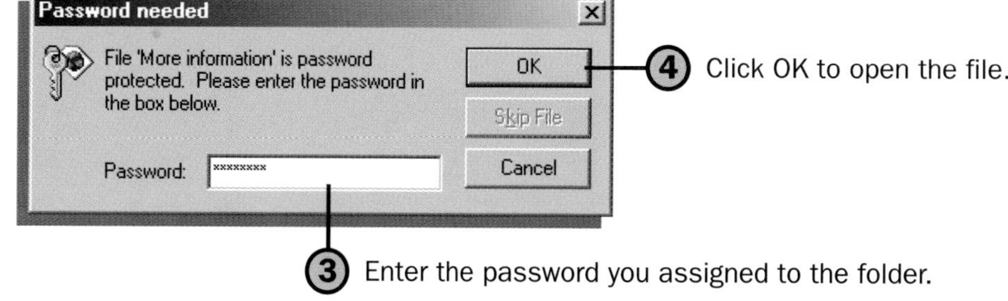

3. Enter the password you assigned to the folder.
4. Click OK to open the file.

TIP: The encryption can't be cracked unless you're a very sophisticated cryptologist, so make sure that you don't forget the password!

TRY THIS: Encrypt a single file by right-clicking it, pointing to Send To on the shortcut menu, and clicking Compressed Folder. Then right-click the compressed folder that's created, choose Encrypt, and assign a password.

TIP: An individual encrypted file can be deleted without using the password, but the password is required to copy the file. Once it has been copied, the file is no longer encrypted.

12 Managing Windows Me

In this section

The beauty of Microsoft Windows Millennium Edition is the flexibility it gives you to make changes, fix problems, and generally make your computer work better. You can install any Windows Me components that weren't included in the initial installation, and you can free up disk space by removing any installed components that you don't use. You can install or remove other programs and add whatever hardware you need. Windows Me makes all such operations quick and easy by providing you with "wizards" that walk through the process.

Windows Me also provides disk-maintenance tools that will help make your computer run better. You can schedule these tools to run periodically (even while you sleep!)—they'll find and re-order bits of files that have become scattered or lost, delete unused files, and so on. You can change the way you log on, and, if more than one person uses your computer, each individual can have his or her own unique settings that are accessed at logon. And, because computers, programs, and peripheral devices are continually changing, Windows Me provides the Updates Wizard that compares what you have with what's available and lets you choose the way in which you want to update your computer. Finally, if you can't get Windows Me to start properly, you'll find several solutions that will either get you started or help you diagnose what's wrong. And if you've made changes to your computer and now wish that you hadn't, you can use the System Restore tool to revert to your previous settings.

Adding or Removing Windows Me Components

When Windows Me is installed on your computer, some—but not all—of its components are included in the installation. If any components you *do* need haven't been installed, you can add them; if there are components you never use, you can remove them from your system to save disk space.

SEE ALSO: For information about updating existing Windows Me components or adding recently released components, see "Updating Your System" on page 184.

TIP: To install fonts on your system, open the Control Panel, double-click the Fonts folder, and choose Install New Font from the File menu.

Add or Remove Items

1. Save any documents you're working on, and close all your running programs.
2. Open the Control Panel from the Settings submenu of the Start menu, and double-click the Add/Remove Programs icon to display the Add/Remove Programs Properties dialog box.

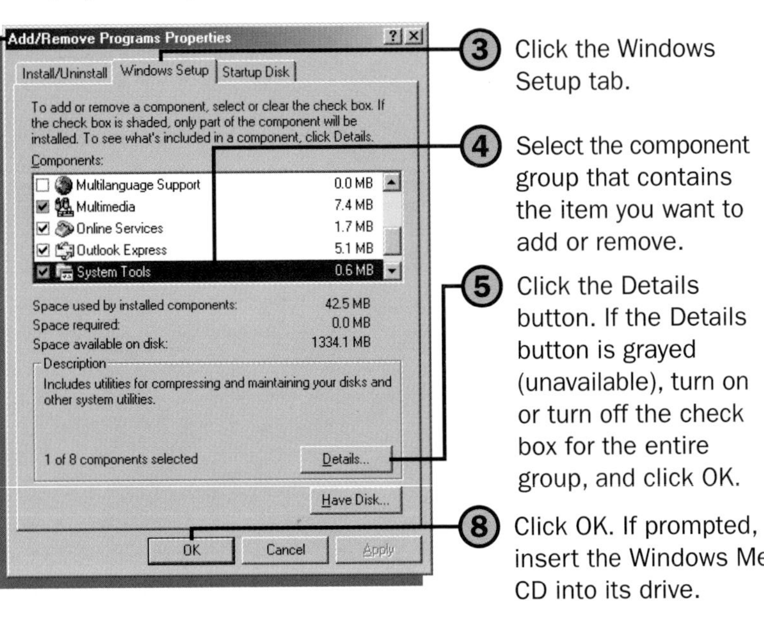

3. Click the Windows Setup tab.
4. Select the component group that contains the item you want to add or remove.
5. Click the Details button. If the Details button is grayed (unavailable), turn on or turn off the check box for the entire group, and click OK.
6. Click a checked box to remove the item, or click an unchecked box to add the item. Continue checking or clearing check boxes until you've specified all the items you want to add or remove.

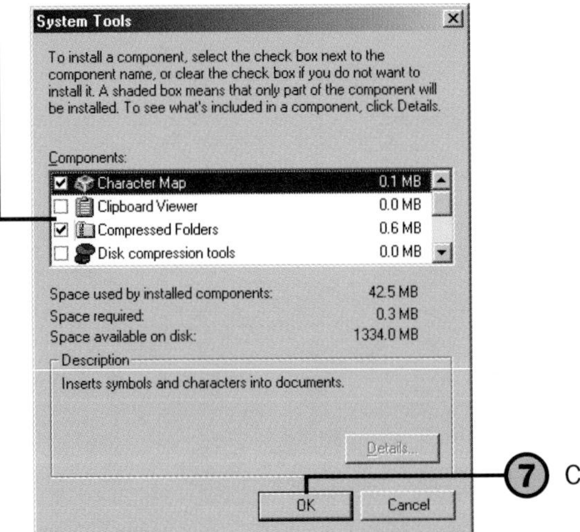

7. Click OK.
8. Click OK. If prompted, insert the Windows Me CD into its drive.

Installing a Program

Most software programs contain their own installation program, which copies the required files to the computer's hard disk and tells Windows Me which files are installed, where they are, and what they do.

> **TIP:** Some programs are only partially installed until you use them for the first time. When you first choose one of these programs from the Start menu, you'll be asked whether you want to install it. You'll see this request if you chose Install On First Use when you installed the program.

> **TIP:** You can also install a program by double-clicking its Setup.exe or Install.exe program.

Install a Program

1. Close all your running programs. If you're installing from a CD, place the CD in its drive, follow the instructions that appear on the screen, and skip steps 2 through 5.
2. If the CD didn't start, or if you're installing from a different drive or from a network location, open the Control Panel from the Settings submenu of the Start menu, and double-click the Add/Remove Programs icon to open the Add/Remove Programs Properties dialog box.
3. On the Install/Uninstall tab, click Install.
4. Place the CD or the installation disk in its drive, and click Next.
5. If the Setup or installation program is found, click Finish. If not, click Browse, locate the Setup or installation program on a different drive or in a network folder, and click Finish. Follow the Setup or installation program's instructions, and close the Add/Remove Programs Properties dialog box when the installation is complete.

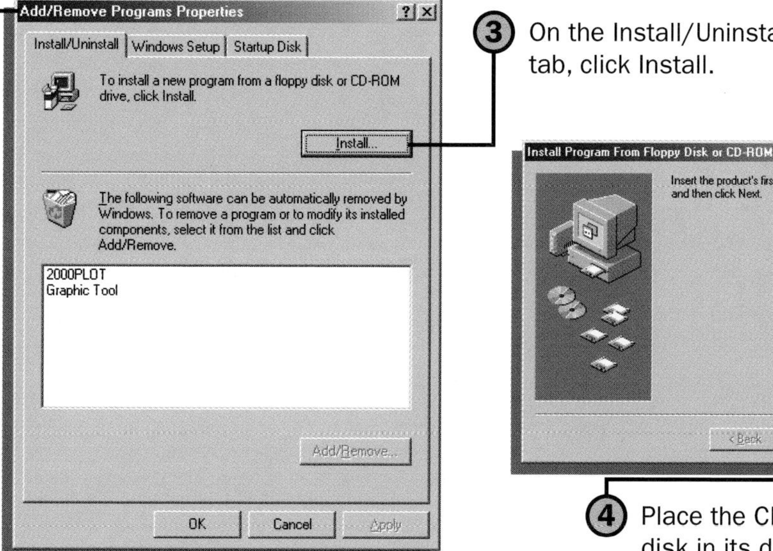

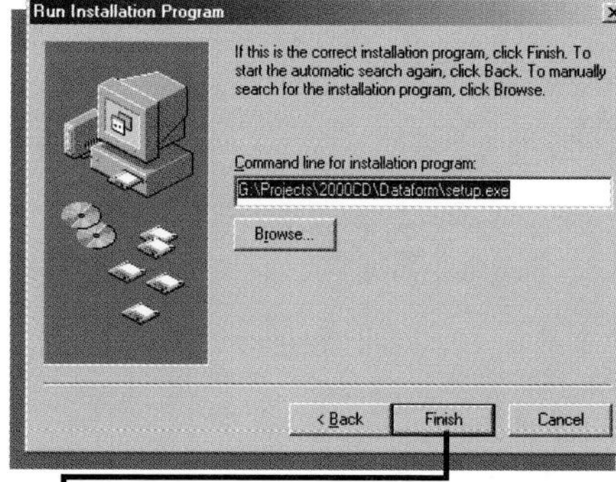

Removing a Program

Most programs are *registered* with Windows Me when you install them. You can—and should—use Windows tools to remove a program. If you simply delete the files, you might leave accessory files you don't need or delete files you need for other programs. When you uninstall a program using Windows tools, Windows Me keeps track of the files, and only when a file is no longer needed by any of your programs does Windows Me delete the file.

TIP: If the program you want to remove isn't listed in the Add/Remove Programs Properties dialog box, consult the program's documentation for information about the tools you need to remove the program.

SEE ALSO: For information about removing programs that came with Windows Me, see "Adding or Removing Windows Me Components" on page 170.

Uninstall a Program

1. Close all your running programs. Open the Control Panel from the Settings submenu of the Start menu, and double-click the Add/Remove Programs icon to open the Add/Remove Programs Properties dialog box.

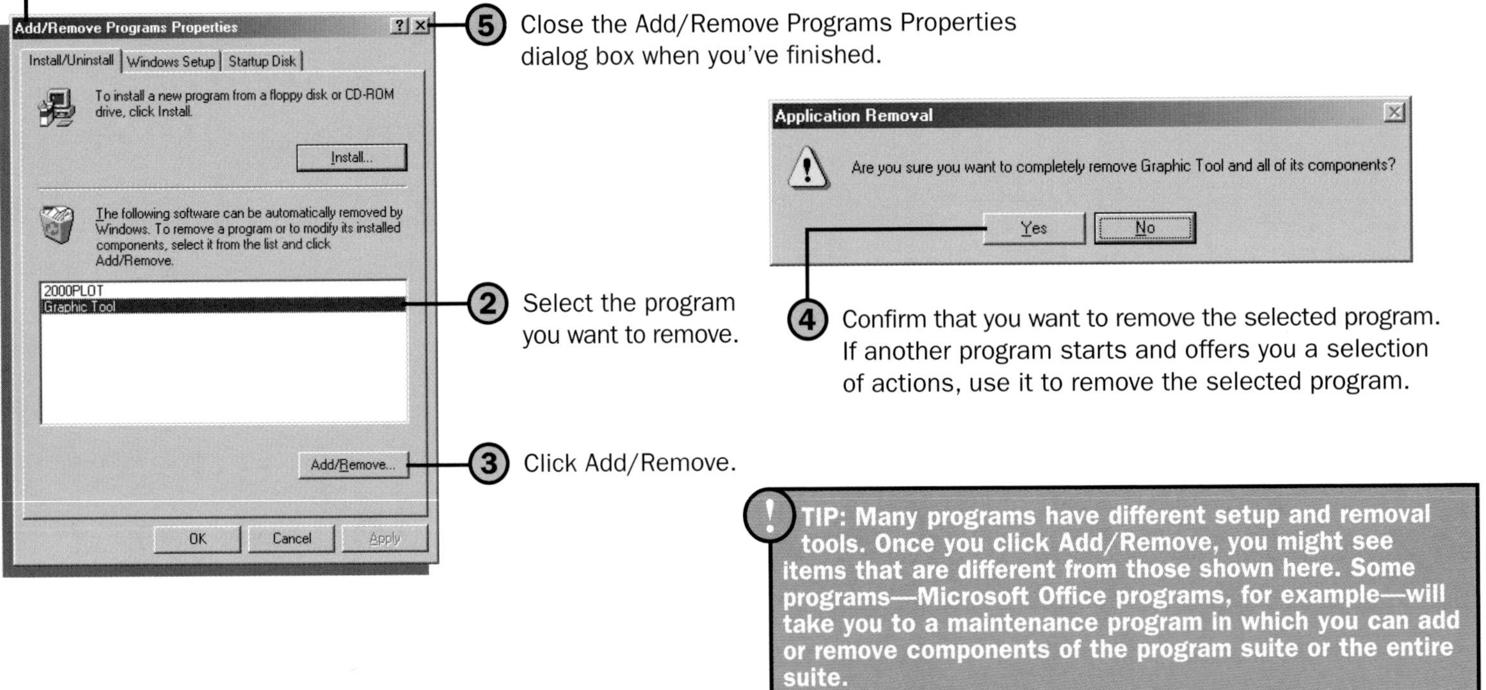

2. Select the program you want to remove.
3. Click Add/Remove.
4. Confirm that you want to remove the selected program. If another program starts and offers you a selection of actions, use it to remove the selected program.
5. Close the Add/Remove Programs Properties dialog box when you've finished.

TIP: Many programs have different setup and removal tools. Once you click Add/Remove, you might see items that are different from those shown here. Some programs—Microsoft Office programs, for example—will take you to a maintenance program in which you can add or remove components of the program suite or the entire suite.

Adding Hardware

Windows Me tries to keep track of its environment, and it usually notices when you add some hardware to your computer. In most cases, the hardware can identify itself to Windows Me, which will immediately add any necessary software and will configure your computer to use the hardware. Some hardware comes with its own software installation package. In some instances, you'll need to inform Windows Me about the new hardware, and, if necessary, provide the required software.

TIP: To see the system settings and the working status of your hardware, right-click My Computer, choose Properties from the shortcut menu, and explore the items on the Device Manager list. Do not, however, make any changes here unless you're certain that you know what you're doing; otherwise, you could cause serious problems to your system.

Add an Item

1. Install the item, following the manufacturer's instructions. If you needed to shut down the computer, restart it. Wait for the item to be detected and for any supporting software to be installed.

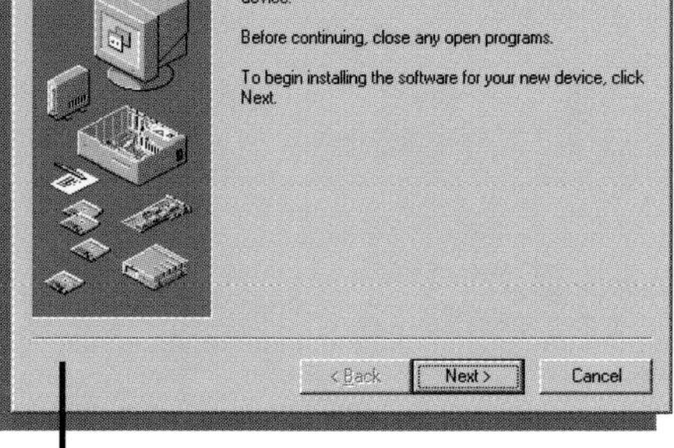

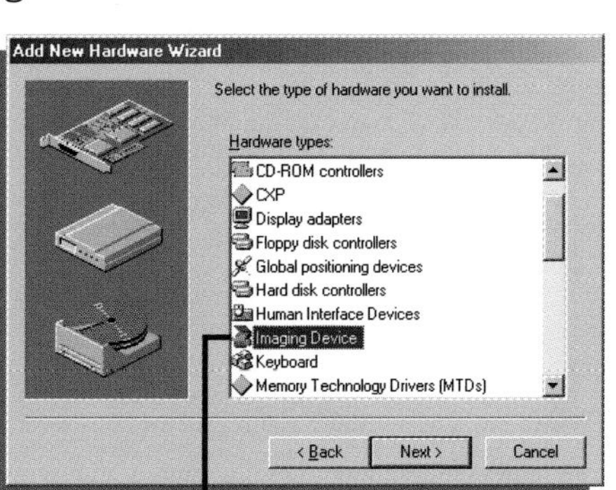

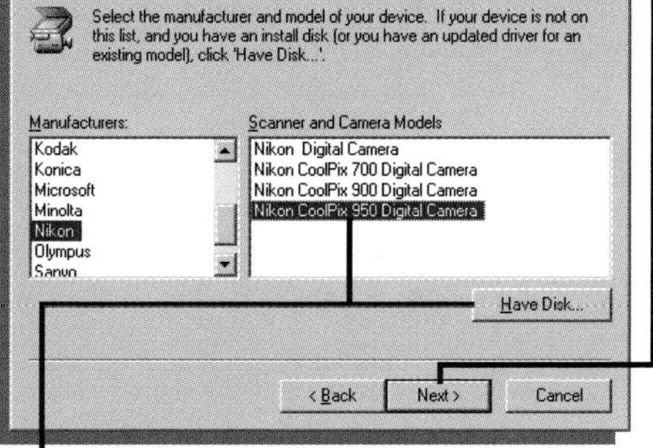

2. If the item wasn't detected and installed, open the Control Panel from the Settings submenu of the Start menu, double-click the Add New Hardware icon, and step through the wizard.

3. If the hardware wasn't detected, select the type of hardware, and click Next.

4. Do either of the following:
   - Select the manufacturer and model.
   - Click Have Disk if you have a disk that contains installation files for the hardware. Use the Browse button to locate the files, and click OK.

5. Click Next, and complete the wizard.

TIP: Sometimes, when you step through the wizard and specify the type of device you're adding, a new wizard will start to help you install that specific type of hardware. For example, if you're installing a printer, the Add Printer Wizard will start.

Changing the Date or Time

Windows Me and your computer keep track of the date and time, and they use the commonly accepted formats in which to display them. If your computer has the wrong date or time, or if you travel with your computer into a different time zone, you can reset the date, time, or time zone.

TIP: To see whether the date is correct, point to the time on the taskbar, and hold the mouse steady until the date appears.

Change the Date or Time

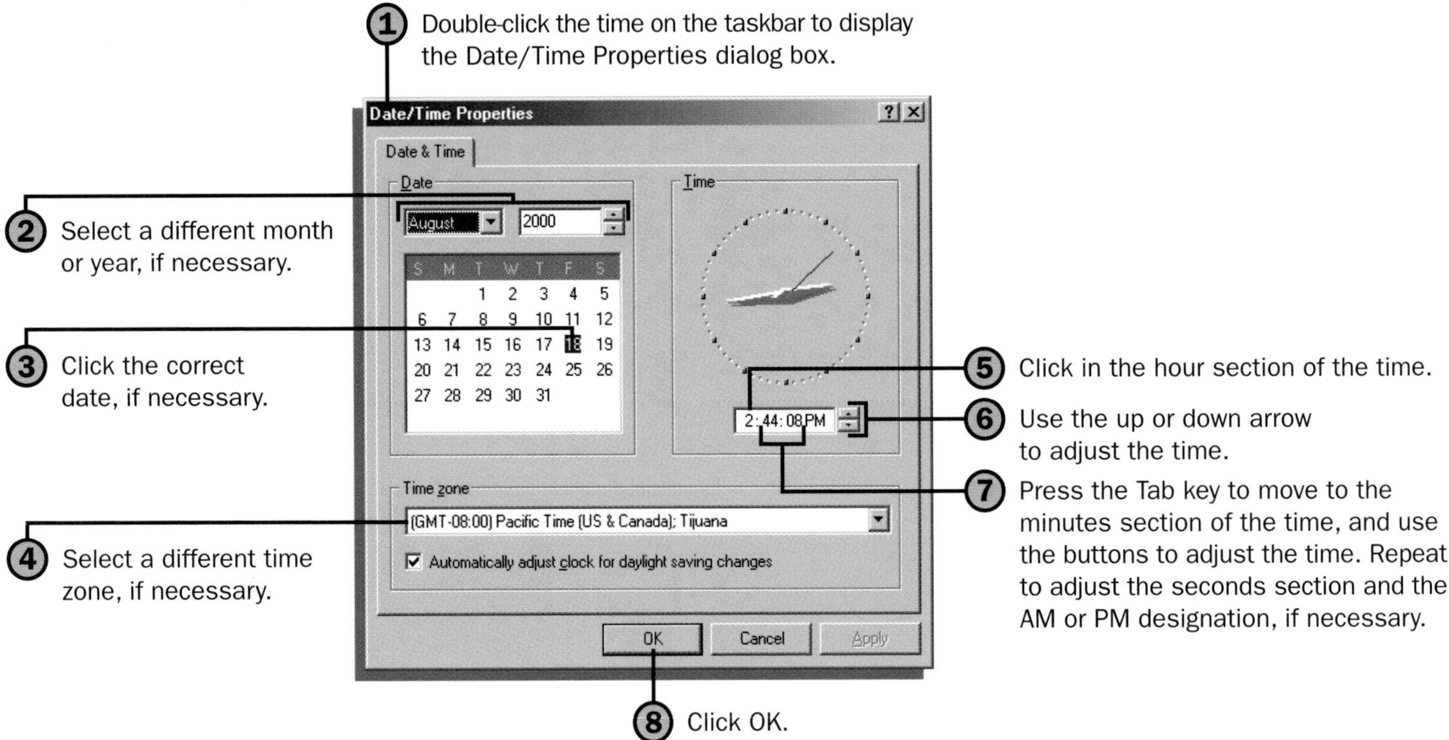

TIP: If the time isn't displayed on the taskbar, right-click a blank spot on the taskbar, choose Properties from the shortcut menu, and turn on the Show Clock check box.

Changing the Display Size

If you want to squeeze more items onto your Desktop, you can change its size…sort of. This is one of those "virtual" realities. You "enlarge" the available space by changing the screen resolution, and thereby the *scaling,* which lets you fit more items onto the Desktop even though its area on your screen doesn't get any larger. Your gain in "virtual" area comes at a cost, though—everything will be smaller and harder to read.

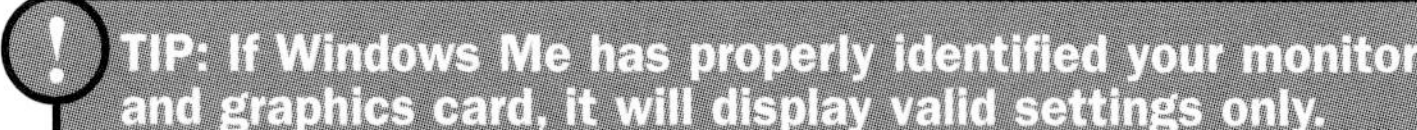

TIP: If Windows Me has properly identified your monitor and graphics card, it will display valid settings only.

TIP: If text is too large or too small after you've adjusted the screen area, click the Advanced button on the Settings tab, and change the font size.

Increase the Screen Area

1. Right-click a blank spot on the Desktop, and choose Properties from the shortcut menu to display the Display Properties dialog box.

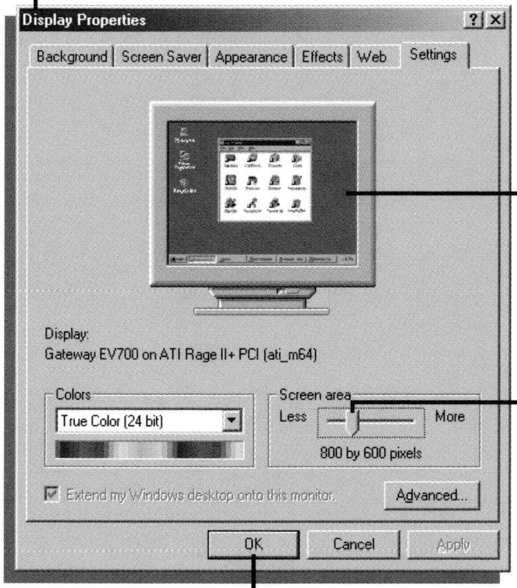

Preview the change in the Desktop area.

2. On the Settings tab, drag the slider to select a screen area.

3. Click OK.

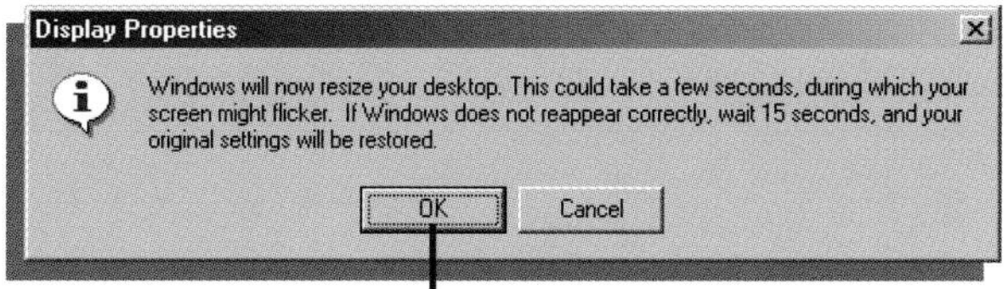

4. Click OK to confirm that you want to resize the Desktop.

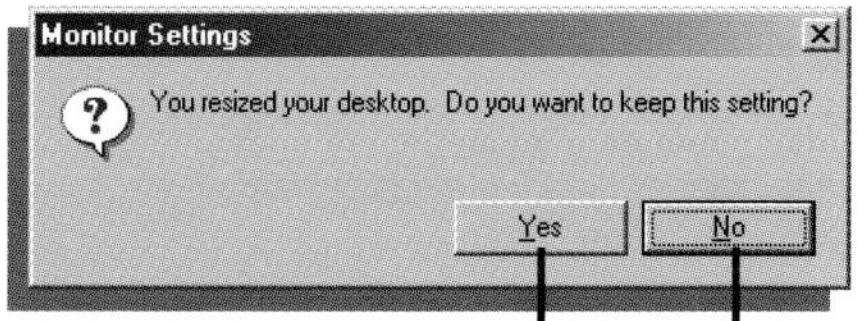

5. After the Desktop has been resized, click Yes to accept the new settings or No to revert to the original settings. If you don't click Yes within 15 seconds, Windows Me restores the original settings.

Setting the Power Options

Different computers often have different power-management requirements and abilities. You might want the monitor on your main desktop computer to shut down after a few minutes of idleness, but you might also want the hard disk to "stay awake" constantly. On your laptop computer, you might want everything to shut down after a few minutes of idleness. Depending on the features and abilities of your computer, you can set these power schemes, as well as some other features.

TIP: You'll see an Alarms tab and a Power Meter tab only if your computer is a portable computer with a battery. You won't see those tabs or the Hibernate tab if your computer doesn't fully support advanced power-management features. Only the items supported by your computer will appear on the various tabs.

Use a Power Scheme

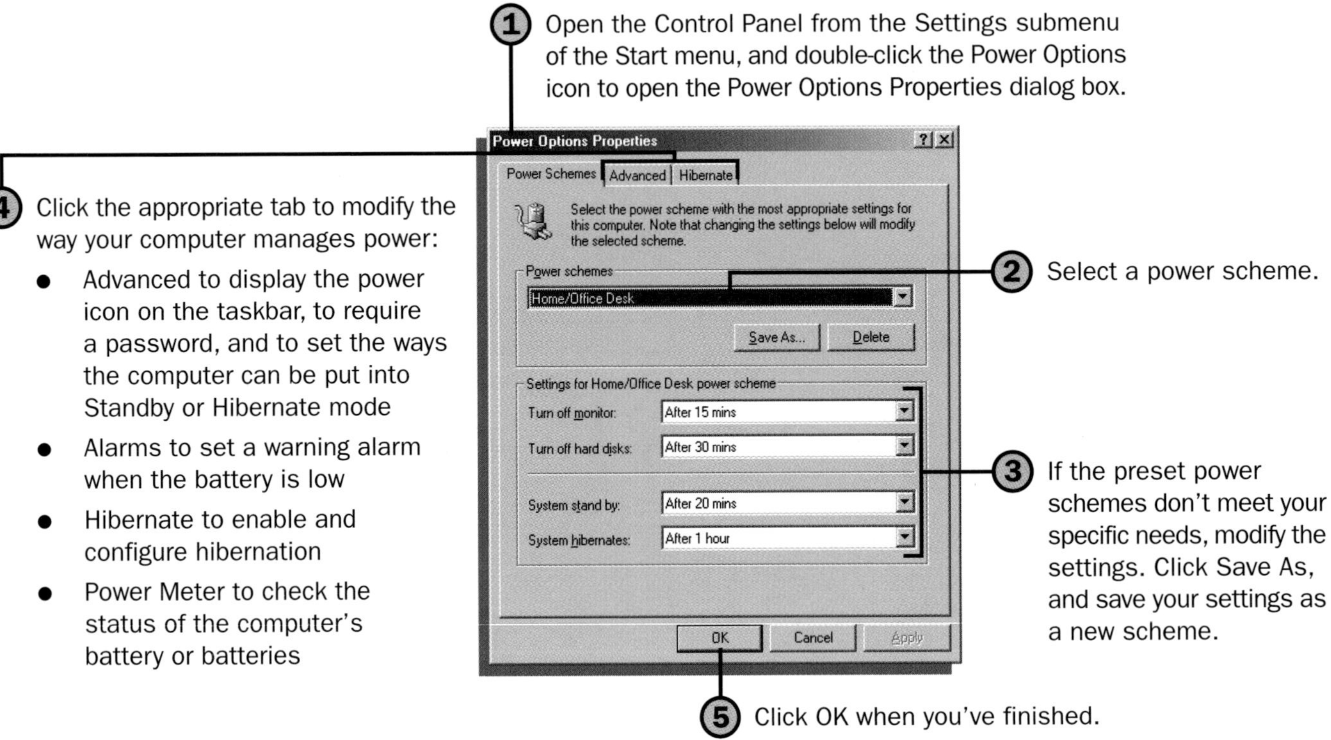

1. Open the Control Panel from the Settings submenu of the Start menu, and double-click the Power Options icon to open the Power Options Properties dialog box.
2. Select a power scheme.
3. If the preset power schemes don't meet your specific needs, modify the settings. Click Save As, and save your settings as a new scheme.
4. Click the appropriate tab to modify the way your computer manages power:
   - Advanced to display the power icon on the taskbar, to require a password, and to set the ways the computer can be put into Standby or Hibernate mode
   - Alarms to set a warning alarm when the battery is low
   - Hibernate to enable and configure hibernation
   - Power Meter to check the status of the computer's battery or batteries
5. Click OK when you've finished.

Common Power-Management Options

Option	Function
Alarm Action	The action that's executed when the low or critical battery alarm is activated.
Always Show Icon On The Taskbar	Shows the power source when pointed to; switches power schemes or shows the battery state when clicked.
Always Use Least Power In Standby Mode	Ensures that as many devices as possible enter low-power state when computer starts Standby.
Critical Battery Alarm	Activates the battery alarm when the battery's power level declines to the level you designate.
Enable Hibernate Support	Enables the computer to write the information in its memory to the hard disk and then shut down. When you turn the computer back on, the information is restored to its memory.
Low Battery Alarm	Activates the battery alarm when the battery's power level declines to the level you designate.
Prompt For Password When Computer Goes Off Standby And Hibernate	Requires your logon password when the computer returns from standby or hibernation.
When I Press The Power Button On My Computer, When I Close The Lid Of My Portable Computer, or When I Press The Sleep Button On My Computer	Determines whether the computer shuts down, goes on standby, or hibernates when the power button (the on/off button) is pressed, when the lid of a portable computer is closed, or when the Sleep button is pressed.

TIP: Standby mode puts the computer in a low-power state that you can quickly bring back to full power by pressing a key or moving the mouse. When you shut down the computer, anything in its memory that you haven't saved (changes you've made to a document, for example) will be lost.

TIP: Hibernate mode stores everything in the computer's memory in a special file on the hard disk, and then shuts down the computer. When you restart the computer, it's restored to the way it was before it was shut down, and everything that was contained in its memory is restored.

TIP: To manually put your computer into Standby or Hibernate mode, choose Shut Down from the Start menu, choose Standby or Hibernate, and click OK.

TIP: Windows Me has strict standards for supporting advanced power-management features. If your computer is designed to support advanced power-management features but they aren't available in Windows Me, contact the computer manufacturer about obtaining an updated version of the BIOS that's designed to work with Windows Me. Also check your computer's documentation to see how to verify that the power-management features haven't been disabled in the computer's setup.

Changing the Screen Colors

If you're tired of looking at the same old screen colors, you can brighten them up—or tone them down. You increase the number of colors available to be displayed, and you can either select a predefined color scheme or define your own color scheme that determines the color of the Windows Me elements.

TIP: If you're not asked whether the computer should be restarted, or if you always (or never) want to restart after changing the color level, click the Advanced button on the Settings tab, and select the action you want in the Compatibility section.

Change the Color Level

1. Right-click a blank spot on the Desktop, and choose Properties from the shortcut menu to display the Display Properties dialog box.

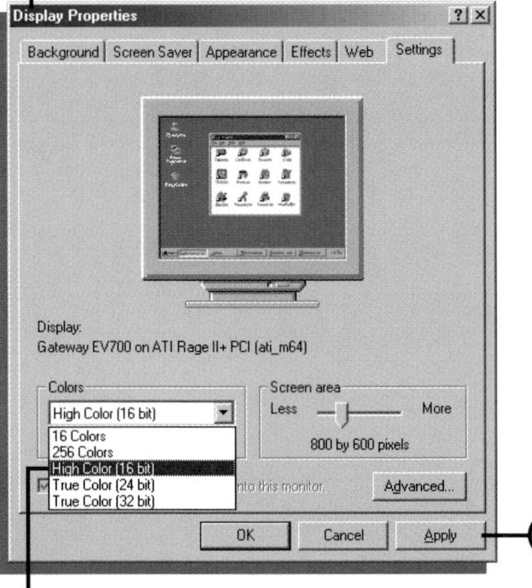

2. On the Settings tab, select a color level.
3. Click Apply.
4. Specify whether to apply the new color settings with or without restarting the computer. You should always restart, however, if the display isn't working correctly after you've changed the color settings.

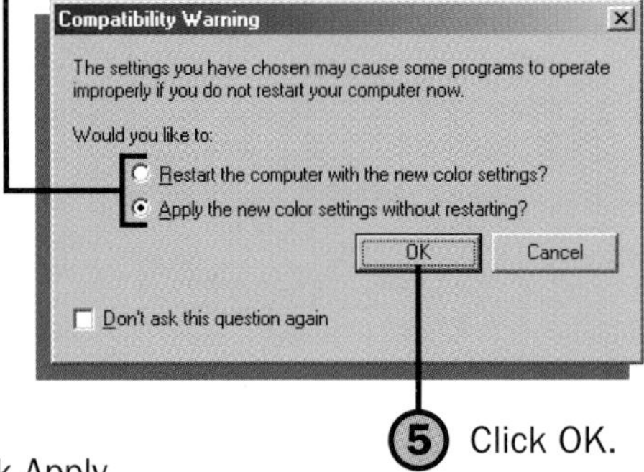

5. Click OK.

TIP: The more colors you use and the higher the screen resolution, the more display memory is required. Therefore, you might need to use a lower screen resolution to display more colors, or display fewer colors to use a higher screen resolution.

Select and Modify a Color Scheme

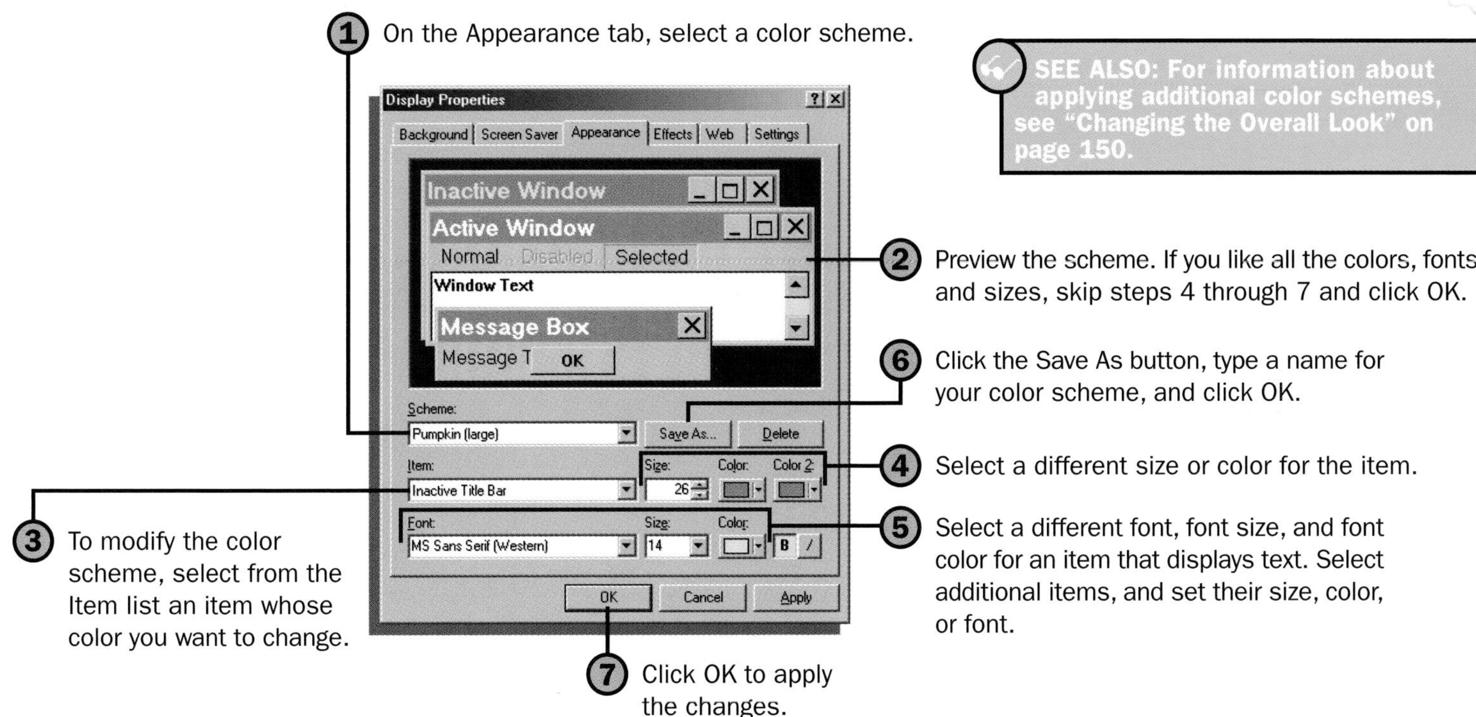

1. On the Appearance tab, select a color scheme.
2. Preview the scheme. If you like all the colors, fonts, and sizes, skip steps 4 through 7 and click OK.
3. To modify the color scheme, select from the Item list an item whose color you want to change.
4. Select a different size or color for the item.
5. Select a different font, font size, and font color for an item that displays text. Select additional items, and set their size, color, or font.
6. Click the Save As button, type a name for your color scheme, and click OK.
7. Click OK to apply the changes.

SEE ALSO: For information about applying additional color schemes, see "Changing the Overall Look" on page 150.

TIP: Change your colors with caution, and be sure to keep enough contrast between a text color and its background. If, for example, you change the menu font color to the same color as the menu itself, you won't be able to see the names of the menu items until you've selected them.

TIP: The High Contrast and the Large and Extra Large schemes provide settings that make the Windows Me components more easily visible on your screen.

Maintaining Your Computer

With time and use, your computer can become a bit disorganized. Fortunately, Windows Me comes with the Disk Cleanup, ScanDisk, and Disk Defragmenter programs to help you reorganize your computer and get it to work a little better. Although you can run each program individually from the Start menu, you can schedule all the tools to run automatically when you're not using the computer.

Set Up Maintenance

1. Choose Maintenance Wizard from the System Tools submenu of the Start Menu to start the wizard.

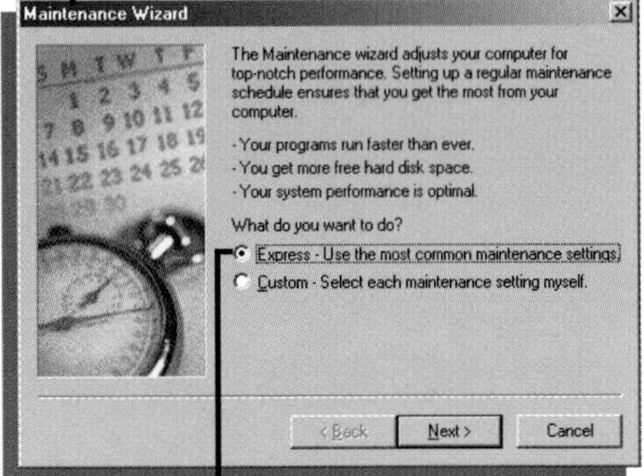

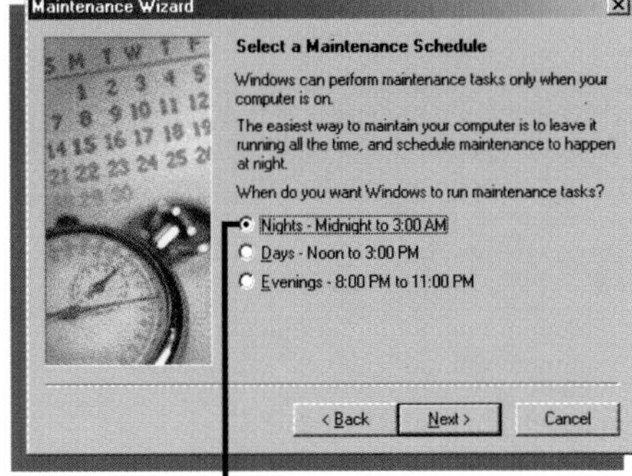

Maintenance Wizard
Windows will perform the following tasks:
Speed up your most frequently used programs.
Check hard disk for errors.
Delete unnecessary files from hard disk.
Remember to leave your computer on nights from Midnight to 3:00 A.M. so that maintenance can occur.
When I click Finish, perform each scheduled task for the first time.
< Back
Finish
Cancel

2. Step through the wizard, and select the Express setup.
3. Specify when you want the tools to run.
4. Click Finish.

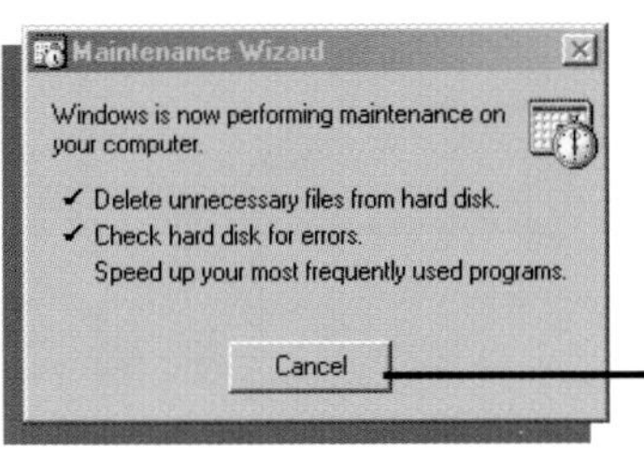

5. Click Cancel if you need to stop running all the maintenance programs until the next time they're scheduled to run.

TIP: To change the schedule, or to run the maintenance programs immediately, choose Maintenance Wizard from the Start menu, and select the action you want. To change how often each program is to run, or to choose different times from those proposed in the Express setup, choose the Custom option when you're running the Maintenance Wizard setup.

TIP: When you schedule the programs, be sure to select times when the computer will be turned on but will not be in use.

Changing the Logon

Windows Me provides three logon options: the Windows Logon, the Microsoft Family Logon, and the Network Logon (identified here as Client For Microsoft Networks). Each logon has a purpose: the Windows Logon identifies you to the computer so that your individual settings can be used; the Microsoft Family Logon simplifies the logon process while using individual settings; and the Client For Microsoft Networks Logon identifies you to your computer and to your network, and logs you on to the network. If you want to change the way you log on, you can select a different type of logon.

SEE ALSO: For information about changing your password, see "Changing Your Password" on page 165.

For information about creating individual settings for different individuals who log on, see "Adding Users" on page 182.

TIP: To start Windows Me without having to use a logon dialog box, change your password, and set the new password to be blank (that is, to contain no characters).

Change the Logon

1. Right-click My Network Places on the Desktop, and choose Properties from the shortcut menu to display the Network dialog box.
2. Select the logon.
3. If the logon isn't listed, click Add.
4. Select Client, and click Add.
5. Select the logon you want to use.
6. Click OK.
7. Click OK. Restart the computer when prompted.

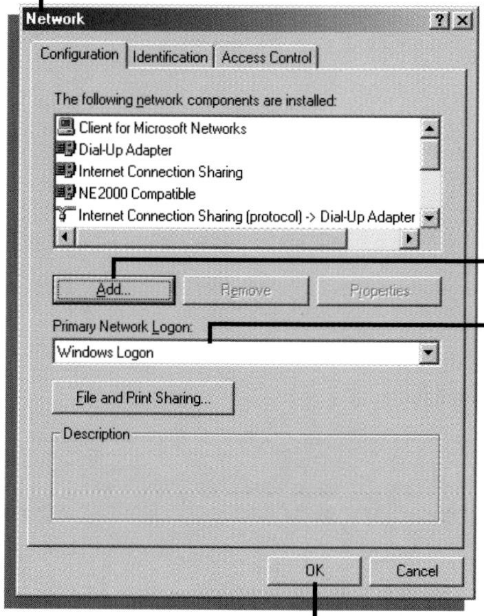

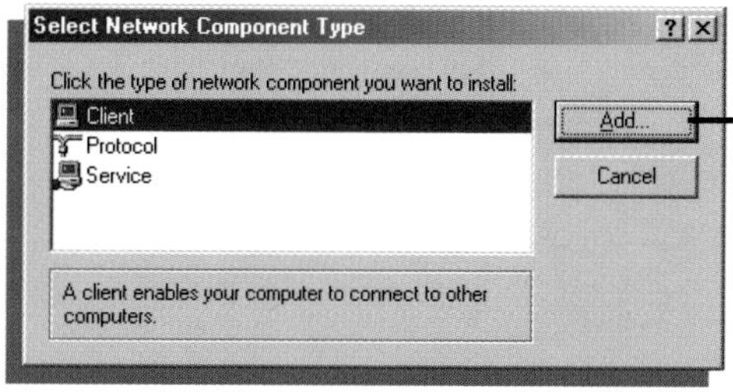

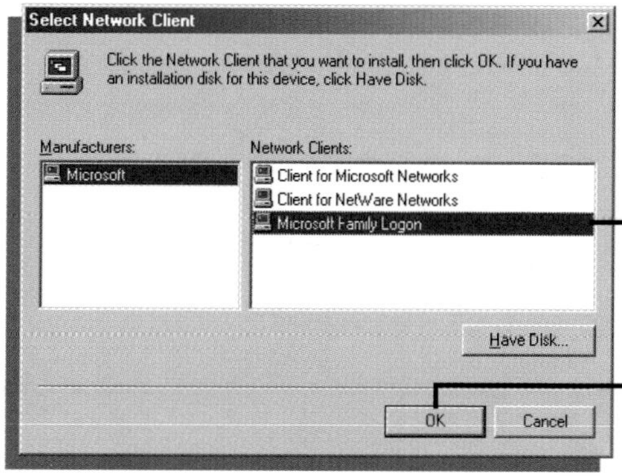

Adding Users

If your computer is used by more than one person, each individual can have his or her own settings—a unique My Documents folder, for example, and different display and system settings. To enter a new user's name and to specify which items are unique to that person, you run the Enable Multi-User Settings Wizard.

TIP: The first time you add a new user, the Enable Multi-User Settings Wizard starts when you double-click the Users icon in the Control Panel. When you add subsequent users, the User Settings dialog box appears when you double-click the Users icon.

Specify a New User

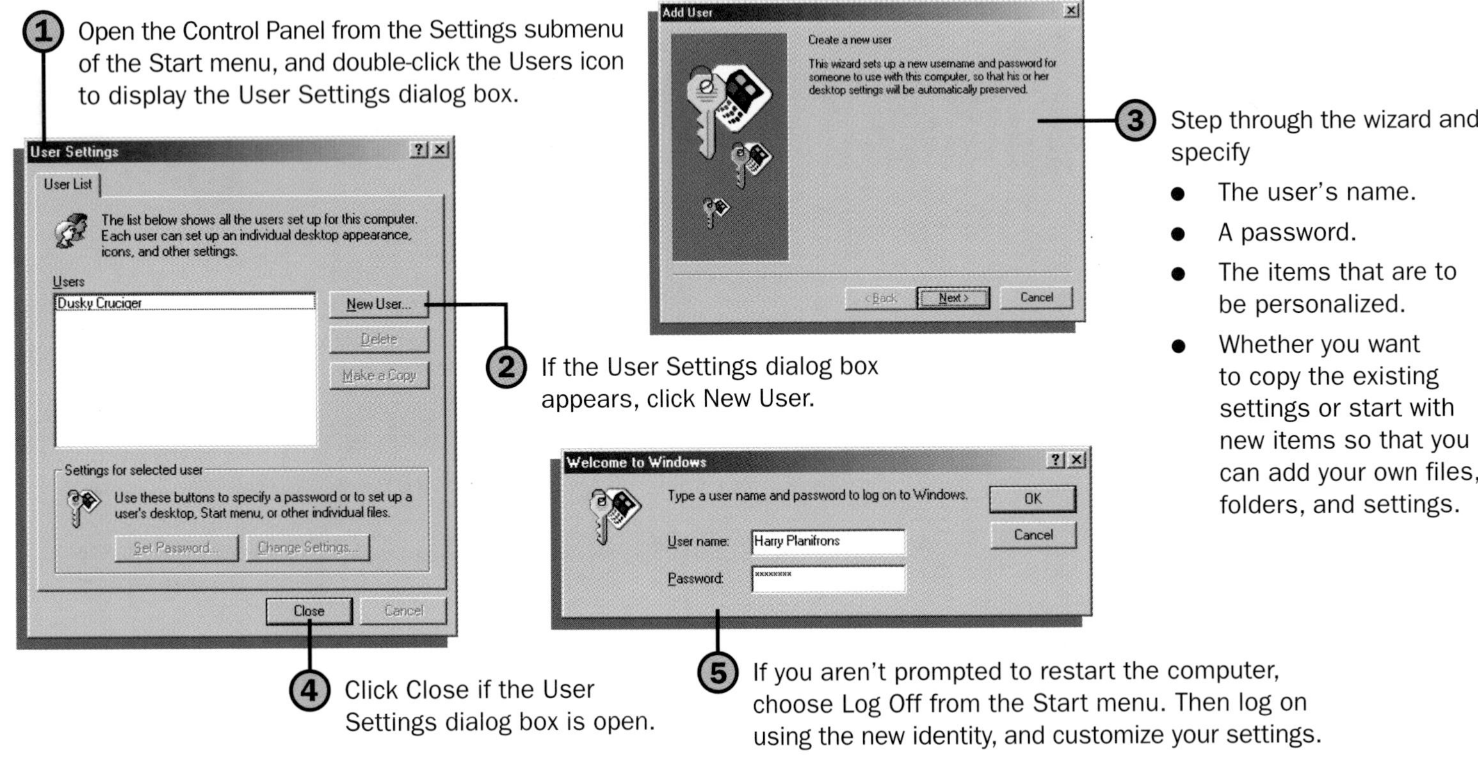

1. Open the Control Panel from the Settings submenu of the Start menu, and double-click the Users icon to display the User Settings dialog box.
2. If the User Settings dialog box appears, click New User.
3. Step through the wizard and specify
   - The user's name.
   - A password.
   - The items that are to be personalized.
   - Whether you want to copy the existing settings or start with new items so that you can add your own files, folders, and settings.
4. Click Close if the User Settings dialog box is open.
5. If you aren't prompted to restart the computer, choose Log Off from the Start menu. Then log on using the new identity, and customize your settings.

TIP: In most cases, you'll want to copy the existing settings. It's usually easier to delete or move items than it is to add them.

TIP: Use the User Settings dialog box to remove an existing user or to change which items are personalized for an existing user.

Fixing Problems

A fabulous feature of Windows Me is the System Restore tool, which makes it possible for you to undo whatever changes you or your programs have made to your system. Periodically, Windows Me records all your system information. If you've made changes to the system but the effect isn't what you wanted, you can tell Windows Me to revert to the previous settings.

TIP: You can run System Restore from Windows Me or when you've started the computer in Safe Mode. You can't run System Restore when you've started up using the startup disk.

Restore the System

1. Start System Restore from the System Tools submenu of the Start menu.

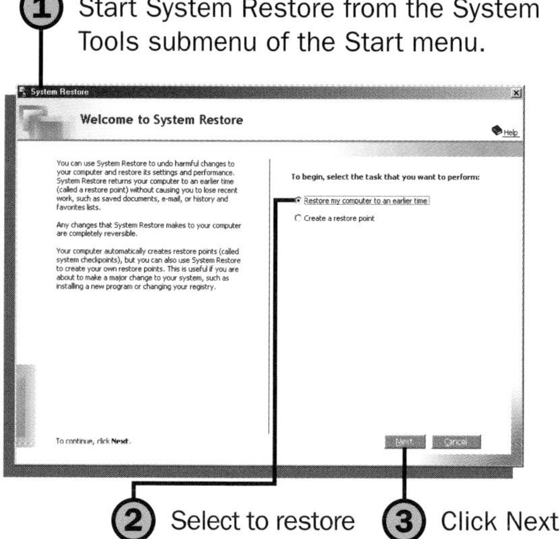

2. Select to restore your computer.
3. Click Next.

TIP: If using System Restore caused additional problems, start System Restore again, and choose the option to undo the last restoration.

4. Select the date that contains a restore point. (Only the dates in bold type contain restore points.)

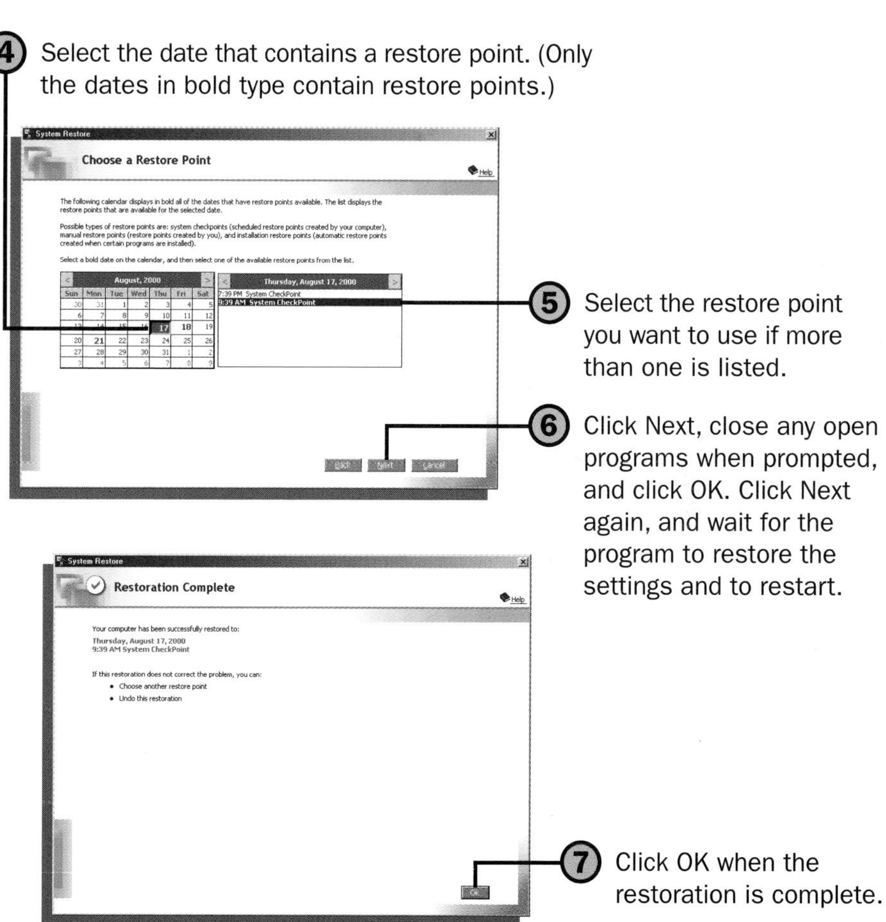

5. Select the restore point you want to use if more than one is listed.
6. Click Next, close any open programs when prompted, and click OK. Click Next again, and wait for the program to restore the settings and to restart.
7. Click OK when the restoration is complete.

Updating Your System

As time marches on, Microsoft continues to make improvements, fix problems, and even offer new features in Windows Me. Windows Me keeps track of which updates you need for your computer. You can choose to have Windows Me automatically check for new updates over the Internet, or you can check for updates by visiting the Windows Update web page. Either way, the updates are downloaded to your computer and then you install them.

Specify How You Want to Update

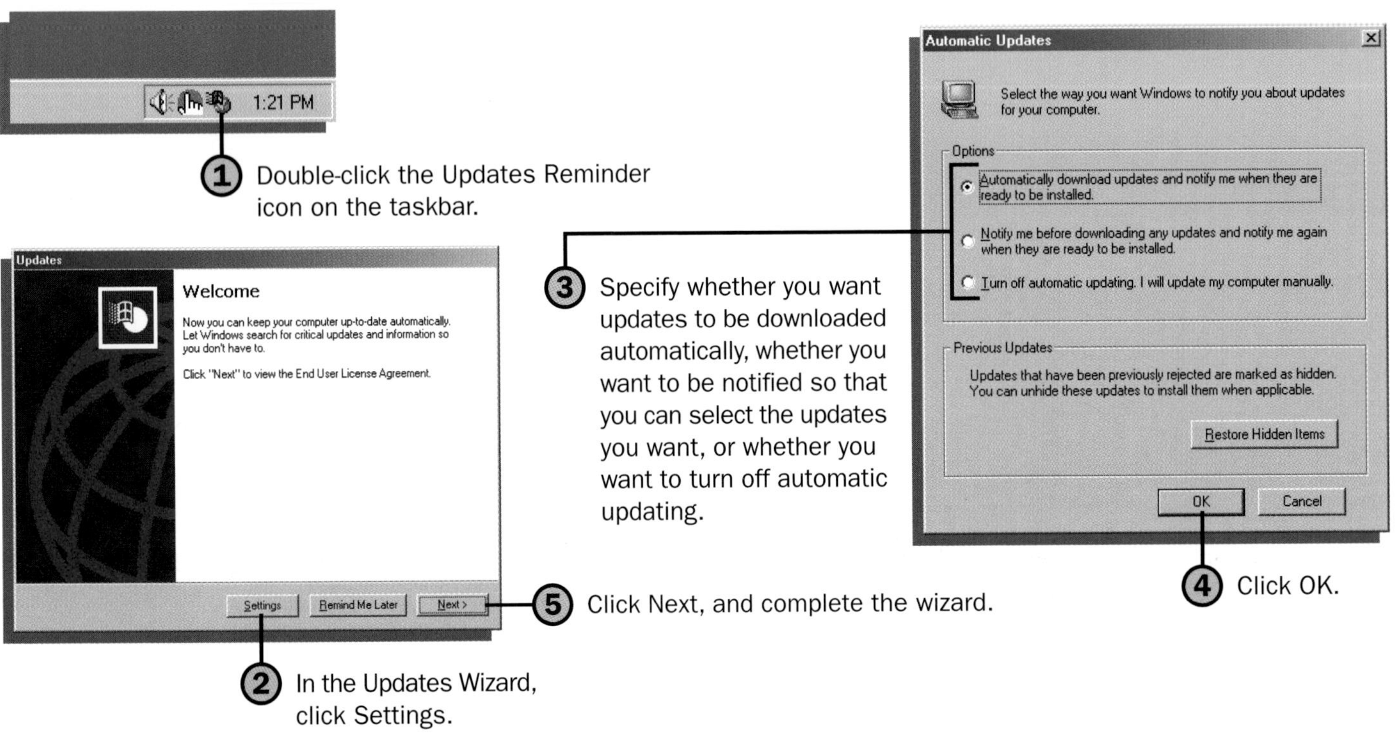

1. Double-click the Updates Reminder icon on the taskbar.
2. In the Updates Wizard, click Settings.
3. Specify whether you want updates to be downloaded automatically, whether you want to be notified so that you can select the updates you want, or whether you want to turn off automatic updating.
4. Click OK.
5. Click Next, and complete the wizard.

TIP: Because Windows Update is a web page, and because web pages change frequently, what you see on the Windows Update page might look different from what you see here. Be sure to read and follow the instructions on the web page to select, download, and install your updates.

TIP: To change the way you receive updates, double-click the Automatic Updates icon in the Control Panel, and change the settings in the Automatic Updates dialog box. To install updates you previously decided not to install, click the Restore Hidden Items button in the Automatic Updates dialog box.

Update Your System Automatically

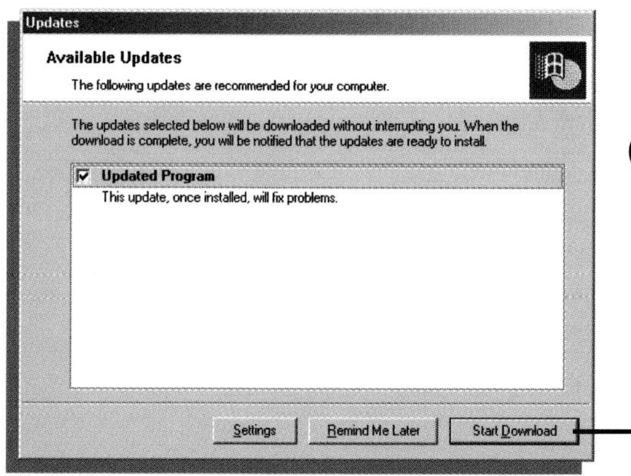

1. If Windows Me notifies you that updates are available, double-click the Updates icon on the taskbar, select the updates you want to download, and click Start Download.

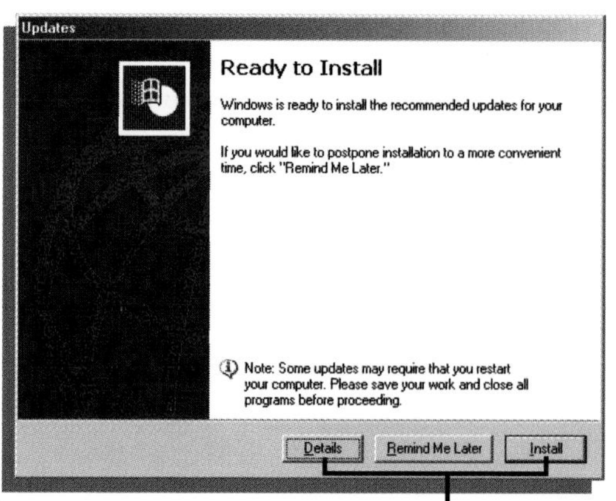

2. When Windows Me notifies you that updates have been downloaded, double-click the Updates icon, and click Install. If you want to select which items are installed, click Details. Wait for the updates to be installed, and follow the instructions if you need to restart your computer.

TIP: Automatic updates work best when your computer is continuously connected to the Internet or when you remain connected for long periods of time. Manual updates are the easiest to use if you dial in for short Internet sessions.

Update Your System Manually

1. Choose Windows Update from the Start menu. Connect to the Internet if you're not already connected.

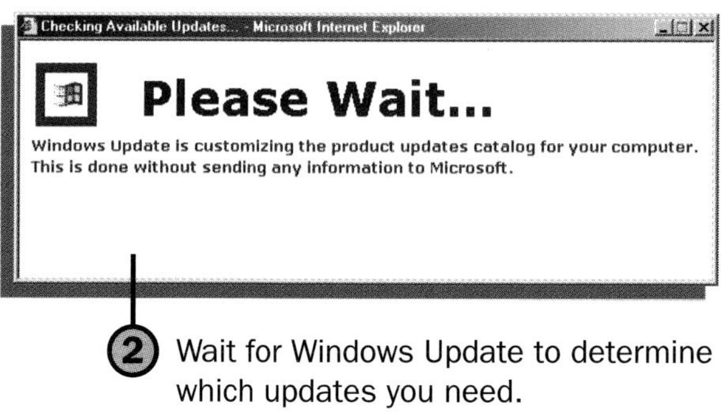

2. Wait for Windows Update to determine which updates you need.

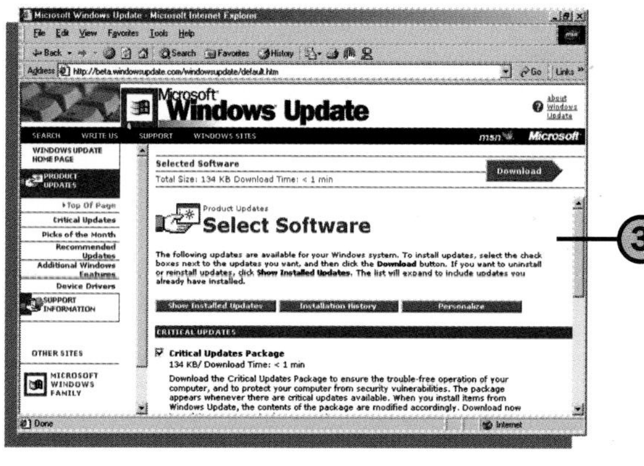

3. Follow the information on the page to select and download the updates.

Starting Up When There's a Problem

If you can't get Windows Me to start up correctly, you can use one of several startup procedures, either to help you diagnose what's wrong or to start Windows Me with minimal features so that you can adjust or restore settings. If you can't get Windows Me to start at all, you could have a major problem caused by a virus, a hardware failure, or software corruption. You can try to fix the problem yourself using the Windows Startup disk, but you should consider getting technical support from your computer manufacturer or retailer.

SEE ALSO: For information about fixing problems by resetting your computer to previous settings, see "Fixing Problems" on page 183.

Control the Startup

1. Restart your computer.
2. As the computer starts, press the F8 key or the Ctrl key when you see the OS Loading message. The Microsoft Windows Millennium Startup Menu appears.
3. Use the Down arrow key to select Safe Mode.
4. Press Enter.
5. Make changes to your system to correct the problem.
6. Shut down your computer and then restart it to see whether it starts correctly.
7. If it doesn't start correctly, repeat steps 1 and 2, and choose a different startup mode to help diagnose the problem.

Startup Options

Option	What it does
Normal	Executes a standard startup.
Logged (\BOOTLOG.TXT)	Starts normally; records startup information in a log file in the root folder.
Safe Mode	Starts with no network connections and without most of its drivers, including no access to CDs. Video settings use a generic driver for VGA display.
Step-By-Step Confirmation	Steps through the startup procedure, asking whether each step should be executed or skipped.

TIP: When Safe Mode starts, the Safe Mode Troubleshooter appears. Use the troubleshooter if you don't already know the cause of the problem or how to fix it.

TIP: If your computer came with Windows Me preinstalled, read the documentation from the manufacturer about fixing problems before you execute any actions.

Start Up from a Disk

1. Turn off your computer, restart it, and use a "boot" disk from a virus-detection program to verify that the problem isn't being caused by a virus.
2. Insert your Windows Me startup disk into the floppy disk drive, and restart the computer.
3. When the Microsoft Windows Millennium Startup Menu appears, press Enter to display Help.
4. Use the Up and Down arrow keys to scroll through the Help file, noting suggested actions. When you've finished with Help, press the Alt, F, and X keys to close the Help file.
5. Note the information on the screen about the drive letter for the CD drive and the temporary drive that contains the tools that have been extracted from the startup disk.
6. Use the appropriate command shown in the table to try and fix the problem. Do any of the following to try and fix the computer:

- Type *scandisk /all* to check for serious errors on the hard disk.
- Type *scanreg /restore* to use a previous copy of the system registry.
- Switch to your CD drive, and type *setup* to reinstall Windows Me.

TIP: To read the Help information on a different computer, open the Readme.txt file on the floppy disk in Notepad or in another word processing program.

Helpful Windows Me Startup Disk Tools

Command	What it does
Attrib	Changes the attributes of programs so that you can copy, move, or delete them.
CDdrive:setup	Reinstalls Windows Me.
Edit	Starts a text editor program to edit system files.
Format *driveletter*	Deletes all content and reformats the hard disk. System files, Windows Me, and all programs must be reinstalled. Use only as a last resort and after reading the manufacturer's documentation and/or consulting a technician.
Help	Displays Help for using the startup disk.
Scandisk /all	Examines the hard disks and repairs errors.
Scanreg /restore	Replaces the current Windows Me registry (the database that keeps track of all of Windows Me's settings) with a previous version.
Sys c:	Copies the system boot file to your hard disk.

TIP: If a startup disk wasn't included with your computer, or if you didn't create one when you installed Windows Me yourself, you should create one before you encounter any problems. To create a startup disk, open the Add/Remove Programs dialog box from the Control Panel, and follow the instructions on the Startup Disk tab.

Index

D

E

F

G

L

M

N

O

P

Q

R

S

T

U

V

W

Z

Author Bio

Jerry Joyce has had a long-standing relationship with Microsoft: he was the technical editor on numerous books published by Microsoft Press, and he has written manuals, help files, and specifications for various Microsoft products. As a programmer, he has tried to make using a computer as simple as using any household appliance, but he has yet to succeed. Jerry's alter ego is that of a marine biologist; he has conducted research from the Arctic to the Antarctic and has published extensively on marine-mammal and fisheries issues. As an antidote to staring at his computer screen, he enjoys traveling, birding, boating, and wandering about beaches, wetlands, and mountains.

Marianne Moon has worked in the publishing world for many years as proofreader, editor, and writer—sometimes all three simultaneously. She has been editing and proofreading Microsoft Press books since 1984 and has written and edited documentation for Microsoft products such as Microsoft Works, Flight Simulator, Space Simulator, Golf, Publisher, the Microsoft Mouse, and Greetings Workshop. In another life, she was chief cook and bottlewasher for her own catering service and wrote cooking columns for several newspapers. When she's not chained to her computer, she likes gardening, cooking, traveling, writing poetry, and knitting sweaters for tiny dogs.

Marianne and **Jerry** own and operate **Moon Joyce Resources,** a small consulting company. They are coauthors of *Microsoft Word 97 At a Glance, Microsoft Windows 95 At a Glance, Microsoft Windows NT Workstation 4.0 At a Glance, Microsoft Windows 98 At a Glance, Microsoft Word 2000 At a Glance,* and *Microsoft Windows 2000 Professional At a Glance.* They've had a 19-year working relationship and have been married for 9 years. If you have questions or comments about any of their books, you can reach them at moonjoyceresourc@hotmail.com.

The manuscript for this book was prepared and submitted to Microsoft Press in electronic form. Text files were prepared using Microsoft Word 2000. Pages were composed by Microsoft Press using Adobe PageMaker 6.52 for Windows, with text set in Times and display type in ITC Franklin Gothic. Composed pages were delivered to the printer as electronic prepress files.

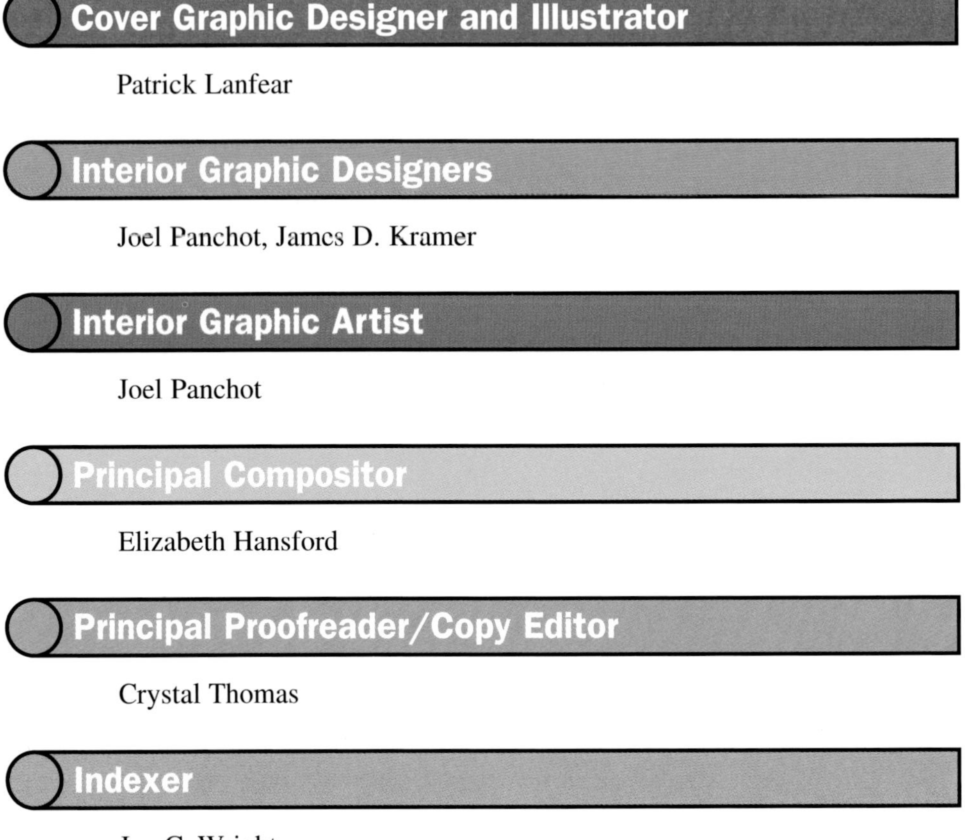

Cover Graphic Designer and Illustrator

Patrick Lanfear

Interior Graphic Designers

Joel Panchot, James D. Kramer

Interior Graphic Artist

Joel Panchot

Principal Compositor

Elizabeth Hansford

Principal Proofreader/Copy Editor

Crystal Thomas

Indexer

Jan C. Wright

Proof of Purchase

0-7356-0970-5

Do not send this card with your registration.
Use this card as proof of purchase if participating in a promotion or rebate offer on *Microsoft® Windows® Me At a Glance*. Card must be used in conjunction with other proof(s) of payment such as your dated sales receipt—see offer details.

Microsoft® Windows® Me At a Glance

WHERE DID YOU PURCHASE THIS PRODUCT?

CUSTOMER NAME

Microsoft®

mspress.microsoft.com

Microsoft Press, PO Box 97017, Redmond, WA 98073-9830

OWNER REGISTRATION CARD

Register Today!

0-7356-0970-5

Return the bottom portion of this card to register today.

Microsoft® Windows® Me At a Glance

FIRST NAME | MIDDLE INITIAL | LAST NAME

INSTITUTION OR COMPANY NAME

ADDRESS

CITY | STATE | ZIP

E-MAIL ADDRESS | ( ) PHONE NUMBER

U.S. and Canada addresses only. Fill in information above and mail postage-free.
Please mail only the bottom half of this page.